Dog Body,
Dog Mind

Dr. Michael W. Fox

CAT BODY, CAT MIND (2007)

KILLER FOODS: WHEN SCIENTISTS MANIPULATE GENES, BETTER IS NOT ALWAYS BEST (2004)

BRINGING LIFE TO ETHICS: GLOBAL BIOETHICS FOR A HUMANE SOCIETY (2001)

EATING WITH CONSCIENCE: THE BIOETHICS OF FOOD (1997)

CONCEPTS IN ETHOLOGY, ANIMAL BEHAVIOR AND BIOETHICS (1997, revised edition)

THE BOUNDLESS CIRCLE (1996)

ST. FRANCIS OF ASSISI, ANIMALS, AND NATURE (1989)

THE NEW EDEN (1989)

THE NEW ANIMAL DOCTOR'S ANSWER BOOK (1989)

LABORATORY ANIMAL HUSBANDRY (1986)

THE WHISTLING HUNTERS (1984)

THE HEALING TOUCH FOR DOGS & THE HEALING TOUCH FOR CATS (2004)

LOVE IS A HAPPY CAT (1982)

INTEGRATIVE DEVELOPMENT OF BRAIN AND BEHAVIOR IN THE DOG (1971)

Dog Body,
Dog Mind

Exploring Canine
Consciousness and
Total Well-Being

Dr. Michael W. Fox

The Lyons Press
Guilford, Connecticut

An imprint of The Globe Pequot Press

To buy books in quantity for corporate use
or incentives, call **(800) 962–0973**
or e-mail **premiums@GlobePequot.com.**

The Lyons Press is an imprint of The Globe Pequot Press.

10 9 8 7 6 5 4 3 2 1

Printed in the United States of America

Designed by Sheryl P. Kober

ISBN 13: 978-1-59921-045-2

Library of Congress Cataloging-in-Publication Data is available on file.

For Deanna, and all we embrace

Acknowledgments

I wish to acknowledge the many dogs and other animals that have enriched my life and taught me much. I am especially grateful for the sensitive and skilled editorial work of Lilly Golden. To my publisher, Lyons Press, a word of thanks for helping me inform and inspire more understanding and compassion in our relationships with dogs and all creatures great and small.

| Contents |

| Introduction |

The primary purpose of this book is to further your understanding of your canine companions and how you communicate with them. This book will help you become more fluent in "dog-speak"—to know what your dog is feeling, intending, and wanting. It will then be easier for your dog to communicate with you, especially when he or she wants to play, is distressed about something and wants your attention, or is possibly ill.

The human-animal bond is not only strengthened through improved understanding and communication. It is also reinforced through better care, and this book offers you precisely what is needed in this regard: a holistic approach to companion animal care and preventive medicine that will help guarantee a healthy and happy animal, and a healthy and happy bond between the two of you.

Many people are convinced that their dogs are psychic and can read their minds. Others contend that their companion animals have helped heal them and have even communicated from beyond the grave. Is all of this sheer fiction? Or are we dealing with a set of phenomena that our loyal dogs are revealing to us—one that calls for a radical change in our concept of reality and in our understanding of these animal companions and indeed all creatures great and small? This book will help you find answers to these and other questions.

For many people—including children and especially the lonely and the elderly—one of the deepest relationships they have enjoyed in their lives has been with their companion animals. This fact has touched me deeply as a result of my consultations with thousands of people over the years who sought my advice as a veterinarian and animal behavior therapist. In this book, I have put together the knowledge, insight, and concerns from this service work for the welfare of animals to provide some basic measures—

some of which are long overdue—to improve the health and well-being of dogs here in the United States and abroad. After all, dogs are very significant others in the lives of millions of people and in countless families around the world.

In times past, when our ancestors lived closer to nature and to wild and domesticated animals, there was no doubt that animals spoke to humans and were recognized as sharing an inner wisdom and connection with the sacred or metaphysical realm. They became guardians, teachers, and healers—provided the people whose lives they touched had an open heart and mind.

Today our hearts and minds are being opened by what amounts to a renaissance (literally, a rebirth) in our rediscovery of these animal powers and a recovery of the ancient wisdom, thanks to the millions of dogs that enrich our lives as family companions, playmates, and soul mates. They have much to offer us.

The only, if not the last, connection with all that is natural and not manmade for so many of us is our connection with domesticated animals. Their presence and spirit makes us feel more whole and secure. For many, companion animals give unconditional relief from loneliness, alienation, depression, and despair. And for others, the animals in their lives give the only affirmation that there is something miraculous and wonderful, even spiritual, in this close relationship with another living being, which can be a source of joy and deep satisfaction from childhood on.

Since our animal companions have been at the sides of mankind from generation to generation, they mirror, in their health and well-being, the sensitivity and compassion of the times. The ideal bond between us and them is one that is mutually enhancing and based as much upon love and respect as upon understanding. The better we understand the dog's mind and have a basic comprehension of how our dogs communicate their needs, intentions, and feelings, the more mindful we will be—and the more satisfying and meaningful that bond will be.

There are people who look down on other people's close bond with their canine companions, seeing the relationship as misguided sentimentalism or some displaced parental urge. They are incredulous over how deeply such people mourn the loss of a beloved dog, and they firmly believe that animals don't have emotions, self-consciousness, and souls. Companion animals are seen by such skeptics as being emotional parasites and, when compared to their wild counterparts, degenerate and inferior.

To regard companion dogs as inferior to their wolf and coyote cousins because they have been domesticated and have been made dependent on us is to reveal a prejudice based on ignorance rather than sound science. In fact, scientific studies have shown that while the brains of domesticated animals are slightly smaller than their wild counterparts (the same is apparently true for modern human brains compared to the skull/brain-case volume of our Cro-Magnon ancestors!), their physiology and psychology have been profoundly influenced in a more positive way. They are less fearful, more trusting, more responsive, and more adaptable and trainable than their wild ancestors; but they have been made more vulnerable to us in the process.

This does not mean that wild animals, especially those born in captivity and raised by caring people, are incapable of establishing a close emotional bond with us. But rather, domestication has made the deep heart of companion animals more accessible to us. With less instinctual fear and more trust, dogs can bare their souls to us and reveal, often to our astonishment and delight, as I will share in this book, some of their higher powers like insight, reasoning, prescience, empathy, devotion, and emotional intelligence—traits and talents we thought were exclusive to only the best of our own kind.

Skeptics have argued that such revelations are all a projection of our own imaginations and of our need to feel loved and understood, and by so doing, we are guilty of anthropomorphizing animals, which means endowing them with human qualities that only we actually possess.

This book demolishes such skepticism, which leads ultimately to *speciesism*: regarding animals like some inferior race of beings. This book provides a wealth of evidence to the contrary and is a testimony to the higher powers of animals; it provides affirmation that those dogs who share and enrich our lives in so many ways are indeed self-conscious, sensitive souls who live more in the present (like good existentialists!) than most of us. They have much to teach us about the nature of love and the love of nature—of all that is natural and spontaneous—through our deep heart connection with them.

My friend and mentor the late Professor Konrad Lorenz, who received the Nobel Prize for his pioneering work in ethology, the science of animal behavior, once told an international gathering of scientists that, "Before you can really study and understand an animal you must first love it." Konrad would agree with me that he is half right, because before you can really love another human or nonhuman being, you must first have some understanding—and the greater the understanding, the deeper the love. Hence the first part of this book deals with what is so often lacking in the human-animal bond: not love so much as an understanding of animal behavior and communication.

As an ethologist, one who studies animal behavior, and a veterinarian who has shared his life with many animals—from dogs and cats to wolves, foxes, and coyotes (which are not pets)—I can attest to the fact that in the research setting of scientific study and in the veterinary hospital animals are less likely and less able to be themselves and show their true colors, compared to when they are in their familiar and secure home environment with their loved ones. It is here, in their familiar surroundings, that insights about their natures abound—their souls and higher powers—can be found. Thanks to consultations, lectures, and communications with people about their animal companions, I have accumulated a treasure trove from the deep heart of our canine and other animal companions that will now be opened and shared with all. I feel privileged to be able to contribute to the advancement of our understanding, respect, and appreciation of fellow creatures great and small and to join others in affirming and celebrating this wonderful bond.

Chapters at the end of this book address the major companion animal health and welfare concerns. They also provide essential information on holistic health and preventive medicine, as well as advice on nutrition, vaccination protocols, basic training, and dealing with some of the most common behavioral problems.

Dog Body,
Dog Mind

Part One
Dog Mind

1.
| The Case for Dog Consciousness |

Dogs as Guides

Dogs can be our allies, guides, and healers—when we are able to be open to them. In American Indian and other traditional aboriginal cultures, animals are as much a part of the culture's spirituality and mythology as they are a part of the ecological community and social economy. In modern society, these animal powers are less understood, but they are still there—even in highly domesticated animal companions such as the dog. We should not take dogs for granted or regard them as lacking in the powers their wild cousins possess. Many of them have the ability to survive and multiply as feral animals and live in the wild by their own wits, quite independent of us.

Millions of people throughout the "civilized" world have one thing in common with aboriginal peoples: they have daily contact with one or more animals, usually cats and dogs. Fortunately, only a few keep wild animals—such as wolves, wild cats, and hawks—in captivity. Unlike cats and dogs, which have been domesticated for thousands of years, wild animals are unable to adapt in body, mind, and spirit to a domestic environment; they inevitably suffer in captivity (including wolf-dog hybrids).

Acknowledging a Dog's Awareness

When we do not understand animals and fully respect them in their own right, whatever feeling we may have for them is, at best, sentimental affection. This is because our ability to empathize with them—to put ourselves in their place and imagine what they are feeling, thinking, desiring, and going to do next—will be extremely limited if our understanding of their behavior and psychology is rudimentary. In other words, the better we understand them, the better we can empathize with them.

Empathy is the bridge of compassion and loving kindness to which dogs are extremely responsive. As our understanding develops, the nature of that love and the quality of our relationships with animals changes. They become even more a part of our lives, to a degree of satisfaction rarely equaled with our own species.

Those who refuse to accept that dogs and other animals have feelings tend to put them down by claiming everything they do is instinctive and automatic. They aren't consciously aware of what they do and feel and, in these individuals' eyes, animals are unfeeling automatons—mere biological machines. It is perhaps no coincidence that people who feel this way about animals often exploit them as a livelihood.

Yet there are many converts. One world-renowned surgeon who transplanted chimpanzee hearts into human patients (or were they human guinea pigs?) stopped participating in the practice when the screams of a female chimp touched his soul after he had taken her mate out of her cage to be killed for his heart. An American hunter put his gun down forever after he killed a Canada goose and saw her mate fly down to defend her as she struggled on the ground in the final throes of death. A scientist I knew who regularly experimented on dogs and other animals in the laboratory decided to quit his research on animals after his daughter brought home a stray dog. The family adopted the stray, and the dog's love and devotion—especially to this man—made him realize how sensitive and intelligent the animals he experimented on were.

I have heard of men on whaling boats sickened by what they do as they watch a harpooned whale die and drown, helped by its companions who sometimes ram the boat. What a contrast to whale researchers who approach these gentle giants and touch them while the whales swim under the researchers' frail little rubber dinghies, careful never to capsize their watercraft.

Those who deny that dogs and animals have feelings may be denying their own feelings, too. Animals do have feelings—and to believe otherwise is to deny our kinship with them and stop empathizing with them. In the process of denying animals their feelings, we become unfeeling toward them—and to be unfeeling is to be inhuman.

It is ironic how some research psychologists raise infant monkeys in total isolation, as a model of separation anxiety in human infants, and others give dogs and other animals inescapable electrical shocks, and then claim such treatment provides a useful model for studying anxiety and depression in humans. They don't feel there is anything morally wrong with what they do; some even claim the animals don't suffer the way a human would, if subjected to similar treatment. Yet, in the same breath, they claim that animal studies are relevant to understanding human emotional problems. If animals were not emotionally similar to us, then such research would not be relevant.

Animals not only have feelings, they also have emotional problems that are very similar to our own. *Separation anxiety* is the term given by animal behavior therapists to the most common emotional problem in dogs, which develops when they are left alone all day in the house. The fact that experts now recognize animals have feelings and emotional problems is paving the way toward a greater respect for animals and their rights.

It is well documented that many zoo animals become depressed when their cage-mates die or are separated from them. Likewise, dogs show depression—disinterest in food and in life itself—when a beloved owner or animal companion dies (see chapter 7), or when they are boarded while their owners are away on vacation.

* * *

What follows is an overview of some of the basic aspects of animal behavior to help stimulate a greater understanding of them, so we will be better able to empathize with animals and be the recipients of their trust, affection, and myriad gifts and powers.

Signs of Distress

Gross changes in behavior—such as flight, screaming, struggling, and defensive self-protective "fear-biting" rather than offensive aggression—won't always occur when a dog is distressed and suffering. One must be alert for more subtle reactions that may, in certain combinations and contexts, be clear indicators of distress. Here are some examples:

1. Changes in the autonomic nervous system, the unconscious homeostatic or balancing control system of bodily functions, are associated

with physical and/or emotional distress. These include: salivation, pupil dilation, increased rate of heart beats (palpitations), respiration (panting), increased body temperature, muscular tremors (shivering) or muscular tension, piloerection (fluffed fur), urination, defecation, and release of anal sack contents.

2. Disruption of normal cyclic and maintenance behaviors, such as not eating, drinking, sleeping, or grooming.

3. Disturbance in social and other behaviors is exhibited when the animal will not explore, play, or interact socially—with its own kind or with humans (may be passive, actively avoid, or show defensive aggression).

4. Abnormal behaviors may develop, such as prolonged refusal to eat, leading to anorexia (wasting), polydipsia (excessive drinking), hyper-aggressive or flight reactions, excessive grooming, redirected (self-directed) aggression and self-mutilation, pacing and circling stereotyped movements, and increased susceptibility to disease.

Displacement Behavior and Redirected Actions
Many dogs and other animals (including humans), when in a state of conflict or anxiety, may suddenly display a particular behavior that, to the attuned observer, gives a clear indication of the animal's emotional state. Self-directed scratching, licking, and grooming are especially common in a variety of mammals, from rats and cats to apes and people. Such actions (for example, thumb-sucking in a child) are self-comforting and are thought therefore to reduce anxiety. But they can become addictive, obsessive-compulsive disorders leading to chronic wounding and infection. Displacement eating and drinking have been observed in many different animals and are two amusing aspects of human behavior at a formal cocktail party or reception!

Some animals engage in displacement or *sham-sleep* when they are scared (like playing possum). Dogs in shelters will sham-sleep as a way of coping with stress; to the naïve observer, the dog may simply seem relaxed.

Sometimes the behavior is not displacement but a redirection. Instead of attacking a rival on the other side of the fence, a dog may instead bite or snap at his owner or at another dog that he lives with. Or the animal may redirect the attack against some inanimate object (the leash or a bush) or even

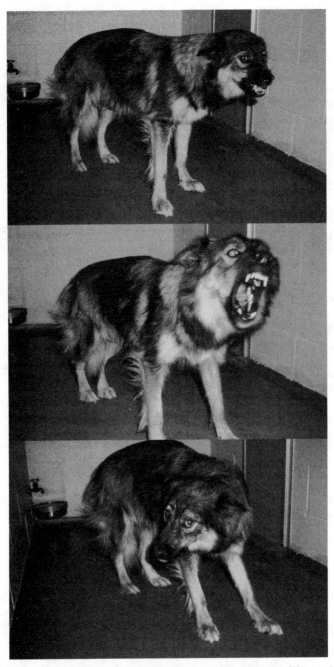

A fearful dog in an animal shelter. This sequence shows the submissive flattening of the ears, tucked tail, and defensive snarl (top); the dog becomes more offensive when approached by me (center); this turns into submission when I squat down and speak softly (bottom); then I can pet her.
Photos: M. W. Fox

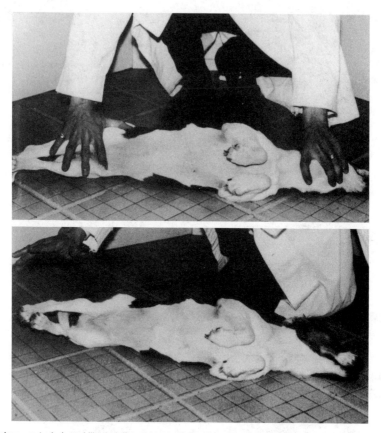

Catalepsy or tonic immobility is induced by simply turning a terrified dog that had no human contact earlier in life onto her side.
Photos: M. W. Fox

against itself, by biting a paw or tail (another cause of self-mutilation). Such redirected actions are common in many animals, including human beings. One human example is when a man or woman comes home after a bad day at work and turns that experience into anger against children or a spouse.

Stereotyped Behaviors

You may have seen zoo animals and some dogs in shelters pacing, circling to and fro in their cages. These are called stereotyped behaviors and they will develop when an animal (or human being) is frustrated, anxious, hyper-aroused, or wholly understimulated in a sterile cage or prison cell. The movements are self-stimulating and may afford a kind of sensory escape from confinement. Sometimes this is self-comforting, such as when an anxious or over-aroused autistic child or adult schizophrenic begins to rock back and forth and either sucks a thumb or "self-clings" with both arms wrapped around the body.

Stereotyped behavior indicates that something is wrong. The animal may want to escape to reach a mate in an adjoining cage, may be excited because it's near feeding time, or is simply bored and needs a cage companion or play objects in the enclosure. Recent studies have shown that stereotyped behaviors result in increased production of natural opiates in the animal's body; this may help the animal cope with stress and distress, but it can make the behaviors addictive and obsessively compulsive.

What Makes My Pet Happy?

This is the title of a brochure published in 2006 by the British Veterinary Association's Animal Welfare Foundation (www.bva-awf.org.uk). This landmark publication acknowledges that happiness, welfare, and quality of life have to do with how animals feel. And that the first thing to do to determine if your animal is happy is to check how you are treating your animal companion against the so-called Five Freedoms, which include both physical and mental health considerations.

These Five Freedoms are:

1. Freedom from hunger and thirst

2. Freedom from pain, injury, and disease

3. Freedom from discomfort (e.g., temperature extremes, uncomfortable floor surfaces)

4. Freedom to express normal behavior

5. Freedom from fear and distress

Most people are not remiss in meeting the happiness criteria of numbers one through three, by providing their animal companions with proper physical care and veterinary attention as needed. But numbers four and five may be more difficult to provide without some understanding of animal behavior. There is much in this book that will help inform and guide people who want their animal companions to be happy and healthy. But when in doubt about numbers four and five, when it comes to having misgivings about your animal's quality of life that is a function of freedom from fear and distress and freedom to express normal behaviors (and I would add freedom from abnormal behaviors that can develop with improper rearing, handling, and training—or lack thereof), then always seek professional advice from a vet or trainer.

An animal's happiness and quality of life are profoundly influenced by the quality time spent with that animal every day: engaging in activities the animal enjoys, especially various games; being groomed and massaged; and having the opportunity to live with or meet members of the same species for social interaction.

Letting You Know

Animals let us know when they are suffering and in pain in ways that are sometimes obvious, and sometimes ambiguous. Some dogs whine and pace and solicit attention. Others become silent, withdrawn, irritable, and may growl or snap when touched.

One of my dogs named Batman simply rolled over and held his two front paws up in the air as he cried loudly at me, refusing to walk any farther because he was afraid of the snow and his feet were cold. He had recently come from India, and this was his first winter in America. Snow boots made life easier for him in the cold weather, plus a winter coat! Another of my dogs named Benji, who came from a St. Louis animal shelter, one day started to act as though he had been scared by something and cowered when I approached him. He would slink around, almost acting as if he was guilty; he wasn't interested in playing and had lost his usually voracious appetite. Tests revealed that he had an intestinal blockage and surgery was performed in time to save his life. Benji did not show the usual signs of abdominal pain and straining associated with this acute condition and was, to some extent, masking his symptoms.

This is a problem with some individual animals and certain species, as I learned working with sheep and various zoo animals. They mask being in pain and being ill, possibly as a strategy to avoid being picked out from the herd by predators. Wolves, for example, will "test" a herd of deer or caribou and with expert observation and precision, detect a weak, sick, or injured animal and cull it from the herd.

Some animals simply go off to be alone when they are ill, which may be their way of healing: finding a quiet and secure place to let natural healing processes work. But this may not always be the best remedy, and any animal who behaves in such a way should be taken for a veterinary checkup. Don't allow him outdoors off leash until you've taken him to the vet, because once outside he may be hard to find. This reclusive, self-cloistering behavior probably underlies the widespread observation that many dogs that are ill and "know their time has come" go off alone to die.

Wild animals will also sometimes seek out human help when they are suffering. One remarkable example was a bobcat that was severely infected and dying from porcupine quills in his face, mouth, and chest; he crawled over to two cross-country skiers and lay down in front of them. He was taken to a veterinarian, treated, and later released back into the wild.

At the Animal Refuge in South India, which my wife Deanna Krantz and I operated for many years, we had several remarkable animal experiences. In two instances, animals in need of veterinary care brought themselves to us for treatment. One was a water buffalo with a severe screw-worm infestation that was eating her alive; the other was a dog that had a broken back and pelvis and dragged himself from where he had been hit by a vehicle over a mile away. Neither of these animals had ever been near our refuge before, yet somehow they knew it was a place where animals were cared for and healed.

In July 2003, the Associated Press reported a similar story about an old black Labrador retriever who was hit by a car and took himself to the Beckley Regional Veterinary Hospital in West Virginia, limping through the sliding glass doors and waiting for assistance in the hallway. He lay down where everyone could see him, and the amazed staff immediately treated him and put the word out to find the dog's owner.

Emotional Intelligence and Sensibility

At our Animal Refuge in India, with over three hundred animals of all kinds, we found some animals were very attentive to sick and injured animals brought in for treatment. It was a touching sight to see a cow care for an orphaned foal with nuzzles and licks; to see a dog provide for an injured fawn with body warmth, licks, nibbles, and a protective growl when any other resident animal came near; and to see an adult male monkey caring for an abandoned baby monkey, holding her in his arms and cooing. One

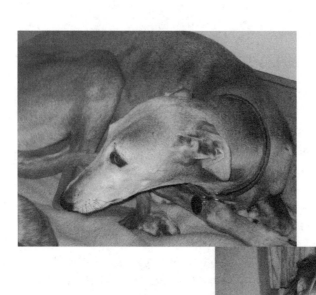

From fear to trust and happy play. A rescued, abused greyhound avoids eye contact
and remains immobile when cornered and
approached (left upper). A rehabilitated greyhound on his back, which is a sign of trust
(right), displaying an open-mouth play-face
while being embraced by my wife Deanna;
the same dog gives me a play-fight happy
"monster" face as we take a break from
wrestling together (left lower).
Photos: M. W. Fox

resident dog named Bruno would insist on observing all surgeries and other treatments of animal patients and would lie protectively at their sides during their recovery and recuperation. Other dogs played important roles protecting, socializing, and introducing new puppies and dogs into the resident pack. These observations confirmed my long-standing belief that companion dogs are happier and healthier when they live with at least one member of their own species in the home, or with another animal species that is compatible. The animals provide companionship and tender loving care for each other, especially when left alone in the home for extended periods during the workweek.

By observing animals' interrelations and reactions, we see they have different temperaments. As we come to know them more closely, we can describe their different personalities in purely anthropomorphic terms. We might refer to a dog as affectionate and outgoing, or fearful and untrusting, or curious and playful, or relaxed and content: this shows our empathic recognition of their emotionality. Just as with humans, emotionality in dogs and other animals is the basis for every animal having a particular temperament, a personality, and therefore, personhood.

(But our judicial system is not yet poised to accept what it must surely now consider: that dogs and beings other than humans have an emotional life more similar to our own than different (including virtually identical neurochemical systems) and therefore interests and rights as moral subjects under our dominion.

I like to give dog owners and people caring for other animal species the following questions to reflect upon.

- What makes your animal happy, and how do you know when she or he is happy?

- How do you show your animal affection, and how does the animal respond to you and show affection?

Having established with convincing examples and observation of behavior that dogs have a highly evolved emotional sensibility and intelligence, the next area of the dog mind to explore is their awareness and the key to our understanding, how they communicate.

Once you understand how dogs communicate, the above questions may be more easily answered.

2.
| Animal Awareness and Communication |

The fascinating work of behavioral scientists has recently hit the popular press. Their attempts to establish two-way communication with animals, such as chimpanzees and dolphins, have provided conclusive evidence that humans are not the only intelligent beings on earth. The old assumption is that nonhuman animals lack any conscious intent (or awareness) to communicate, making humans the only species who know what they are doing when they communicate.

Some philosophers have argued that a creature cannot think if it has no verbal language; thus, since only humans have a verbal means of communicating feelings and intentions, only humans can think. This is a ludicrously anthropocentric view indeed—and one that any dog owner would certainly object to. But this view has prevailed in science for many decades; it is perhaps the kind of attitude that underlies so much abuse of animals in society today.

One of the reasons why the inner mental realm of dogs and other animals hasn't been well researched is likely because few experimenters develop a close-enough rapport with their animals to be accepted by them and to become "at one" with them socially and emotionally. I did no less with the captive wolves I studied in the 1970s; like J. A. Boone with the German shepherd dog Strongheart (in his book *Kinship With All Life*, Harper & Row, NY, 1954), the wolves became my teachers.

It would seem that an all-important key to communicating with these and other highly social mammals—from captive primates and elephants to whales and dolphins—is to establish a bond of affection. A subjective, empathetic mode of investigation has been lacking to date—or at least has not been integrated with the detached objectivity of the scientific investigator. Pet owners who have the kind of relationship with their animals whereby the species barrier is broken should perhaps be emulated more by scientists of animal behavior. Take, for instance, one of Dr. John Lilly's research dolphins, who, knowing which colored balls to retrieve when given a verbal command by her trainer, deliberately began to retrieve the wrong ball, in a pattern that revealed that she was communicating the strategy of the game or test in reverse—a clear sign of a highly evolved intelligence and sense of humor. This is not unlike the dog whose owner refused to give her any cheese from the coffee table and the dog returned from the kitchen with one of her big doggie biscuits and laid it in her owner's lap and then looked longingly at the cheese.

These examples show us that animals can reason and sometimes express their ideas or intentions. A more familiar one is the dog who is ready for a walk and brings his leash and drops it in front of you; or when soliciting play, he drops a ball or stick at your feet. A dog will do exactly the same to solicit play from another dog.

Word Recognition

I remember being singularly impressed by a well-trained shepherd dog at a dinner reception. He had been put on one side of the room in a sit-and-stay, but on three or four occasions during the conversation at the table, the dog suddenly appeared by his trainer's side. She had inadvertently mentioned the dog's name, and over he came. Clearly, the dog had been tuned in to his owner's conversation all the time. We should not underestimate the attention span of animals—and the possibility that their word comprehension is much greater than we think.

A well-trained dog can learn anywhere from twenty to forty words and up. It's rather like being with a preverbal child who astounds his parents by switching on the TV or a reading light, or finding a particular toy when asked to do so, even though all he can say is "Mama" and "Dada."

A ten-year-old Border collie named Rico was the subject of study by Dr. Julia Fischer and other scientists at the Max Planck Institute for Evolutionary Anthropology in Leipzig (Germany) in 2004, because of this dog's renowned "vocabulary" of nearly two hundred words. Rico learned the names of various play objects and could remember three out of six new names after one learning session one month earlier, a learning rate equivalent to that of a three-year-old child, according to the scientists.

Dr. Fischer noted that this was not simple conditioning but independent thinking. Rico would retrieve the objects he knew by name; but if a new name was given, seven times out of ten he would pick out and retrieve an object he had never seen before. This discloses a high level of insight and logical thinking. Rico's rate of learning was equivalent to that of a young child, and his capacity to memorize different words and sounds was on a level of that seen in apes, dolphins, and parrots.

As for birds, it is not always simple conditioning when they mimic certain words. Mary Whitby of Highland, California, wrote about their Edgar Allen Crow, which had had a broken wing and became a member of her family. He especially loved her mother and said to her in a guttural voice, "I love you."

The most educated bird on record is an African gray parrot named N'kisi that appeared on BBC TV *Wildlife Magazine* in January 2004. He astounded scientists not only with his 950-word vocabulary, but N'kisi could invent his own words and phrases when confronted with novel ideas that his existing repertoire could not handle. He also used words in context, with past, present, and future tense. One of his invented phrases was "pretty smell medicine" to describe the aromatherapy oils his New York–based owner used. When he first met my friend Dr. Jane Goodall, after seeing her picture with apes, he asked her, "Got a chimp?"

No less remarkable, and a subject explored further in chapter 8, was N'kisi's psychic power of clairvoyance. In an experiment, the bird and the owner were put in separate rooms and filmed as the owner opened random envelopes containing picture cards. Analysis showed that the parrot used appropriate key words to describe the pictures the owner was looking at in the other room, three times more often than would be likely by chance!

And what about talking dogs? There are a few reports of dogs that can form distinct word-sounds. Two of my own dogs, Tanza and Batman, learned to turn their excited, ready-to-go-out barks into barks that sound like the word *out*. One dentist wrote and informed me that his dog could articulate six different words, which were only "spoken" at appropriate times. The dog could vocalize the word *hamburger* while standing beside the refrigerator.

Like the parrot that says hello when you come into the room and good-bye when you leave, we must not be so parsimonious as to say all this is simple conditioning and mimicry. The animal *is* aware of the appropriateness of the sounds in relation to specific contexts—no less than with its own silent language of body displays. To presume that these are automatic instincts or conditioned reflexes and that the animal has no awareness and no inner mental imagery is illogical. Yet this view is widespread today, thanks to the mechanistic view of animals held by many "authorities" in the behavioral sciences.

Body Language

Few people have tried, or are inclined, to mimic some of the behavior patterns of their canine companions. This is not as difficult as it may sound, once you become familiar with some of the animals' communication signals. I have described these at length in my book *Understanding Your Dog*,[1] many of which you may try to mimic.

If you try this, what happens very often is something akin to a revelation for the human, especially for a child, and sometimes one for the animal as well. Suddenly a human being is communicating with the dog in his own "language" and is consciously attempting to break the species barrier. Judging by the responses of receptive animals, this is a highly rewarding experience. Mimicking a dog's open-mouth panting play-face combined with a play-soliciting bow is a good beginning. Or pretending to dodge one way and then the other, leading up to a game of tag or catch-me-if-you-can, is a game that humans and many other animal species play.

Humans and animals often use similar signals, too. A direct stare, for example, is virtually a pan-species threat signal. The human smile is not only pan-cultural (i.e., common to all human races), but it is also shared by other species such as wolves, dogs, and chimpanzees. In some species of primates, however, such as the macaque monkeys, a toothy grin may signal fear and defensive aggression rather than friendly submission—so the Dr. Dolittle animal mimic must be cautious, as interspecies ambiguity of signals could lead to considerable confusion!

We should also remember that with animals, just as with people, the same communication signal can be given in different contexts but the sender and receiver are aware of the social context they share, so they don't

1. Michael W. Fox, *Understanding Your Dog*, (New York: St. Martin's Press, 1992).

Classic canine embrace by a malamute courting a wolf, who displays an open-mouth happy play-face when she is hugged by the male, who wears a submissive grin.
Photo: M. W. Fox

misread each other. For example, avoiding eye contact in humans can be a submissive signal in one context, a rude cut-off by a social superior in another, and a sexual coquettish come-on in yet a third context.

Animals have also shown they too use the *same* signal in various contexts, but the signal has different meaning depending on which context it is given in. A good example is the bark of a dog: a dog will bark in one context as a threat, in another as a warning, and in a third for attention. What this means is that an animal's awareness of itself and others is far more developed and sophisticated than many human skeptics might think.

Sometimes, though, a person might misread you because he or she may not be sharing the same context or set of expectations as you. A friendly laugh or smile may be mistaken for derisive laughter or a sneer; an admiring gaze may be taken as a rude stare or sexual invitation. This becomes a particular problem when the other person is paranoid or psychotic.

The same goes for animals. They too have this context and signal-related awareness and can get into misunderstandings. A playful, excited wolf with back-hair and tail erect may be misread by a dog as readying to fight. Similarly, a friendly spitz-type dog with a permanently up-curled tail may be misread by a wolf or other dog as signaling a challenge. A direct,

With a piercing stare, dominant, tail-up Benji intimidates a Golden retriever who dares not to look, and then rolls over into passive submission as my dog struts and sniffs.
Photos: M. W. Fox

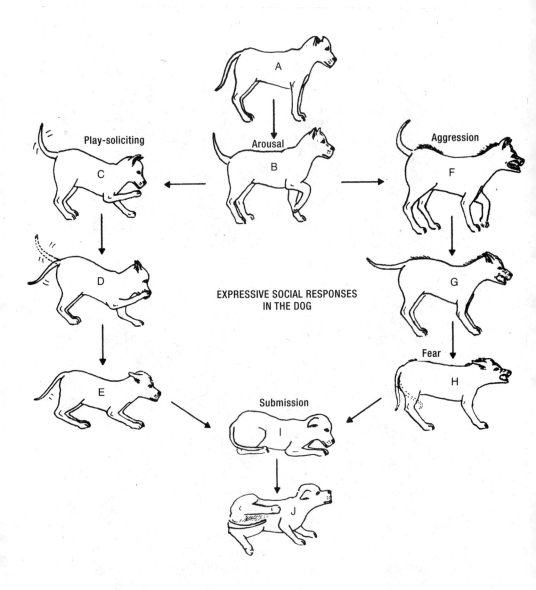

**EXPRESSIVE SOCIAL RESPONSES
IN THE DOG**

Play-soliciting

Arousal

Aggression

Fear

Submission

From an alert posture (A), a dog becomes aroused (B) with tail up, ears erect—a display of confidence. In F, a display of dominance-aggression with hackles raised and a snarl turns into defensive aggression (G–H) as tail and ears are lowered and weight shifts backward. Passive submissive displays include crouching and avoiding eye contact (I) and rolling over (J). The dog may go from aroused posture (B) into play-bow (C) to solicit play, or to display a submissive, friendly greeting (D–E).
Illustration: Foxfiles

curious, but friendly stare from a person can be misread as a threat and intimidate a dog.

One amusing misreading of signals was related to me by a lady who had a sporadic but chronic cough, especially in the evenings. When she coughed, her resting dog would alert and bark, the latter misreading his owner's signal as a warning bark! A friend of mine's dog learned to sneeze repeatedly when he wanted a treat. Therefore, when animals or people do not share the same conceptual space in a given social context, signals can be ambiguous and misunderstandings will arise. This again indicates that animals are intelligent and aware, as does their ability to mirror or mimic some of our behaviors.

Learning Dog-Speak

Dogs have a rich and varied repertoire of communication signals. Recognizing these signals will help us communicate more effectively with them and understand their intentions, needs, and emotions.

Communicating Dominance

When a dog wants to communicate dominance, she will give a direct stare, raise its shoulder hackles and tail, and walk stiffly erect, growling or pushing the lips forward into an aggressive, tight-lipped "pucker." Humans give very similar signals—we stare threateningly, stiffen up, raise our shoulders, and growl or purse our lips—so a dog can understand when we're angry or asserting our dominance.

Much of dog-human communication is facilitated by the fact that dogs and humans use several very similar nonverbal signals or *displays*. One should always give a direct stare when disciplining a dog and add a growl tone to one's voice to mimic the growl of a dominant dog.

A dog will occasionally physically dominate another by seizing and shaking the scruff of the neck. Or he may seize the other around the muzzle or cheek and pin him to the ground. These two methods—shaking (or pulling up on the leash and shaking) and pinning—are highly effective psychological ways of dominating a socially maladjusted dog. They should be used sparingly, however.

For a hyperactive or hyperaggressive pup, such gentle judo is effective in establishing dominance and in teaching the animal to be gentle. But there is never any need to strike a dog! Hyperactive pups are best treated by

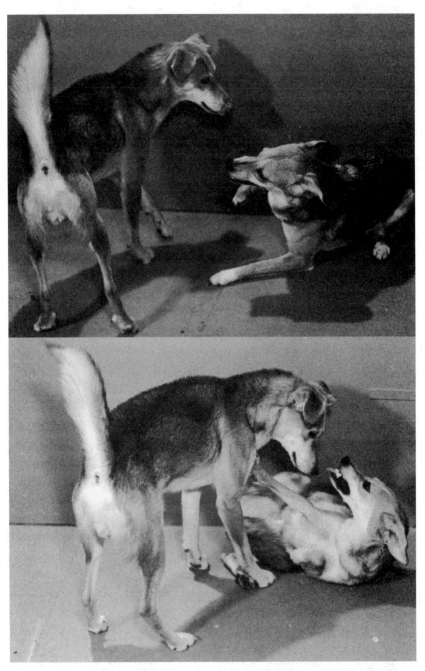

Classic canine postures of dominance, with tail up, ears forward, a direct stare and stiff, upright posture in the dog on the left; and of submission, with paw-raising, ears back, lowering of body, and eventually rolling over onto one side with defensive snarl coupled with anxious licking/extrusion of the tongue.
Photos: M. W. Fox

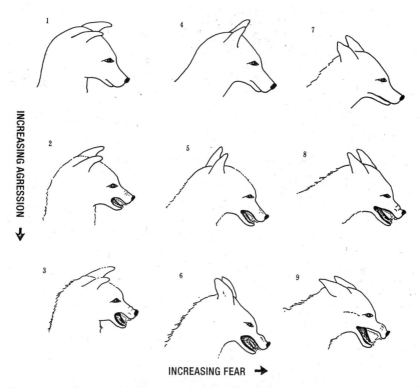

INCREASING AGGRESSION ↓

INCREASING FEAR ➡

Basic canine facial expressions: Views 1–3 show increasing aggress
direct stare; views 1, 4, and 7 show increasing fear/submission with ears back and lips pulled into
a submissive "grin." Expressions of aggression and fear/submission can be super-imposed in varying
intensities, as in 1–5–9 or 3–5–9. View 9 is the typical expression of a fear-biter.
Illustration: Foxfiles

being held firmly in one's arms and only released when they submit to the gentle restraint. This way they learn self-control. Never use a choke-chain collar and leash to dominate and control a dog; such abusive handling can make dogs more fearful and aggressive and can cause severe damage to the neck and throat.

Communicating Submission

A dog signals submission by breaking eye contact, looking away, crouching, slinking, lowering the tail and ears, and pulling the lips back horizontally into a submissive grin. Our own submissive grin is almost identical. Also, a slight backward movement of the body is given by dogs and people alike in time of fear.

Additional signals of submission include raising one fore-paw, rolling over onto one side and, especially in young dogs, releasing a little urine. Most dogs grow out of submissive urination and to punish the dog would not only be cruel: it would probably reinforce the behavior.

Greetings

All dogs will present their hindquarters as a friendly, submissive gesture. Dogs will nuzzle each other in the flank; we can mimic this simply by placing one hand gently on the dog's groin area. This is the canine equivalent of the human handshake.

The greeting display between dogs includes excited barking and yapping, jumping up and "hugging" with the forelimbs, face-oriented licking ("kissing"), and tail-wagging. Humans can reciprocate this hug with a large dog, and most dog owners return "kisses" one way or another. Face-to-face contact does have obvious health risks, and children should not be encouraged to let a pup kiss them all over until the animal is clear of worms and otherwise in good health.

When two dogs meet and investigate each other, one remains still while the other sniffs. Remaining still is a show of canine good manners,

A typical canine display of friendly submission entails rolling over onto one side, a submissive grin with ears back, and raising the upper hind leg to invite groin/inguinal contact. In assuming an open, vulnerable posture, this dog is displaying absolute trust.
Photo: M. W. Fox

which people should respect. If a strange dog comes over to investigate, it is advisable to remain still. A sudden movement, especially running off, may make the other dog chase and even attack. Children should be instructed accordingly.

Invitation to Play
A dog tells when she wants to play by extending her front legs and "bowing" with a bright-eyed, open-mouth play-face expression. She may also bark, pant excitedly (equivalent to human laughter), and skip backward and forward. A person, especially a child, mimicking these actions—bowing, panting, and grinning—will establish immediate rapport with a friendly and familiar dog.

The Tail of the Dog

To deny animals consciousness and intentionality can lead to the absurdly mechanistic and reductionistic interpretations of their behaviors, which one can find in scientific journals and in some books that purport to increase our understanding of animals. The reductionist end point of mechanomorphizing is to believe that the tail wags the dog. The other end point of ignorance is superstition. Some rural Americans believe that cutting off a roaming dog's tail and burying the tail in the backyard will make the dog stay at home. Feeding dogs gunpowder, they claim, will make the dogs mean. Masai pastoralists in Tanzania told me that they cropped some dogs' ears to make them fierce. I recall reading about a veterinarian in New York City in the 1970s who cropped the lips of Doberman pincher guard-dogs to give them a more fearsome look.

Of course, most veterinarians would never mutilate a dog's face in this way, though many still crop dog ears, puppy tails, and declaw cats. There are veterinarians, such as those with the American Association of Veterinarians for Animals Rights, who are seeking to make painful ear-cropping and declawing illegal. Many, including myself, are also opposed to docking dogs' tails because the tail is so important to dogs as a means of communication.

I always taught my students to try to put themselves in the animal's place. Certainly this would be impossible if animals were irrational, unfeeling machines. One way to begin was to start observing how animals behave and what they do (and how and why in various situations). Dog tail-wagging was a good start for them to learn to observe and interpret animal behavior.

Dogs' Scent-Lines: Understanding Canine Urine Markings

Dogs have their own scent-lines. Male dogs mark areas with less of their urine and many times more often than female dogs. Females puddle a lot in squats, rather than squirt a little like the boys do. The boys have to calculate how to make a bladderful of urine go around the neighborhood so that there is enough for all habitual marking spots, and new ones that must be made over, or aside, the marks of others dogs. The boys also mark new spots that are needed if a new terrain is explored for the first time. Sometimes the boys run out of urine before their walkabout is over. Then they engage in shadow-urination, the sometimes amusing habit male dogs have of lifting their legs to urinate after their bladders are empty. They also engage in marking for other reasons that only dogs know best.

My three dogs Batman, Xylo, and Lizzie have taught me a lot about their scent-lines in both familiar and unfamiliar terrain. All three have been spayed and neutered. Lizzie comes from Jamaica, and Xylo and Batman from India. They are quite territorial, marking more often when close to our home, especially when another dog has been by and they scent his or her mark.

Each mark is a signature of a dog's sex, personal identity, and probably the dog's emotional and motivational states, intentions, and overall health and age.

My female dog Lizzie often carefully urinates over where Xylo has made her mark. Does this make Lizzie the boss over Xylo, or is Lizzie telling boy Batman that she is with Xylo, so look out! Lizzie never marks over Batman's little squirts.

All three of my dogs scrape the ground with their hind feet, kicking the dirt backward toward where they have marked. I interpret this behavior as laying down a very clear arrow on the ground, which includes scent from the dogs' paws, pointing out to other dogs that may pass by exactly where they have marked.

Dogs urinate more often when they are sick, as with degenerative kidney disease and diabetes, and mark more often when they are insecure and need to reassure or assert themselves. For example, a German shepherd mix of a friend of mine cocks his leg and urinates on her boyfriend's legs, clothes, and baggage!

I wish for a cool, moist night and for my nose to be like a dog's from dusk to dawn! Maybe I'd lose my mind and come to my senses. So I try to be patient when my dogs are on their evening walk and respect my dogs' need to read the fine print multi-markings of countless other dogs, including themselves, placed in the same spot over many seasons. Whatever they are deciphering seems to be very important, if not also highly enjoyable: the essence of canine social-chemistry, I'm sure.

I would say that a dog's ability to wag his tails is inborn. Instinct determines how they wag their tails when they are being playful, submissive, assertive, or when they are generally excited—but not entirely. Otherwise the intensity—frequency, amplitude, and duration—of the tail wag would be a mechanical constant and never vary. But it does vary from context to context, and in terms of who the animal is communicating with. The variation is due to conscious modulation, when a mother dog wags the tip of her tail for one of her pups to catch; and to emotional influences, such as love and fear, that the animal—while in such an affective state—is not necessarily consciously aware of wagging her tail; and to social influences like allegiance, dominance, and subordination that often involve complex learning rather than simple conditioning; and to the ability to recognize others as individuals and understand their emotional states and intentions. How, to whom, and when and why dogs wag their tails therefore entails both instinct and learning, and also consciousness (or mindfulness) and emotion. This is a long way from René Descartes' interpretation of the behavior of dogs on the vivisectors' laboratory tables. Some of these dogs certainly wagged their tails. They were fully conscious but were not conscious of the reason for their suffering, if reason there was.

Now scientific rationalists would say, how can you prove that tails are important to dogs? They would call for experimental investigations and empirical evidence. Scientists would amputate dog tails, give prosthetic ones to already docked ones, and amputate puppy tails at different ages, even implanting electrodes into brain regions that regulate the wagging of the tail. This would all be called justified and sanctified by science's hollow mantra "knowledge for knowledge's sake" to determine if removal, replacement, and artificial stimulation of dogs' tails affected their communication, social behavior, and relationships.

Tail Play

The canine and feline species come naturally with a tail, a highly evolved, biologically adaptive organ of expression, communication, and intention. I once observed two Arctic foxes playing together. Their full bushy tails, that they would tuck their faces into to keep warm in the bitter winter Tundra nights, played a major role in their play-fighting. Their contact sport was a ritualized dance of chasing, wrestling, leaping, and biting—gaping and gargle-screaming, panting, grinning, and bowing, with tails up vertically or arched over their backs.

Tanza rolls over and solicits little Lizzie to attack playfully, then playfully attacks her, later engaging in a sustained tug-of-war with a sock.

Photos: M. W. Fox

One would rush at her partner and at the last moment twist and whisk her tail across his face. This was his cue to grab her tail, and only then would she take off and then literally have a tug-of-war wrestling match with her mate for her tail. They took turns, each using the other's tail as an object of play, a social tool-using behavior, where the tail was a catalyst for fox fun and games. A mother cat will tease her kittens, inciting them to attack the tip of her tail that she twitches to get them to respond, possibly to activate their natural hunting instinct, and to learn self-control because they will be disciplined if they bite too hard! Dogs will often use a rag or sock as a pull-toy instead of their tails.

I am surprised and saddened that many scientists are such doubting Thomases that they have interpreted the play behavior of dogs, cats, and other animals in purely instrumental terms (reflecting a mechanistic orientation) contending, for example, that through play, puppies and kittens are simply learning how to improve their fighting and hunting abilities and establish dominance. There is no place or space in this orientation or paradigm for considering the possibility that animals play together because they enjoy it. Of course, there are other benefits from social play: not only physical exercise, but also establishing and maintaining affectionate ties and reinforcing social rank. There is also an element of creativity as animals make up new games, sometimes using inanimate objects as toys, and orchestrate variations in the frequency and duration of various actions and sequences. There are also role reversals, as when a socially dominant dog or cat allows a subordinate to playfully "kill" him or mount him.

Observing dogs at play, and identifying and describing various actions and displays (like play bow, face-snap, open-mouth play-face) and then making shorthand notes to document the content of a bout of play between two or more dogs was one of my more popular student assignments.

Some who first see dogs or cats at play think they are acting aggressively. One student, house-sitting for my two cats, called me while I was on vacation in panic as to what he should do the first night with them because he thought they were going to kill each other. I explained to him that they did this most nights; they were play-fighting, and this was their "evening crazies." I have seen more than one novice dog owner in our local dog park protectively intervening when their dogs got into rough play-fighting, thinking that the dogs were actually fighting. Some purported dog behavior experts follow the reductionist path of interpreting play-fighting merely as a way of asserting social dominance and rank and of testing other dogs'

Play has a bonding function, and these two dog buddies playfully attack each other with conscious control of bite intensity, enjoying a bout of "jaw wrestling."
Photo: M. W. Fox

strength. More will be said later of an almost cultish adherence of some interpreters of dog behavior and sociality to the following view: That almost all dog-dog and dog-human interactions are based on dominance and submission, as seen in the rigid hierarchy and rules of the wolf pack, the domestic dog being regarded as a degenerate, infantilized descendant of wolves.

But just as when young boys are playing together and things start to fall apart and a fight erupts, so it is with dogs at play. This is especially true with young adults, usually male and often neutered dogs between eighteen to thirty-six months of age. Sometimes dogs that are normally best buddies will get into a serious fight that may well result in one or both dogs requiring veterinary attention. But the next day such dogs are good buddies again and engage in their usual rough and tumble play-wrestling and running/ chasing, catch-me-if-you-can games. If these altercations were simply linked with assertion of dominance and social rank, then one would expect these dogs, after their fights, to display dominance and submission according to who won. On the contrary, they greet each other as equals.

Dog Fights

Sometimes even dog to dog communications break down. I once witnessed a fight between best buddies in our local park—two large neutered males, both mixed-breed and about eighteen months old. It was a wild and noisy fight, both dogs growling, yelping, snapping, rolling, and smashing each other into parked cars for some time until they were exhausted enough to let their screaming human companions pull them apart. I told the people later that their yelling and protective agitation helped to incite their dogs further, making each dog react as though their people were egging them on.

Egging on is a very dog-pack thing that ethologists call social facilitation. A dramatic example of this is when a couple of dogs start picking on a third, playing too roughly and frightening her, and she starts to yelp, cringe, and display defensive aggression and submission. Quickly, other dogs will join in, including pups, all taking turns to nip at the victim who is being treated like prey cornered by the pack.

This is the one aspect of dog behavior that I don't like and one I see in my own far-less-virtuous species: street gangs and schoolyard gangs. I was once a victim of such a gang and felt like hunted prey.

During these ganging-up attacks on other dogs—that are not strangers to the group—one can see another feature of "agonistic" behavior, and this is called redirected aggression. This is when one of the attacking pack is too scared to bite or snap at the victim and so turns and bites or snaps at a gang member. Redirected aggression can turn a relatively coordinated pack-attack into a melee where gang members start fighting amongst themselves. The victim may then be able to slink away unscathed.

Redirected aggression is often seen in human-human interactions: a spouse has a bad day at work and gets chewed out by the boss, then goes home and kicks the dog and takes it out on his or her partner and children.

Breaking Up a Dog Fight

Although your dog is probably easygoing, chances are that sooner or later he or she will get into a scrap. You can take measures to prevent dog fights, such as neutering a belligerent male to reduce his aggressiveness, giving your dogs obedience training, or not allowing them to roam free. Nevertheless, fights do occasionally erupt, usually over territory, or in males, especially over a female in heat. If you know what to do, you can keep your dog—and yourself—from getting hurt.

The best ways to break up a dog fight is not to yell and panic, but to stay calm, throw a bucket of water over them in the yard (or a jacket or coat), and for each person, if they are physically able, to grab the tail and hind leg of their dogs at the same time, pull them apart and get them leashed.

Most important rule: Never pick up your dog when he's fighting. You then become the object of the other dog's fury and are likely to get bitten, even by your own dog as he tries to defend himself.

If the attacking dog is larger than yours and seems vicious, or if the dog is smaller and could get hurt, hold your dog's leash tightly and yell at the adversary, staring threateningly and raising one arm as though you were holding a rock or stick. If your dog is frequently attacked when you take him for a walk, you may want to carry a walking stick with you, which you can try to insert into the attacker's mouth. Do not beat the dog. Pain could make the dog even more aggressive.

While you should always keep your dog on a leash, you should be aware that a dog on a leash is more aggressive since you are now part of his territory. Being leashed may also make the dog feel more vulnerable. If the rival dog is about the same size as yours and ignores your commands to stay away, drop the leash, especially if there is no one around to pull the other dog off. Then let them interact. More often, the dogs won't fight. If there is a fight, the fighting is often highly ritualized with growling, rearing back and snapping at each other's scruffs, and neither dog gets hurt.

The Language of Scent

Perfume can be an ambiguous signal, especially for animals with a very sensitive sense of smell. Dogs, for example, are sometimes clearly disturbed, and sometimes even sexually aroused, by certain perfumes and aftershave lotions their owners put on. What signals might they really be giving to their pets, one may well wonder!

Interestingly, many dogs have perfumed areas on their furry heads, cheeks, groins, and sometimes diffusely over their entire bodies, the precise function of which has yet to be determined. Owners have told me that their dogs smell like baby powder on the top of the head or all over, or like butterscotch on the temples. One woman found her dog's baby powder–like smell gentle and soothing to her. Possibly such natural odors of pheromones convey information to other animals of the wearer's identity, emotional state,

My dog Lizzie invites over a husky cross at their off-leash park with a flop-over display of submission, finds a stick, and invites him to chase her and try to grab it. They then become buddies and the larger dog lets the smaller one embrace and play-bite.
Photos: M. W. Fox

and personality. French scientists have isolated the pheromones from the skin scent glands of cats and from around the breast skin of nursing dogs and have found that dispensing these aromas to their respective species can help reduce some behavioral problems, especially those associated with loneliness and separation anxiety. (Better to get another animal, in my mind, instead of a comforting yet ghostly vapor!)

Stroking a dog is akin to one dog grooming another. Playfully but gently pawing her head or pretending to catch her tail (especially if she is playfully twitching it for you) are play actions one dog will do to another. Many of these species-characteristic actions and signals we mimic with our dogs because they are part of our own repertoire—but also because the dog "teaches" us (or shapes and reinforces our behavior) to use certain signals in preference to others, by virtue of their appropriateness and effectiveness.

Shared Language

Even without further documentary evidence, it is obvious that animals have a very sophisticated sense of awareness and undoubtedly a much higher degree of consciousness than we might think. They know their own "language"—elements of which are shared with other species, including us— and they can learn, as in the case of a domestic animal, to understand and sometimes mimic the other's communication. It is fascinating, for example, to observe a dog and a horse, or a cat and a dog, relating with each other.

Harvard University anthropologist Dr. Brian Hare recently reported that compared to highly intelligent chimpanzees and wolves, domesticated dogs far outperform these wild species in learning to interpret human gestures, such as being signaled where food has been hidden. This superior ability of dogs, which leads some people to feel their dogs can read their minds (because of unconscious signals being given to the dog), has been honed over thousands of years of living with people and being subject to artificial selection.

When learning about an animal's communication repertoire, the human observer becomes increasingly sensitive to very subtle signals that might not otherwise be recognized as being of any significance. Your dog simply turning and looking briefly in one direction can be a general but context-specific signal that may mean "Look over there," "Follow me," or "My water bowl is empty." When a human being does not correctly interpret the meaning of such subtle signals because he or she is unable to understand the context, the animal must experience some frustration and wonder if the human companion is the dumb one.

For example, a dog that woke its owner up by whining and pawing on the bedroom door was immediately put outside to relieve herself. The woman hadn't paused to ask the dog, "What do you want?" and then waited to see if the dog would lead her to the door to be let out (as she usually did). After the dog was allowed in again and continued to whine, the owner eventually, after some recriminations, discovered what was disturbing the dog: she was intensely thirsty and was suffering from an illness, which her veterinarian later said could have been aggravated further if the dog had been deprived of water for an extended period.

A heightened sensitivity toward animals' signals will also be transferred to one's relationships with people, giving an added depth of awareness to the subtleties of human communication. Shifts in posture, in eye contact, and gesture emphasis while speaking and being spoken to as well as tension in the shoulders, nervous swallowing, fist-clenching, and self-clasping will be noted with greater clarity—affording more effective interpersonal relatedness through empathetic understanding.

Becoming a Student of Dog Language

I have been fortunate to have spent much of my life with dogs and to have been able to observe their behavior and development from controlled laboratory environments and animal shelters to the less controllable, if not more real, natural environments of the home, my local dog park, and our animal refuge in India. Located in the Nilgiris, in South India, my wife has a resident pack of some thirty local "country" dogs. The animal refuge is an ethologist's dream because these animals are free to interact with each other, with new dogs in recovery from sickness and injury, and also with other species: a herd of nearly a hundred donkeys; a half-dozen ponies and horses; and several cattle, calves, goats, sheep, water buffalo, orphaned monkeys, and fawns.

I have found it particularly instructive to observe how dogs communicate with other species and with other injured animals. Some are simply curious, others are afraid or ready to attack, while a few are especially concerned, protective, and clearly empathetic; they actually provide comfort to new animals coming into the refuge, speed their recovery from sickness or injury, and help them settle down in this new environment.

An attentive young adult Bonnet macaque monkey, showing compassion and concern, comforts an orphaned infant monkey being treated for an electrical burn.
Photo: M. W. Fox

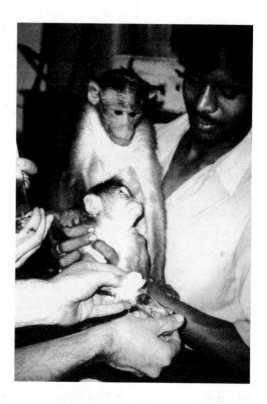

As Professor Nikko Tinbergen, another Nobel Laureate and founding father of ethology, said, "Every time you have two animals together, you have an experiment."

But my best teachers have been the dogs themselves. When I first began to study their behavior, I made the novice's mistake of being an intense observer instead of being a seemingly indifferent bystander. My behavior made some dogs apprehensive; being observed meant being looked at, and that is very threatening to some dogs. Since I was raised with dogs and spent more time with them than with my own kind as a child, I was surprised when I was bitten by a dog in the veterinary hospital. I had been staring at him while the senior veterinarian was in conversation with the dog's guardian. The dog made eye contact with me and I locked eyes with him but remained otherwise motionless and expressionless. I was just beginning to learn how dogs use their eyes to communicate with each other. In the "eye language" of dogs, as I soon after deduced, the look I gave this dog was an extremely threatening, challenging signal.

Some years later, I gave this same stare and hunched my shoulders slightly forward to a very large malamute. I was having lunch with my first PhD student, Marc Bekoff. His dog leapt at me and grabbed my arm; I moved it as though he was shaking it and made some sounds as though I was being hurt. Marc leapt from his chair to intervene and I laughed as his dog let go of my arm and pranced around the table barking, bowing, and wildly wagging his tail.

Certainly it appeared to Marc that his dog had launched an unprovoked attack on his professor. Marc was quite upset until I told him that before I locked eyes with his dog and raised my shoulders slightly (both threatening actions), I had caught his gaze, grinned, and gave a couple of pants, which is a dog play signal, meaning what is to follow isn't serious—like staring, snapping, leaping, and so forth.

Soon Marc was recording behavior patterns, signals, and sequences as he observed my wild and domestic canid research associates: foxes, coyotes, beagles, wolves, and wolf-dog and coyote-dog hybrids. As Marc discovered, once you learn the rudiments of canid body-language communication, you can "talk dog" to some degree, being able to let dogs know your intentions and feelings and being able to understand theirs.

* * *

The time is ripe for people to break through the species barrier and learn to relate more effectively with their animal companions by observing and mimicking their behavior. For too long, perhaps, animals in our homes have sat around learning all our nuances, signals, and direct commands: let's equalize things and establish real two-way communication.

Intelligent Thinking and Insight

For those who believe animals lack the vestiges not only of human feeling but also of insight, reasoning, and foresight, the following examples of such capacity in dogs should dispell such ignorance and prejudice.

- *Insight.* A dog sees its owner setting cookies out on the high kitchen counter and moving a stool away from the counter so the dog can't get up. The owner comes back later and finds the stool pushed back to the counter and all the cookies gone.

- *Reasoning.* A dog sees its owner break ice in his water bowl with an old boot. The next morning, the owner finds ice broken by the dog and boot in the water bowl.

- *Foresight.* A dog becomes restless every evening during the week around 6:00 p.m., around the time his owner comes home. The dog becomes agitated and hides under the bed when the wife packs her suitcase.

I have long held the belief that animals do experience guilt and remorse. But again, people who *mechanomorphize* animals—see and even treat them as if they were unfeeling machines—believe otherwise. They believe animals don't have any conscience or moral sensibility, yet we have all seen the guilt on our dogs' faces when they have messed in the house during our absence. Such apparent guilt or remorse may be compounded by fear/anxiety over the owner's anticipated reactions. Pure guilt/remorse/concern may be evidenced by some dogs, but not by others that seem indifferent or lacking any "conscience."

My funniest anecdote is of the old Doberman who, on two occasions when he defecated in the house downstairs (which was almost a unique occurrence in itself), covered the mess with a blanket he pulled off one of the beds upstairs. He acted as though nothing had happened when the owners came home but became apprehensive when the blanket was lifted!

And what of the dog in New Zealand who, in 1992, saved his master's life by bringing water to the man? The man had just had a stroke in bed and was badly paralyzed. The dog kept soaking a towel in the toilet for several days, then took the towel to the man who sucked it and was rescued after many days to tell his tale!

A farmer told me the story of a tame coyote he kept in a kennel on a long chain, where it could do no damage. When, over a period of time, a number of his chickens mysteriously disappeared, he became suspicious. Hiding out near the barn, he saw the coyote take some of its own food and some corn cob (from a stored cache). The coyote put them out at the end of the chain, then ran back into the kennel and waited in hiding for its prey. No human hunter using bait could have shown more reasoned insight.

The ability to reason entails making logical associations. Recently a sheltie named Muffin went on a short plane ride. The trip must have been very unpleasant for her, because now, any time a plane flies over her home, Muffin has an anxiety attack, barking and racing all over the place until the plane has gone. Such associative phobias are common in animals. One of my friends has a dog that starts to whimper when she puts on perfume. The reason? From past experience, the dog knows its owner is going out for the evening.

Do animals sit and wonder or worry about things as we do? That is difficult to know, since they can't speak, but it is quite clear when a dog or cat is anxious or apprehensive. They will also have nightmares, crying and running in their sleep after a particularly traumatic day, such as being attacked by another animal or after an upsetting trip to see the veterinarian.

Playful Insights

Child psychologists learn much about children's emotional state, imagination, and creativity from observing them at play. Likewise, closely observing how an animal companion plays with toys can provide similar insights into the psyche. Here are some examples for you to interpret, followed by my own interpretations.

1. A dog carries a sock or another toy all over the house, is highly protective of the object, and "hides" it in a closet or buries it under a carpet or a pillow.

2. A dog adopts an old slipper a few weeks after coming out of heat, becomes very protective of it, even sleeps with it.

3. A dog brings out all its toys when visitors come, chews and paws them vigorously, but growls protectively when approached.

4. A dog brings a sock or another toy to you; but instead of placing it at your feet or in your lap, drops it some distance from you and then walks away and sits staring at you.

5. A dog brings a favorite toy to a houseguest, places it in the guest's lap, and looks with anticipation at the guest.

My interpretations are as follows.

My dog Tanza teaches my daughter Mara that play-bites are okay because they don't hurt; mask-play for intelligent dogs like her is always fun.
Photos: M. W. Fox

1. The dog is "fantasizing" about carrying prey or food around, and hiding it.

2. The dog is having a false pregnancy, and the slipper or other toy is a puppy substitute.

3. The dog feels insecure, is jealous of the attention being given to the visitors, and needs the security of his toys.

4. The dog is training you to retrieve, or is inviting you to get the toy and have a tug-of-war, or is daring you to take it.

5. The dog is making friends—being a good ambassador and soliciting play and attention.

The more we observe our animal companions at play (and also play with them and give them suitable and safe toys to play with), the more they can communicate with us, and the more we can overcome the barrier of verbal language and learn about their psyches. The profound bonding function of play—animals that play together stay together—is critical for all who wish for a close relationship with their dogs.

Beginning at an early age, regular play sessions are as important as regular feeding, grooming, and exercise. Through play, animals learn to be gentle, develop self-control, and refine various actions associated with fighting, prey-chasing, killing, and so forth. During social play and play with a toy, they can also show a sense of humor, creativity, and imagination—as well as joy in physical contact and in various activities, such as chasing and being chased, hiding, and ambushing.

*   *   *

Professor Donald Griffin, in his controversial book *The Question of Animal Awareness*, observes that, "behavioral scientists have grown highly uncomfortable at the very thought of mental states or subjective qualities in animals. When they intrude on our scientific discourse, many of us feel sheepish, and when we find ourselves using such words as fear, pain, pleasure, or the like, we tend to shield our reductionist egos behind a respectability blanket of quotation marks."[2]

To doubt if an animal can experience pain, fear, anxiety, satisfaction, and pleasure is to doubt the very existence of our own consciousness. And to reject the possibility that our most recently evolved animal kin—the carnivores and primates—cannot or do not experience comparable states of joy, depression, guilt, remorse, and love is as illogical as denying that you or I have such experiences.

---

2. Donald Griffin, *The Question of Animal Awareness* (New York: Rockefeller University Press, 1981).

3.

Correcting Behavioral and Communication Problems

Obedience Training

All dogs should have basic obedience training. You can start as soon as you get your pup, training the pup to "Come" when you call his or her name, especially when you're ready to take the pup out for a walk and play. After eight weeks of age, the pup can be taught to "Sit" and know what "No" means when the pup bites too hard.

Always be consistent with both praise and discipline. Never let your dog get away with anything or, eventually, the dog may become top dog in the house and therefore uncontrollable. Basic obedience training helps dogs develop self-control, to learn what behaviors are acceptable, and to learn the boundaries of unacceptable behavior.

All dogs should be taught to "Stay" and should understand the command "Down," to facilitate handling them when crossing the road and to control overly enthusiastic greeting, jumping, and barking. Anyone with a large dog, especially of a protective guard-dog breed, should attend obedience school.

Naturally Bothersome, but not Serious, Behaviors

There are many aspects of dog behavior that seem odd to us but are natural to dogs. Dogs have emotions similar to ours; they can experience and express pain, fear, anxiety, depression, guilt, happiness, playful humor, anger, submission, and affection. But while they have some moral sense of right and wrong and can reason to some extent, and sometimes show remarkable empathy and insight, they are still dogs and often seem to act irrationally. This is because they also act out of natural instincts. Some instinctual reactions can be a source of annoyance to owners, and can even be regarded as abnormal or perverse behavior.

Pups often engage in sex play, mounting and clasping another pup (even of the same sex) or a person. They are not homosexuals or sex maniacs. They are simply acting naturally. Such behavior that can sometimes lead to fighting can be inhibited by simple discipline, such as making the pup sit and stay, or by cradling (see p. 46).

I was bemused by the man in my local dog park in Washington, D.C., who would get very upset and say "It's disgusting" when my East Indian village dog Batman engaged in sex play, mounting and thrusting against the man's sheltie. But both these neutered males clearly liked each other immensely—greeting each other excitedly every time they met, before they engaged in racing, chasing together, and the contact sport of sex play instead of the more usual wrestling and fight play.

Our expectations of how dogs ought to behave are often based on a lack of behavioral understanding and biased by anthropomorphic comparisons, values, and judgments. Crotch-sniffing dogs notwithstanding, the ways of animals can be inspiring, educational, and sometimes highly amusing. This occurs when they are free to be themselves and their ways are not grossly distorted by human interference and abuse. (Especially horrible is selectively breeding and training them to fight and kill, or be killed. This is one of the greatest perversions of the dog-human relationship; it is worse than raising dogs for food and killing them for their skins—which in some Eastern countries is a common practice today.) As with most spontaneous canine behaviors that essentially do no harm—except perhaps to some dubious fundamentalist moral sensibility—my attitude is to let be and let's see. Unbiased observation, devoid of either prejudice or expectation, can lead to greater wisdom. As for dog trainers who would discipline pups for engaging in sex play (which can be a first step to assertion of dominance and a possible fight), again, I would say back off and wait and see. Too much control can spoil a dog's spirit—just as it can a child's.

The one thing I especially liked about the late dog trainer and TV celebrity Barbara Woodhouse, a fellow Brit, was her enthusiasm: it was contagious to her canine students and their owners. Make learning fun! What a contrast to the old school of domination and control. The lack of empathy shown by many dog trainers can lead to cruelty and much animal suffering.

The first step I take with a healthy dog, in order to get to know him or her, is to solicit play after showing friendly intent and allowing the animal to first sniff me, as I encourage close contact by squatting and remaining passive and nonthreatening—even avoiding eye contact with very shy dogs and those that react to my presence with fear and defensive-aggression.

I avoid overtly and directly aggressive dogs, leaving such potential canine psychopaths (often with a history of abuse) to remedial care. That care entails the most judicious approach of offering food, water, security, and a quiet environment, and later toys, grooming, walks on a leash, and short-term medication with psychotropic drugs and pheromone therapy coupled with the company of an easygoing dog (if the aggression problem is not dog-directed).

Aggressive dogs that have become so because they have been over-indulged and are engaging in dominance-aggression rather than full-blown attack behavior are more easily dealt with not by intimidation and domination, but by playful redirection, remotivation, and, if small and easy to handle, by cradling, as described on page 46.

A well-socialized dog, properly raised during the first few critical weeks of social and emotional development, should never develop serious behavioral problems unless he or she has been mistreated or misread, or has an inherent, often inherited quirk in temperament such as timidity, attention-deficit disorder, hyperactivity, and aggressivity. One of the most potent ways to discipline a dog is what I call *shame and shun*. If a dog steals something off the coffee table, for instance, stand up and shame the dog in a chastizing, growly voice, and then point your arm in the direction you want the dog to go and say, "Go away now." Then ignore the dog for five to ten minutes, then call the dog over and make up.

When dogs chase and nip at joggers, cyclists, and automobiles, dogs are not expressing aggression but rather a natural prey-chasing reaction. When two or more dogs are active together, their pack instinct is awakened—making them more strongly motivated to chase and even attack. Obedience training will usually control this instinct.

Nearly all dogs like to roll in obnoxious and smelly materials. Being so smell-oriented, wearing a novel odor may give them pleasure as well as an aesthetic kick! A little perfume or aftershave lotion on the dog will often satisfy and therefore inhibit its need to roll.

Another natural behavior that can be a problem is the male dog's (and tomcat's) drive to be free and roam the neighborhood in search of females. Sometimes, they are searcing for males to fight. Neutering will greatly reduce this drive, lessen the animal's frustration, and make him easier to control.

Dogs kept in backyards often like to dig holes to alleviate boredom. Sometimes, however, they're making themselves cool pits to lie in during the summer. Dogs that spend a lot of time outdoors should be provided with toys, exercise, water, and shade.

Grass eating is a natural instinct in both cats and dogs. The grass probably helps clean out the digestive system by stimulating vomiting, and it is not necessarily a sign that the animal is sick or has worms.

Coprophagia (stool eating) is likewise not necessarily a sign of worms; nor is it likely to cause the dog to get worms. It is most often a vice that needs some disciplining. But in some instances, the behavior reflects a nutritional deficiency. A change in diet to one that is more complete in nutrients and of top quality, giving the dog B-complex vitamins and/or a multivitamin and multimineral supplement, or sometimes unpasteurized yogurt or acidophilus pills, sees an end to this behavior.

Many dogs will eat soil and rotting wood on occasion, possibly finding a source of natural nutrients missing in their regular diets that may well need supplementing with essential trace minerals, such as zinc and selenium and vitamin B complex.

On his own territory, a dog is usually dominant over all intruding dogs (dogs seem to respect the other's territorial rights). Dogs will therefore naturally defend their territory or home-base against strange dogs and people by barking and/or attacking. Owners should be aware of this and control their dogs through obedience training and physical restraint, if necessary.

Male dogs especially like to mark their territory with urine. This is analogous to leaving a calling card for other dogs. Scraping the ground afterward is not a burying action: it is the dog's way of leaving an additional visual mark in the torn-up ground.

Often, when female dogs are not bred after they come into heat, they will go into what is called a false or pseudo-pregnancy. They may look pregnant and will behave protectively toward a favorite toy or adopted slipper. Some dogs will even go through false labor! This psychological distress is best prevented by having the bitch spayed.

More Serious Dog Behavior Problems

Although the above-mentioned problems are sometimes a nuisance, they are nonetheless natural to dogs. But there are other more serious behavior problems. Understanding these can help in their prevention and treatment and give a deeper appreciation of the fact that animals, just like humans, can have psychological problems and suffer emotionally.

Aggressive Behavior

For serious problems such as aggression toward other dogs or other people, I strongly advise a referral from the veterinarian for a behavioral therapist—after the dog has had a thorough medical examination for a possible physical cause. Older dogs can become more irritable and aggressive when they are suffering from a chronic, painful condition such as arthritis or have hypothyroidism.

It is important to distinguish between *defensive aggression*, or fear-biting; *dominance aggression*, which is common in adolescent dogs resisting control by their owners and wanting to have their own way; and overt *directed aggression* toward other dogs (sometimes after an altercation with a particular breed, which can become generalized toward all dogs of that breed) and toward certain people, especially "territory-intruding" delivery and home-service people.

Techniques of desensitization, behavior modification, and basic obedience training may be employed by experienced dog trainers/therapists to correct this most common behavioral problem in dogs, which only too often results in dogs being put up for adoption or euthanized. Since prevention is the best medicine, proper socialization and handling early in life can be the best insurance against later problems of aggressive behavior in its various forms. One technique that I call *cradling*, described below, is especially useful.

Cradling Therapy and Training

Simply cradling a puppy in one's arms is part of the process of animal socialization that is as gentle as it is profound. Puppies and dogs soon learn to accept being picked up and gently held in one's arms without struggling, and they learn to enjoy the intimacy and security of close physical contact.

Submitting to and accepting such handling is integral to effective and proper socialization or bonding with the human caregiver. It greatly facilitates subsequent training and communication. If and when the animal struggles while being cradled, the gentle embrace becomes firm resistance that immediately softens and yields as soon as the animal ceases to struggle, begins to relax, accepts cradling restraint, and starts to trust.

This gentle psycho-physical "judo" can help in the behavior modification of adult, hyperactive, snappy, poorly socialized companion animals—often with a history of being overindulged and having no sense of boundaries and limited self-control.

Cradling conditions the animal to accept restraint, to develop what the Russian scientist Pavlov called *internal inhibition* or self-restraint; above all, it helps the animal to develop the kind of trust that is the keystone for a strong, sustaining human-animal bond.

The Home Wrecker

The left-at-home dog is a very common problem today. Out of boredom and frustration, he will bark and whine excessively, become unhousebroken, and turn into a house wrecker—chewing and tearing up furniture, books, drapes, etc. People who go out to work all day should think twice before getting a dog, since many dogs do not adapt to being left alone each day.

Getting a companion pet, leaving the radio on, or hiring a day sitter or dog-walking service are possible solutions. Training the dog to accept being

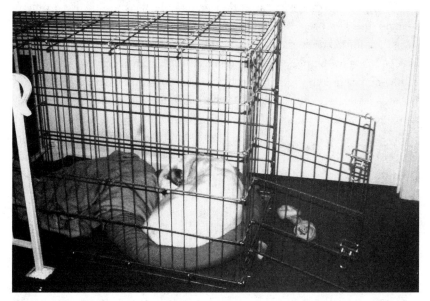

Dogs should never be confined in a crate much of the day, except for medical reasons. Early crate training can lead to dogs enjoying the open crate as their "den," and can help them cope better with separation anxiety.
Photo: M. W. Fox

confined in a large dog crate is a popular method to prevent home wrecking. But keeping the dog in a small crate all day is inhumane and unacceptable.

Proper crate use should be a pleasurable experience. When crate training, the dog or puppy should be fed occasionally in the crate, which should be left open when the animal is not alone. When done correctly, the crate becomes the dog's den—a place of security that helps it cope with separation anxiety when left alone, during which time the crate is closed.

Young dogs who are teething and want to chew things and are anxious and bored when left alone can be very destructive. Crate confinement for two to three hours maximum is acceptable. Again, no dog should be confined all day in a crate.

As pups mature, they usually don't need to be locked in a crate. If they have been correctly trained, they will see the open crate as a den in adulthood.

The Jealous Dog

A new pet (or a new baby or spouse) can create other problems: jealousy and rivalry. Many dogs will sulk, stop eating, and act aggressively when they feel that a newcomer is threatening their security and taking attention from them. Giving the dog extra attention generally solves the rivalry problem. Getting the dog prepared for a new baby ahead of time is a good idea. A life-size doll that cries and can be swaddled and held will help both dogs and cats get used to the presence of a real live baby in the home at a later date. When taking in a new dog or puppy, let the dogs first meet on neutral territory—a park, a neighbor's yard—otherwise the resident dog may jealously guard his territory. He should be reassured with plenty of love and care.

The Neurotic Dog

Because dogs are such astute observers of their owner's behavior and moods, they frequently get the upper hand and they can manipulate their caretakers in order to get their way. Some will refuse regular food and eat only what they like (which may not be healthy) or protest being disciplined by urinating or defecating on the rug or bed. Some dogs act sick—by pretending to be lame, for example—in order to get their owner's undivided attention.

To be certain the dog is not being manipulative, a veterinarian must rule out physical disease and make a thorough differential diagnosis. Dogs will also develop psychosomatic disorders—asthmatic-like attacks, seizures, excessive scratching, and diarrhea—as a result of emotional stress. The loss of a companion (human or animal) can depress a dog so acutely, he may refuse to eat.

The Poorly Raised Dog

Other serious problems can arise when owners do not raise their dogs correctly. An owner who is inconsistent in discipline and erratic in moods and behavior will often end up with a neurotic, unstable dog.

Indulging a dog excessively and catering to every whim and whine will make him either an overdependent hypochondriac or a spoiled brat that sulks or snaps when he doesn't get his own way. And overpermissive rearing (with no discipline or obedience training) will often produce a canine delinquent. Such dogs rule their owners and may even attack them as well as well-meaning strangers (including veterinarians) whenever they feel that their dominance status is being challenged.

Improper rearing may aggravate inborn temperamental peculiarities, which are a product of bad breeding. Hyperactivity, shyness, hyper-aggressiveness, and fear-biting, for example, can be partially remedied by more careful selective breeding. Prospective dog owners should be advised to locate a local, reputable breeder and see the pup's mother and father, if possible, before they make their decision. They should also consider adopting a mixed breed or "natural" dog from the local humane society, since such dogs are generally more resilient and stable than those that have been highly inbred.

Fear of Thunderstorms

Dogs (and to a lesser degree, cats) are often afraid of thunderstorms. Their thunder phobia can be so intense that the animal panics and, if left untended, may do damage to your home. The solutions include understanding and simple behavior-modification techniques.

If your dog reacts with fear but not hysteria during a thunderstorm, put him or her in a relatively quiet place, such as a basement, or play a battery operated tape recorder or CD player with loud music to mask the sound outside (a radio will probably crackle during a storm, exacerbating your pet's fear). Placing a blanket over the dog can be extremely calming.

If your dog becomes extremely upset during thunderstorms, have your veterinarian prescribe a tranquilizer to quiet your dog. Xanax (Alpralozam) is especially effective if given about half an hour before a storm or Fourth of July fireworks are set off.

If tranquilizers don't work, try making a recording of heavy rain or thunder next time there is a storm. Or, you may be able to find prerecorded tapes of rainfall. Then gradually expose your dog to the recording, increasing the volume each time. Undertake these desensitizing sessions when your dog is hungry, and soothe him with food and petting to help your dog associate the storm's sounds with a pleasant experience.

Behavior Therapy for Dogs

If your dog has a disruptive emotional or behavioral problem, you may want to seek help from an animal behavior therapist. Most animal behavior therapists are well-trained professionals who perform a legitimate and valuable service. The phobias and psychological problems of pets are just as real as those of humans. These range from fear of strangers (or of ringing doorbells and telephones), to depression, anorexia, and self-mutilation.

To find a qualified animal behavior therapist, it is important to first consult with your veterinarian for a referral. Your vet will need to examine your pet before recommending a therapist, to rule out the possibility that the animal's seemingly psychological problem has an underlying physical cause. For example, a dog that becomes a fear-biter when petted may not have an emotional, anti-social problem, but an infected ear that hurts when touched. Some dogs act lame on one leg in order to get attention when there's nothing physically wrong with the leg.

The animal behavior therapist may ask for an interview with the entire family. Friction between spouses, the arrival of a new baby, or the presence of a hyperactive child can have adverse effects on a family dog. Some therapists make house calls. Others have the family and the pet come to the office. Follow-up visits are often necessary to modify the treatment. If you give your full cooperation and follow the therapist's recommendations carefully, behavior therapy is usually not long-term, and it's a good investment, since it allows you to enjoy your dog's presence more.

Psycho-Pharmaceuticals for Dogs

A variety of psychotropic drugs have proven to be beneficial for treating people with various emotional and behavioral problems, such as anxiety, depression, and obsessive-compulsive disorders. Veterinarians are discovering that these drugs can help in treating similar problems in dogs. These clinical findings support my contention that the inner world of dogs, their consciousness and emotionality, must be similar in many ways to ours—otherwise these psychotropic drugs would not result in clinical improvements that are similar in dogs and human patients.

Veterinarians are well advised to use behavioral-modification techniques such as reward training, desensitization, changing the dog's environment, and evaluating the dog-human relationships in the home before prescribing these kinds of drugs. Some have potentially harmful side effects. Then there is the ethical issue of giving drugs to dogs to help them cope with a way of life, such as being left home alone for many hours, often in a crate, during the workweek—a treatment no animal should be subject to. Turning a dog into a chemically dependent zombie is ethically untenable.

The benefits of these mind- (brain-chemistry) and behavior-altering drugs to dogs are being documented in the veterinary literature. Before the advent of these new drugs, many dogs would suffer years of distress (along with their owners), or be euthanized.

Fluoxetine (Dista's Prozac) has helped many dogs suffering from *obsessive-compulsive disorders*, including compulsive licking, pacing, tail-chasing, and self-mutilation.

Selegiline (Pfizer's Anipryl) is now being prescribed for old dogs suffering from the "old dog's disease" of disorientation and anxiety called *cognitive dysfunction syndrome*.

Amitriptylene (Zeneca's Elevil) is one of several medications that can help dogs showing *dominance aggression*, coupled with *underlying anxiety*.

Buspirone (Bristol-Myers Squibb's BuSpar) and Clomipramine (Novartis' Clomicalm) have proven beneficial to dogs suffering from *fear-related aggression*.

Separation anxiety is one of the most common emotional disorders to afflict dogs today. If behavior-modification techniques, providing another dog as a companion, or using an open crate as a safe den do not work, the treatment with any of the above drugs, or with Imipramine (Novartis' Tofranil) or Alprazolam (Pharmacia and Upjohns' Xanax) can provide significant relief for the dog, emotionally or symptomatically—which will help the distraught owners feel better as well.

I find it ethically questionable to drug a dog that is suffering from boredom and loneliness and becomes a house wrecker. Wherever possible, a dog's basic needs should be met and the environment should be changed for the dog's benefit, rather than changing the brain chemistry to help a dog adapt to a relatively deprived existence. Is it more ethical to breed dogs selectively to better adapt to such conditions? Or would they then become *virtual dogs*, dispirited facsimiles of the once-real that our children may never know, respect, and cherish—with no remnant of the wild that we recognized in their original presence?

Many behavioral and emotional problems in dogs have a complex genesis, including the animal's genetic background and basic temperament, the dog's rearing history and experiences earlier in life, and current factors in the dog's immediate environment and family relations—including other animals, as well as people in the home.

I believe the judicious use of psychotropic drugs, with careful monitoring and individual dose-adjustments, is appropriate—but only as a last resort for those conditions when behavioral counseling and modification procedures have failed. Often the dogs can be slowly weaned off these drugs and, in the process, they seem to learn to cope better with the conditions or stimuli that caused their behavioral disturbance in the first place.

The worst side effects of some psychotropic drugs (other than dependence, liver damage, and paradoxical reactions), which lead me to caution against overprescribing, are disturbing consequences that may be hard to detect in the animal, but which humans report when on similar drugs. These may include disorientation, increased feelings of vulnerability, anxiety or depression, fatigue, loss of appetite, and disturbed sleep patterns.

Another often-overlooked factor that can affect behavior is diet. Nutritionists are beginning to discover how dietary habits cannot only affect the immune system and other vital body functions, but also influence behavior, emotions, and cognitive (learning) abilities in humans. Recent work by a team of veterinarians[1] at Tufts Cummings School of Veterinary Medicine, Boston, revealed that for dogs showing *territorial aggression*, their aggressive behavior was lowered when they were fed a low protein diet supplemented with Tryptophan (10 mg/kg per meal, twice daily). Dogs showing *dominance aggression* were less aggressive when fed low or high protein diets supplemented with Tryptophan, compared to when they were fed a high protein diet without the extra Tryptophan. These different diets had no appreciable effect on hyperactive dogs.

---

1. See J. S. DeNapoli, et al., "Effect of dietary protein content and tryptophan supplementation on dominance aggression, territorial aggression and hyperactivity in dogs," *Journal of the American Veterinary Medical Association*, 217 (2000): 504–508 and Correction, 217: 1012.

4.
| Animal Affection and Attachment |

Imprinting and Dependence

There have been numerous studies on the development of emotional bonds (social attachments) in animals, and they give us a closer understanding and empathetic appreciation for the social and emotional relationships between animals and human beings.

The phenomenon of *imprinting* is seen in most birds and mammals that are relatively mature when they are hatched or born. Because their ambulatory and sensory (smell, sight, and sound) abilities are so well developed, as soon as they enter the world they respond immediately to their parent(s) and become attached in a matter of hours. According to the species, the smell, visual configuration (body shape, colors, etc.), or sounds (calls) made by the parent—or a combination of such signals—are the cues that bring about imprinting.

For a chicken or duckling, the movement, shape, and call of the mother evoke following and attachment. Once the attachment imprint is made, the offspring will ignore the calls of the other mothers and only respond to their own. The same goes for the mother. Mammals that are mature at birth—sheep, pigs, and goats, for example—also rely on the smell of the mother. A caribou calf or a lamb can quickly find his mother among hundreds of others within hours after he has been born, because the imprint of his mother's call has been established.

In most species the mother is also imprinted onto the specific sound and/or smell of her offspring. It is for this reason that a mare or goat will refuse to nurse another's foal or kid, but may accept an orphan if he is first rubbed down with a moist cloth that is tainted with her own body odor or her offspring's odor. Similarly, shepherds will skin a dead lamb and tie him onto an orphan lamb so the dead lamb's mother will not reject the orphan.

Imprinting is remarkably rapid and enduring. Sometimes, but not always, the attachment with the parent breaks at sexual maturity. Yet, ironically, the initial social imprint will often determine later social and sexual preferences. Mary's little lamb that followed her to school was imprinted onto Mary.

Any presocial (mature-at-birth) animal raised by a human foster parent, or some other alien species, *before* she has ever become imprinted onto her own parent will cause the animal to become attached to her foster parent. For example, a bottle-raised fawn will quickly become attached to people. This imprinting phenomenon is one of the major reasons for the difficulties and hazards of attempting to reintroduce a hand-raised orphan animal into the wild—be it a quail or a deer. The human attachment means that the imprinted animal regards human beings as kin and the imprint may be virtually impossible to erase. In some species, the attachment may break at full weaning or sexual maturity, but it is not unusual for the animal, even as an adult, to behave in a dependent, infantile, and solicitous way toward human foster parents.

Two other problems can arise in such human-attached animals. With maturity, their sexual behavior may be directed toward people—with predictable confusion, conflict, and frustration. Occasionally possessive (sexual) rivalry may occur, as when the human-attached animal is jealous of another human being who is close to its human-parent-mate. Actual sibling rivalry can occur (with a human child or other young around), with status conflict and fights for social dominance. Here again, the human-imprinted animal will respond in similar ways toward people as it would toward its own kind in the same social contexts.

An imprinting-like attachment in various animal species has also been observed in relation to a place or location (termed *philopatry* in humans), to certain kinds of food, and in birds, to certain sounds and complex songs.

Socialization
The social imprinting detailed here is analogous to a more prolonged process of attachment that takes several days or weeks in other birds and mammals that are relatively immature at birth; starlings, eagles, rabbits, cats, dogs, and humans belong to this group. The attachment in these animals is

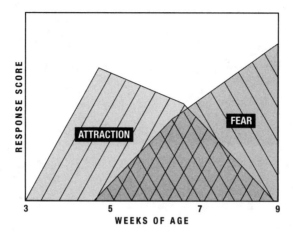

Pups show increasing attraction toward humans around five weeks of age, after which time they show increasing fear after seven to eight weeks of age if never given prior human contact.
Illustration: Foxfiles

called socialization. The same problems described for imprintable species can arise between a human-socialized animal and people.

The other most important practical aspect of imprinting and socialization is that there is a *critical period* for attachment—an optimal time when the bond with its own species and/or with humans can be established. For example, in the dog this is between six to twelve weeks of age; if no human contact is given until a pup is twelve to sixteen weeks of age, he will not make a good pet since he will not bond well to his human companion. Consequently, lacking that dependence, the animal will be difficult to train.

An understanding of imprinting and socialization—which "cement" affection and allegiance in animals, including humans—can help us break down the species barriers and discover the richness of relationships, indeed a kinship, with animals other than ourselves.

Touch and Love

Several years ago, noted pediatrician Dr. Rene Spitz became involved in the care of orphan infants. He found that in orphanages where babies received little tender loving care but had all their survival needs attended to (clean diapers, baths, regular feedings, etc.), outbreaks of disease were common. Also, the babies didn't seem to thrive and some even developed a wasting disease known as marasmus.

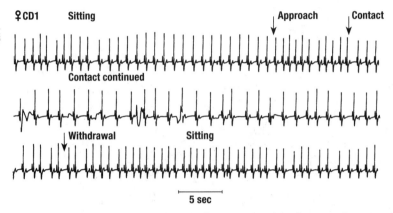

Biotelemetric (remote) recording of a dog's heart rate first at rest, then sitting, increases when approached and slows down dramatically when the dog is stroked.
Illustration: Foxfiles

Today, we have an analogous condition with many commercial animal breeding facilities. Young monkeys, puppies, and calves that are separated from their mothers, even if given plenty of food and warm quarters, don't thrive as well and are more likely to succumb to diseases. Now we are beginning to understand this phenomenon. Part of the answer is related to the creature's heart.

When an animal is petted or groomed or licked by a companion, there is a dramatic decrease in heart rate. When you stroke a dog, provided she's not too excited, her heart rate slows down. This means that the parasympathetic side of the autonomic (vegetative or autonomic visceral nervous system) has been activated. Your touch can evoke such profound changes in the animal's physiology. These changes must be pleasurable for a dog, too, since she will work hard for her master just for the occasional reward of a few gentle strokes. (And we all need to get our strokes too!)

When the parasympathetic system is stimulated, an infant animal relaxes, begins to secrete more digestive juices, and her alimentary system is activated to absorb food. Maternal deprivation, or lack of tender loving care, can therefore be detrimental to survival.

If food isn't properly assimilated in a young animal, susceptibility to disease increases. It would seem that they are born with two physiological dependencies, which the mother normally rectifies by giving affection. Food and a warm bed simply aren't enough.

Dr. Spitz instituted a program of frequent cuddling for the orphaned crib-bound infants, and their health and growth rates immediately improved.

This physiological need for TLC also has another important consequence: attachment. The inborn physiological dependence upon the mother leads to attachment (since TLC is pleasant and rewarding), which in turn leads to an emotional or psychological dependence upon the mother, foster parent, or caretaker.

Through this attachment process, imprinting or socialization takes place and an enduring bond is formed. This bond persists even in adult animals, and this is why socialized dogs enjoy being groomed and petted.[1] It is through touch that humans and animals can appreciate and share a depth of nonverbal communication that transcends the species barrier so they can reaffirm their kinship.

Two South African veterinarians, Drs. J. S. J. Odendaal and R. A. Meintjes, have shown that when a person pets or gently plays with a friendly dog, "feel-good" and beneficial healing neurochemicals are released in both the people and the animals—but with one big difference. Significantly elevated blood serum levels of beta-endorphins, prolactin, oxytocin, dopamine, and beta-phenyl ethylamine were found in both species; but only in humans were levels of the stress hormone cortical decreased. These neurochemicals have a profound bonding function, are associated with pleasure and the improved functioning of the immune system, and provide proof of the benefits of companion animals to us—and of our benefit to them: I call this a mutually enhancing symbiosis.

Other studies[2] have shown that children raised with animals have fewer allergies later in life; couples with companion animals have closer, more satisfying marriages; heart-attack sufferers who have a dog better their odds of surviving one full year eight-fold, compared to patients who have no animal companion; people with companion animals have lower blood pressure, lower triglyceride, and lower cholesterol levels than people with no animals; daily medication costs were halved for patients in nursing homes that allowed animals to visit and kept plants in their patients' environment.

---

1. For details of the therapeutic benefits of touch in animals see Michael W. Fox, *The Healing Touch for Dogs* (New York: New Market Press, 2004).

2. These studies are reviewed in *Veterinary Economics* (August 2002).

Invisible Barriers

When you approach a wild animal at a certain distance he will be quite relaxed and unafraid. If you approach closer, he will take flight because you have crossed an invisible threshold and have penetrated his flight distance. If you were to approach even closer and the animal's flight is blocked, he may even turn and attack you. This happens at close proximity when you enter either his critical distance or attack zone.

A bottle-raised wild animal that has been socialized to people will not show these reactions: socialization essentially eliminates the flight and critical distance reactions.

When this personal space is entered, there are certain laws or rituals to adhere to. Animals are like humans in this regard: People can only do certain things at close proximity; some parts of the body may be touched, for example, while others are taboo or are exclusive to intimate relationships.

During social investigation, dogs and wolves enter the close personal olfactory zone (to sniff anus, mouth, and genitals) and such an intrusion on personal space increases the probability of conflict. Displays of intention have therefore evolved: submissive tail wagging signals friendly intentions, while an erect tail and direct eye stare signal dominance status.

There are accounts of remarkable people who can, like St. Francis of Assisi, approach wild animals and evoke no fear; wildlife may even come to such people spontaneously. What magnet attracts them and what vibrations emanate from such rare individuals? Very often, as in the case of the circus lion tamer, the animal has been bottle-raised and is attached to and trusts the person. Consequently, the social and personal distances may be crossed without flight or attack.

When we raise dogs from infancy, socialization creates the emotional bond that enables us to make contact with them and, in turn, makes them approach us for affection. If deprived of such socializing human contact, a dog will react like a wild animal toward people.

Sometimes, though, we can all be like St. Francis with animals, when the animals have no fear of humans or of being hunted by other animals. On the Galapagos Islands, many of the resident fauna can be approached and touched by humans. Often, the animals of the Galapagos will come close to investigate human visitors. Explorers who discovered vast rookeries of seabirds and seals, wild canids like the Falkland Island wolf-fox, and the now-extinct Dodo bird were amazed at the lack of fear these animals showed. Sadly, the early human visitors to the islands clubbed the curious

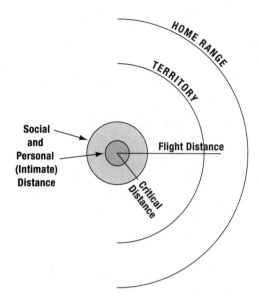

HOME RANGE

TERRITORY

Social
and
Personal
(Intimate)
Distance

Flight Distance

Critical Distance

With a dog in the center, surrounded by conceptual spheres of *Territory* and *Home Range*, one can enter the animal's *Social Distance* if there is trust and make physical contact on entering the *Personal* or *Intimate Distance*. With a wild/feral dog, entering within the *Flight Distance* will trigger escape; if the animal cannot escape and one continues to approach, one enters the *Critical Distance* and the animal may freeze or attack.
Illustration: Foxfiles

little wolf-foxes to death along with the Dodos, and the seals were pounded to death, as they are today, for their skins. Today, surviving seal colonies have learned to be wary of man and they take to the sea—leaving behind their helpless calves, the skins of which are worn today in ignorance of the bloody slaughter.

Many observers have noted the similarity between the flight distance of animals—how close one can approach before the animal flees—and the reactions of some violent, paranoid, and schizophrenic patients. Some of these patients feel that what is happening outside their flight distance is actually happening *inside their own bodies*. Their reactions include panic, escape, social withdrawal, and a need for solitude.

How wonderful it would be if all animals and people could come close in trust and love. Human beings have been hunters for thousands of years, and I believe this factor alone led to a selection of animals that were wary of humans. They would flee and therefore survive and bear offspring of similar temperament, while the curious and the friendly would be killed. But today, only a small percentage of the world population still hunts; perhaps in a few hundred years more animals may come to trust us again. Such trust is seen today in the wild animals in sanctuaries in the United States and in areas in Africa, where hunting is prohibited. But don't get out of the jeep! The big cats are habituated to eco-safari tourists inside the jeeps, but one step out to pet them could be fatal.

Animals as Mirrors

I am not sure by what process it occurs, but it is a fact that dogs often "take after" their owners emotionally and temperamentally. This may be due to sheer coincidence, to careful choice, or to unconscious identification and selection by the owner. Developmental and socialization factors play a part also: namely, how an animal is raised, and thus affected by the owner's emotionality and temperament, and how emotionally dependent it becomes toward its human companion.

I have known companion animals that are emotionally affected by their owners' rage and depression—becoming fearful, aggressive, or withdrawn, and depressed themselves. The more sympathetically attuned the animal is to the emotionality of its human companion, the more it can be harmed or benefited, as the case may be.

I call this emotional phenomenon of mirroring *sympathetic resonance*, where the emotional state of one being affects another. This is easily demonstrated by a person scolding or playfully soliciting an animal who is emotionally attached to him, or to people in general. The closer or more symbiotic the attachment, the more vulnerable and responsive the animal will be.

Considering then that our emotional states can harm or benefit animals, more attention, therefore, needs to be given to two aspects of the human-animal bond. One is the bond of stewardship (as within laboratory and farm animal husbandry). If there is no empathetic bond and the attitude toward the animals is negative (demeaning, controlling, detached, and objectifying) rather than positive (nurturing, compassionate, patient, playful, and understanding), then the animals may suffer or be harmed.

The other is the bond of companionship, as with a companion dog. This bond can be emotionally exploitative, such as when a person is overly controlling and therefore harmful. The sympathetic resonance may be either beneficial (as with a playful and attentive owner) or harmful (as with a depressed, angry, paranoid, overdependent, hypochondriac, or otherwise emotionally disturbed and insecure person). The dog may feel rejected, depressed, afraid, and perpetually anxious and uncertain. Or he may become a fear-biter, or develop psychosomatic disorders and possibly other diseases—ranging from epilepsy and heart disease to cancer and colitis—that the owner may also experience, even in the same organ systems. This correlation should cause little surprise since it is know that the emotions and temperament affect the body—the physiology, metabolism, disease resistance, and organ/system diathesis or susceptibility. Genetic and other environmental factors, such as nutrition and allergies, also play a significant role in such problems, but they do not mitigate the significance of the emotions and of relations (human and animal, as the case may be) in the etiology of health and disease.

On a recent lecture tour of the Philippines, one veterinarian and anthropologist told me that some people in that country believe that dogs take on and thus take away sickness in the family. This belief leads them to not take a sick family animal to be treated, because if it is cured, a family member would then be likely to become ill instead of the dog!

With these thoughts in mind, we should perhaps take extra measures when "prescribing" animals for the emotionally handicapped, and for an emotionally disturbed public at large, since animals can be harmed and suffer. I do not mean to imply that such people should be prohibited from keeping companion animals—though some radical animal liberationists might hold to this ideal. Rather, I would suggest that in recognition of animals' rights and of the tenets of basic common sense and moral sensibility, all animals that are used for psychotherapeutic/pet-facilitated cotherapeutic purposes be under the care of a sensitized veterinarian, ideally in collaboration with a qualified animal psychologist/behavior therapist. Likewise, veterinarians in general practice need to appreciate the clinical significance of sympathetic resonance.

Some animals may be more susceptible to the adverse effects of sympathetic resonance than others. It would be prudent, therefore, to develop objective criteria to screen out such animals that might be harmed if used in pet-facilitated therapy programs.

Our emotions, temperament, and attitude do affect the physiology, behavior, emotional state, and well-being of others—be they other humans or animals under our care. An important aspect of empathy is knowing how we affect others (through sympathetic resonance) and how others perceive us. This is, I believe, a long-neglected yet fundamental area of veterinary medicine and animal husbandry that warrants far more recognition and careful study.

In the next chapter I will give a more personal account of my experiences with one of my most beloved and special animal "teachers" and behavioral co-researchers. Her name was Tiny, and she was a wolf.

5.
| Lessons from a Wolf |

After I completed my doctoral dissertation on the behavioral development of the dog in 1967, I resolved to learn more about the nature of wolves and other wild canids in order to determine how domestication might influence canine behavior. I did not expect to meet a wolf, that I called Tiny, on this research quest. Tiny would help me come to know a wolf as closely as another person.

I was fortunately placed at Washington University in St. Louis where I found several wolf-devotees in the community. There was the late Dick Grossenheider, a wildlife painter who kept several wolves in a large compound, and the late Marlin Perkins of TV's *Wild Kingdom* fame, who was director of the St. Louis Zoo. We all worked together to establish the Wild Canid Survival and Research Center out in the Ozark Hills on university property. I was soon bottle-raising a variety of wild canid cubs from different sources, including "surplus" zoo stock and orphan animals from the wild. I had a menagerie of different kinds of foxes, coyotes, and wolves who regarded me as their parent-provider and who taught me how to communicate with them. Each species had its own distinct repertoire of vocal sounds, body postures, and facial expressions they used in greeting, to solicit contact and play, and to show fear, affection, and submission.

I had a pair of wolves, Lupey and Lulu, living in a wooded enclosure at the university field station, and they needed at least one more cub to make more of a social group for observation. Through the "wolf-network" I received a six-day-old cub from a couple in Wisconsin who had a number of wolves on their farm for educational and conservation purposes. I picked "Tiny" up in a small crate at the airport. She looked more like a bear cub with tiny ears, and her eyelids were not yet open. She took readily to the bottle and was nursed around the clock until weaning at four weeks. By that age she was already a strong, active, curious, and playful little soul who enjoyed being petted and playing with my children. But wolves don't make pets. As she grew older, she became ever more agile and dexterous—and destructive. A squeak in the sofa springs meant something to find, her natural hunting instinct resulting in a torn up sofa. Any object within her reach was to be examined and chewed, or rolled in if it bore any scent, like bathroom soap or an infant's diaper. Any object in her possession was hers and hers alone, and growls and snarls were a clear sign for us to respect her property rights. Even things we thought were well out of her reach and secure on a high shelf or tabletop would, with a leap, be in her jaws.

During her adolescence her wildness manifested itself as an increasing wariness in strange places and fear around strangers, but she never displayed any aggressiveness. She learned things much faster than any dog her age and had no difficulty opening doors and the latch on her pen-door, to which I had to attach a padlock. I also had to put a roof over her large pen because she would get into one corner and climb out as easily as a cat.

When she was about six months old, I introduced her to Lulu and Lupey and they got on like long-lost friends. Her pack-mates, whom I had also bottle-raised, had been zoo-bred for several generations while Tiny was only one generation removed from the wild. Her particular wolf-race or subspecies was from the Mackenzie River region of northern Canada. This is probably why, by the age of one, she became the pack leader of a group that now included two other young wolves, as well as Lulu and Lupey.

Over the next several years I learned and published much about the behavior of wolves and other wild canids; but the time came when I had to disband the wolf pack. Through the wolf-network I found excellent homes for all but Tiny, who was the wildest and youngest of the group. So she came to live with me, accepting a wonderful stray dog named Benji from the animal shelter as her cage-mate.

For their first twenty-four hours, together in the covered enclosure I put up for them in my backyard, Benji tried desperately to mate with her. But he was a little too short for the order. Tiny would simply turn and look at him quizzically as he kept mounting her, quite unperturbed by his behavior.

They became the best of friends and an integral part of my life for the next ten years. They have given me a depth of understanding of canine

Tiny in her prime.
Photos: M. W. Fox

behavior and an appreciation of the soul and spirit of wolf and dog beyond measure.

My first lesson from the wolf was one winter's day at a frozen lake. Tiny knew about ice, having cracked and pounced on it over puddles since her first winter. We had also swum together in Missouri rivers and lakes, so she knew all about water. She became very agitated and began to pace and whine when Benji went out on the ice to chase the ducks in the middle of the lake where the water had not yet frozen over. As usual, Benji ignored calls to come back and the inevitable happened: he fell through the ice.

The poor dog immediately panicked, scrambling unsuccessfully to get back onto the ice and swimming in circles. He would soon be exhausted. I called to get his attention, to encourage him to swim to the far side of the lake where ice had not yet formed, as I ran in that direction. My actions only confused him, until the wolf took off and in moments was jumping up and down on the shore of the lake where the water was deep and unfrozen. Benji understood and turned and swam toward her, receiving a shower of face-licks from Tiny as he pulled his cold and exhausted body onto firm ground.

Tiny demonstrated her insightfulness and empathy on another occasion when she and I had been swimming in a water hole. Benji was too scared to join us, but he was able to walk across the river over some shallows to the far bank. After a while, he wanted to come back but couldn't find the shallows. He started to whine and pace up and down the far bank, as Tiny and I rested in the shade beside the water hole. She took one look at Benji, dove into the pool with her eyes locked with his, and then slowly turned and swam until she reached the shallows, clearly showing him where to cross. Benji gave a happy bark and came splashing across, close on Tiny's heels.

One morning I witnessed a dramatic difference in their behavior that reflected how domestication had blunted Benji's instinctual wisdom. We were out running in an open meadow when we all caught the pungent scent of a black snake somewhere close in the long grass. Tiny immediately froze and began to circle cautiously, closer and closer; but Benji just put his nose down and made a beeline for the snake. He was on top of it before he knew it. Had the snake been venomous, Benji would probably have been killed. Neither had met a snake before, and Tiny's obvious apprehension was an impressive demonstration of the wolf's inborn wisdom.

After the snake had slithered away, Tiny cautiously investigated where the snake had been lying and warming itself in the morning sun. Then in true wolf fashion, she did a nosedive and a roll into the grass to cover her neck and shoulders with the snake's musk.

Tiny was extremely protective of Benji. One day Benji was the victim of an unprovoked attack in a park by the local bully, a huge German shepherd called Niger. He had Benji on the ground by his throat in a second, and so I let go of Tiny's leash. In one bound she struck Niger with her front paws, knocking him off Benji. She snarled and glared ferociously and Niger leaped at her to strike her neck, but she simply twisted her shoulder and he went careening past her. He turned and attacked her again, only to find himself rolling over into the bushes after she deftly deflected his attack with a quick flip of her hips. He picked himself up and snarled at her and she stood her ground, tail and hackles raised, her yellow eyes piercing with a power that made him lower his tail and run whining back to his owner. I was studying the martial art of aikido at the time and realized that Tiny was an exemplar of the technique of deflecting your attacker's force without effort.

I never knew her to use her powerful jaws against any living being, although once she deliberately used her canine teeth to teach me a lesson. I had lost my temper with Benji, who, covered in mud, had for the third time jumped into the front seat of the car after they had been out for a romp at the field station. I had to keep getting in and out of the car to open and close gates and I just lost my cool and too roughly stuffed Benji onto the backseat with Tiny. Tiny growled at me for being so rough, and when we got back home, I went and petted Benji and apologized. Then I went to Tiny. She growled again and with a quick twist of her head made a half-inch incision with her upper canine tooth on my cheek. I had been properly reprimanded and shamed by a wolf.

Tiny clearly had a moral sensibility and a sense of justice. One time I disciplined her for lunging at a dog she didn't like on our morning walk; afterward, she growled at me every morning for over a week, clearly holding a grudge and expressing her disapproval of my behavior.

Tiny had many joys: sniffing and licking puppies and human babies, rolling in deer droppings and dead fish, dancing in the snow, biting at ocean waves and ripples of water racing across a wide meadow, stalking me and playing hide-and-seek in long grass or deep woods, and jaw wrestling. Wolves engage in this ritualistic game—pretending to be savage and, with the most horrendous snarls, flash and clack their jaws and "fence" with their long canine teeth. Tiny and I would shock visitors when we engaged in this sport, and her expression was indeed terrifying. Quite often one of my tiny canine teeth would clash against one of her fangs as we twisted our heads with our mouths wide open and our eyes glaring, trying to look as hideously savage as we could.

In the language of wolves, stiff movements and a direct stare can mean a challenge or be a display of dominance by an alpha wolf. It took several years for Tiny to learn that people were not threatening her when they became stiff with fear and stared at her when they realized she was a wolf. On several occasions someone would be petting her and ask what kind of dog she was. When I told them she's a wolf, instead of saying "Wonderful!" and continuing to pet her, they suddenly backed off, froze, and stared. Tiny would immediately spook.

The fear of wolves is a deeply ingrained cultural phenomenon. With folktales like Little Red Ridinghood notwithstanding, wolves have more to be fearful of from us than we of wolves.

Being in a lecture hall with many pairs of eyes staring at her was just too intense for Tiny to deal with when she was young. She was a living example of how domestication had selected out such sensitivity and fearfulness in dogs and generally tuned down the canine nervous system to create a more stable, tractable, less reactive, if not less intelligent, psyche.

Tiny got on well with most dogs, tending to be friendlier toward large male dogs than toward females. She did, however, show some ambivalence, if not confusion, toward male dogs that had been neutered. She did not approve of adult dogs running right up to her to play, as opposed to puppies doing the same. To enter her personal space, she expected an adult dog to follow the wolf etiquette of slowly approaching and making and breaking eye contact—breaking eye contact being a signal of submission or deference. The tail should be held low and wagged in a friendly greeting. She was almost invariably disapproving of spitz-type dogs whose tails are always held up high and curled up toward the back. Such a tail position in wolf-talk is either a threat or a display of dominance. The same went for the upright ears of these dogs, which they keep up when they are excited, and the cropped ears of schnauzers and Doberman pinschers, which Tiny evidently interpreted as a possible challenge. These dogs would keep their ears up when they approached Tiny, which in wolf-talk is a sign of dominance or aggressive intent. Proper wolf-etiquette entails pulling the ears back as a sign of friendly submission, which Tiny would reciprocate.

She had serious problems interpreting the behavior of dogs such as Old English sheepdogs—with no tails and a face so covered in fur that she could not see their eyes or any facial expression. Wolves, like dogs, display a clear submissive grin, pulling the lips back horizontally as a display of nonaggression and friendly intent. They also share the open mouth play-face, where the mouth is opened and the lips are pulled back horizontally. She especially liked "wolfish" male German shepherds, malamutes, and natural mixed-breed dogs whose body language was similar to hers. With perpetual puppies, as I call them—dogs such as Golden retrievers that, as adults, behave like playful puppies and grovel submissively at the drop of a hat—she would, if I did not pull her back (she was always leashed around other dogs), have terrified their owners by her wolf response: pinning them to the ground with her jaws around their muzzles, heads, throats, or shoulders. Young wolves solicit such reactions from the alpha wolf. It is more a complex display of trust, allegiance, and obeisance to the leader and parent figure than a simple display of submission. There is much more that keeps the wolf pack together than dominance and submission.

Tiny's gentleness and sense of humor reflected such a remarkable intelligence and awareness that I stopped seeing her as a wolf and began to view her simply as a soul mate embodied as a wolf. When she was about nine years old she added a whole new category of behavior to her rich and variable repertoire: grinning. Wolves—like dogs, coyotes, and foxes—retract their lips horizontally, just like humans and other monkeys do, as a sign of friendly greeting and submission. But I had never seen a wolf grin like a human being to display the front teeth in friendly greeting to each other. Tiny started doing this to me, mimicking my expression with obvious understanding of its meaning. Dogs learn to do this, but one should not be surprised after thousands of years of domestication; but what about a wolf who does this, after only a few years of human affection?

Wolves move so differently from dogs. They glide, they dance, and they can fly. Their movements are liquid and effortless. I commented on the incredible mobility and agility of wolves and coyotes to tai chi master Al Chung-lian Huang, adding that most dogs have lost these qualities. "Most dogs are like people," he advised. "They are too achievement oriented." Upon reflection, wolves, however, are often intensely achievement oriented—as any wolf-handler who has tried to restrain their excitement and curiosity beside a new stretch of river or a fresh deer trail will attest. But unlike dogs, they still remain *centered* in so far as they rarely stumble and are always alert for danger, such as a strange human suddenly appearing in the woods or a snake in the long grass.

My son Mike greets Tiny, both boy and wolf displaying a friendly smile.
Photo: M. W. Fox

Tiny was a very aware creature, sometimes in ways that were baffling and awe-inspiring. She had some instinctive sense of how and what people were feeling, probably because of her nonverbal visual imagery that was based on reading the other's body language. She was therefore a superb ethologist and, as she matured, an extraordinary psychic or psychoanalyst. She could tell at a distance, from a person's body language—which she would often double-check by either sniffing them or the breeze, if it was in her favor—if that person was friendly, afraid, indifferent, unaware, angry, mentally unstable, or drunk and disorderly. She was always afraid of any person whose behavior expressed some physical handicap, such as a bad limp or having only one arm. Unusual hats often spooked her. When I spooked her once with a Halloween mask, she rolled over in submission after I took off my mask; and as I bent down to nuzzle her, she urinated in my face.

In the Taos pueblo in New Mexico, she really spooked when a bent figure wrapped in an Indian blanket suddenly came out from the shadows between two buildings. So did I. The figure did not even turn to see whose path, whose life-paths, he or she was crossing. Tiny sensed, as I did, that such a being was to be avoided because it was so self-involved and moving so swiftly and silently. Perhaps it was a brujho or shaman who thought he was invisible. A moment later, a very tall, blue jean–clad Indian in high boots, tall black hat, and aviator rim glasses came by and Tiny alerted—not yet fully recovered from her brujho spirit vision. I held tightly onto her leash, expecting her to spook again, but she relaxed completely. I couldn't understand it, since she hated sunglasses, uniforms, tall hats, and people who strut. From then on, she seemed better able to deal with strangers.

Over the years, I have appeared many times on various television talk shows with animals. Sometimes, I would bring Tiny. Once in her youth, she all but demolished the set of the *Regis Philbin Show* when she spooked after seeing one of the camera lenses, upon which she was momentarily fixated, suddenly dilate and move toward her. After that I rarely took her to a TV station; both of us preferred to be filmed outdoors in familiar territory, on which occasions I would talk about the need for better wolf protection and habitat restoration. I too had feelings similar to Tiny's the first time I was in front of a "live" camera. I never destroyed a set in my panic, as Tiny almost did. Once when I was on the Dick Cavett show I almost rendered a poor Basset hound bald from ear to ear. I was so nervous that I stroked Bassie between the ears through the entire show. I realized this, to my chagrin, when three of my animal behavior class students showed me the tape they had made of my appearance. As an example to the class, we used my behavior as an example of displacement behavior that reflects a state of high anxiety or conflict.

Tiny could be a sneak-thief when her mood and opportunity coincided. Whenever Tiny came into the house she would always make a dash for the bathroom, where she would grab whatever perfumed soaps and toiletries she could reach and either put them in the bath or scatter them on the floor and then roll in them, to wear the scent on her neck, cheeks, and shoulders. Tear-out paper perfume samplers from magazines were special treats for her. Sometimes, when she was out of her enclosure running free in the high-fenced backyard with Benji, she would test the two rear doors into the house—one basement, one kitchen—and on several occasions she would break in. We would find her either in the bathroom or in a bedroom lying flat out on the soft quilts, perfumed, and looking as though she had been there forever.

While on vacation in New Mexico, Tiny had an experience that did not help her learn to trust people. It was quite to the contrary: she was shot. I was staying with friends who had a pack of two other dogs with whom Tiny had a great time. They liked to go off and roam at night, and Tiny slipped her collar and joined them one night. The dogs returned the next morning, but Tiny was gone for three days. We all called and searched day and night; eventually, we gave up. As we were tearfully packing to leave, Tiny dragged herself into the yard, with two large holes in her hip. The children ran out to embrace her as she collapsed by the doorstep. I examined her and was relieved the bullet had only gone clean through her hip muscles and had not hit any bone or major blood vessel. I would have to irrigate the hole with peroxide and antibiotic and she was clearly in great pain, as well as exhausted. I accomplished this excruciating task with her lying quietly looking at me. Her trust was so complete that she needed neither forcible restraint nor a muzzle. The reassuring voices and gentle hand-strokes of my children was all she was given as I patched her up.

I had hoped that Tiny would be like the late John Harris's wolves Jethro and Clem, in whose van I sometimes traveled to give educational programs to schoolchildren about the plight of the wolf in North America. It was not until she was some ten years old that she would tolerate an audience. Her alert presence always evoked a silent awe from people of all ages who did not see her as a trophy or a cattle-killer.

On my first trip with John Harris, I gave a talk about wolves at the Explorers Club in New York, where all kinds of wildlife killed by explorer-trophy hunters are still on display. There I met the musician Paul Winter, with whom I recently had the pleasure of playing my didgeridoo in concert, and I learned he was making music with wolves and other creatures and essences of nature.

Paul gave me a Japanese shakuhachi flute that, after six months striving to play it, I played for Tiny. She first sniffed the bamboo flute and started to chew the end until I got the first note; then she cocked her head and looked intently at the instrument, and then at me. Then she walked away from me, made a half-circle, then raised her head and howled—striking the same note as I played. I found that she liked one particular note (B tritone) and would hit it as soon as I found it on my flute. Then she would soar an octave and sing like a diva.

This became our evening ritual. An opera singer friend came by to hear my lupine diva one late afternoon and he was incredulous at her musical sense. He pointed out to me that she was *chording*, singing two notes at the same time, like Tibetan monks, and in perfect harmony with me. A Wailaki American Indian friend, Ben Coyote, heard us harmonizing together. Coyote had some herbs in his medicine pouch that he sprinkled in front of

An older Tiny on her recliner smiles at me, then mimics a toothy human smile, and then gives her "monster" face in playful mock-fighting.
Photos: M. W. Fox

himself when he first met Tiny. She liked him immediately as I detected the scent of pines and wild sage. This was good, because she would never sing if she was unsure about who was there. He said that our music said, *Mitakye oyasin*; We are all related.

That was Tiny's gift to me: the gift of her wild soul and living presence that showed we are all related, all one in spirit. It was after she died that Tiny seemed to be in my dreams more often than when she was alive. Perhaps that was because I missed her so much. Or perhaps she was actually communicating with me from beyond the grave.

If all people felt that we are all indeed related, all one in spirit, and could feel this and know this truth, then this world would be a very different place. How different an attitude from those who shoot wolves for sport, catch and skin them in steel-jaw traps, wear their furs, and poison their cubs.

Tiny was expert at exposing frauds—and by that I mean people who pretend to like animals, to understand them, and respect them for what they are; but in reality, they are deeply challenged, if not troubled, souls who are incapable of being authentic and open and therefore trustworthy, empathetic, and truly caring. One of Tiny's visitors, a media-hyped animal psychic or "channeler," misread Tiny's submissive greeting and told me Tiny "said" she was the weakest and most-bullied in her pack. Another visitor, purportedly a world-renowned scientific authority on wolves, equally misjudged her. Tiny was running free in the yard at a small reception for a former student of mine from India. Tiny greeted everyone who greeted her, but the scientist just looked at her as though she were an object. And that was precisely Tiny's response to her. Tiny ignored the scientist completely. With wolves, you get exactly what you give.

6.
| True Communication with Animals |

Animal communicators and healers have always known that when you give out love—as compassionate action with loving concern for the well-being of all whom we embrace—good things, and then better things, begin to happen.

I have been following with interest, and some scientific trepidation, the recent advent of mostly nonveterinary trained people who offer their services as animal healers and communicators.

Animal Communicators and Healers: Hoax or Phenomenon?

Several books and countless workshops are offered to people living with dogs, cats, and other animals who wish to better communicate with their beloved companions. Some veterinarians endorse the communication skills and healing abilities of certain so-called animal communicators and healers. Is this for real, or hocus-pocus?

I sometimes have difficulty when these generally well-intentioned and sometimes gifted and deeply feeling people claim to be able to teach others to become animal communicators. I'm skeptical of animal thoughts being put into words. This is because the language of the heart is from the realm of intuition and empathy, but the words they use are too often pseudo-scientific jargon coupled with unsubstantiated claims and promises. Then there are the dangers, in psychological terms, of projection, countertransference, and introjection—as when the animal communicator attributes his or her own feelings, thoughts, or desires to the animal and then "channels" them back, as if it was all from the horse's mouth or the dog's soul. Sometimes a pecuniary element creeps in: the promotion of a new book or video, a patented or trademarked technique or product.

There is nothing mystical, occult, and—for some fearful skeptics—demonic about being able to communicate nonverbally with animals. Humans are animals and have been communicating with other animals since we first became human millennia ago. Our distant ancestors developed the ability to empathize—to feel others' feelings, anticipate their intentions, and understand their needs.

Communication and communion with creatures are ancient traditions that have been recently adopted by the so-called New Age movement. I see this as one of the more valid aims and visions of this movement. According to British philosopher Robin Waterfield, one of the basic principles of this movement is, "the purpose of all existence is to bring love and enlightenment into existence." Another is, "all of life is interconnected." Waterfield adds a third: "We are jointly responsible for the state of ourselves and our environment. . . . We are now at a time—the New Age—when fundamental change is taking place, and things are evolving toward a more spiritual future."

One might wonder, is this all illusion and wishful thinking—animal communication, channeling, remote sensing, and healing? Does being a doubting Thomas mean joining others of little faith? If our hearts are not open to such transformative possibilities, then our minds and lives remain forever closed, especially by rationalism—unless we perhaps have a life crisis that breaks our hearts and we become open to the world at last, as most of us once were as children.

Perhaps I am skeptical of those who publicly claim to be specially gifted with an ability to converse with animals, living and dead, because I think it unremarkable for us to be able to at least communicate with the living. We do this through what I call the *empathosphere*, the realm of fellow-feeling that is before words and beyond rational empiricism and deductive reasoning. I believe this realm is the same as biologist Rupert Sheldrake's morphic field theory strongly supports, where dogs had the ability to predict accurately when their human companions were coming home.

These dogs were not psychic or possessing extra-sensory abilities: they were demonstrating a quality of being and consciousness that is natural,

My dog Tanza contemplates her image in a mirror, and knows much more than I may ever know.
Photo: M. W. Fox

highly adaptive, and shared by many different species—a concept I empha-sized in my books *Supercat* and *Superdog* and one I discuss in detail later in this book. But we modern humans have just about lost the ability to engage this dimension of effective, empathic communication. Some who have not lost it also know the dimensions of ecstatic communion and of agonizing suffering caused by fellow humans who are ever more disconnected from other animals, from nature, and from life itself (except as a resource or commodity).

A Genuine Connection

Animals are not commodities or unfeeling, unintelligent beings. They are living souls like us. If genuine animal communicators and healers can help us restore our sacred connections and become reoriented in a mutually enhancing way with our animal companions—and with the Earth and all who dwell therein—then praise and gratitude to them. Their adoption of body-mind exercises, meditation, transpersonal and existential psychology, and aboriginal spirituality can be extremely helpful to many in this regard, as I have suggested in my book, *The Healing Touch for Dogs*. We may find ways to cope with our empathic suffering for animals. However, if these ways do not translate into compassionate action but instead induce a kind of feel-good spiritual dissociation, then what is called communication and communion with animals, both wild and domesticated, will be but another form of selfish animal exploitation.

Animals and nature can play such a role in our lives, as St. Francis of Assisi preached: through creatures and creation one can realize divinity. This means that animals and nature can help heal us, since wholeness and connectedness have been long recognized by traditional healers as cardinal elements of the healing process. Humans can likewise play an instrumental role in healing animals and nature, especially in terms of our attitudes toward all living things and the quality of life and environment we provide for them.

Do No Harm

The exploitation of animals for purportedly spiritual purposes—such as the trade in wildlife parts for quasi-shamanic purposes, and eco-tourism's touting of soul-enriching communion with nature and indigenous peoples, which can have harmful socioeconomic, environmental, and cultural consequences—are points on the ethical compass of compassion that concern me deeply. The road to hell will always be paved with good intentions until the consequences of our actions, motives, and values are considered and confronted.

We do not need to be telepathic to know when an animal is being treated cruelly and is suffering, or to know when an animal is feeling secure and experiencing pleasure. We do need to find ways to respond more effectively to the holocaust of the animals and to the plight of the planet without becoming overwhelmed and paralyzed by the complexity and enormity of the consequences of our collective inhumanity—and of the dominant culture of materialism, industrialism, and consumerism. Until we give equal consideration to every living and nonliving entity who shares our home the Earth, we will not succeed—and humans and animals will never be well but will suffer ever more, with most animals becoming extinct.

Above all, we need to redefine what it means to be human in relation to the rest of the Earth community and awaken those attributes, virtues, and values that bring ethics to life and make us human and whole.

In the chapters to follow, deeper realms of animal behavior and awareness will be explored. Reference will be made not only to dogs, but also to cats and other species. This is not done because many are close cousins and often share the same home, but because insights about the ethos or spirit of one species, as in the case of Tiny the wolf, can throw light on the nature of other species—on their deep psychology, their souls.

7.

| How Animals Mourn and Express Grief |

There is a beautiful bronze statue in the city of Edinburgh, Scotland, in memory of a little Cairn terrier named Bobby and erected by loving citizens who knew the dog. Bobby was revered by all who knew of him, for after his beloved master died in 1853 and was buried in the small graveyard, Grey-friars Kirkyard, Bobby took up his lonely vigil, lying beside the man's grave until he died of old age in 1872—a vigil of devoted loyalty of some nineteen years, according to the brass plaque on the memorial statue.

Outside of a subway station in Tokyo, Japan, I was shown a statue commemorating the vigil of another dog local people knew well, because the dog would wait at this station every evening for his master to come home from work. For several years after the master died, this dog kept up his patient vigil, waiting for his beloved human companion to accompany him home.

The fact that people put up monuments to dogs in these far corners of the world says something about us, and something that is good: we recognize, across cultures and time, the good that dogs can embody—namely the virtues of faithfulness, devotion, unconditional love, and selflessness. These qualities are seen by some as the domain of saintliness in our own kind, since these qualities seem all too rare in contemporary society. But perhaps they are not rare, as long as we continue to let the animals help us become more fully human—their well-being under our domination being a mirror of our evolution as a compassionate, humane species. As the Australian aborigines say, "Dingo (dog) makes us human."

Bobby's statue in Edinburgh, one of the world's most famous memorials to canine devotion and fidelity.
Photo: M. W. Fox

Archaeologists have found, in Stone Age burial sites from Denmark to Cyprus, the remains of humans curled around an evidently beloved dog or cat. So clearly, from before the recorded, written history of humankind, companion animals were important to our kind and were venerated for their gifts of soul and spirit, presence and prescience.

Witnessing the Grief of Animals

The following selections from the scores of letters and personal stories I have received over the years spell out in moving detail how many, but not all, companion animals often react to the loss of a human or animal companion and loved one. There is nothing sloppily sentimental, nor is there evidence of anthropomorphized projections of people's grief onto their animals in these testimonies. The scientist and secular materialist could reject these accounts as being subjective and unverifiable anecdotes and cast them into the fires of rational objectivity. But the animals, in their behavior, clearly speak for themselves in the ancient and authentic language of the heart that we share with them. Being true to their natures, they cannot lie.

Anyone feeling discomfort about the emotional depth and intelligence of animals will be moved to bear witness and to accept that we humans are not the only ensouled, sensitive, and intelligent beings on this little blue and green planet. The animals, in their grief, and in their longing for the return of the loved one, show us that the nature of love is an inborn quality that we share with them. We are moved to a deeper understanding and respect for them, since this means that they too must also suffer loss and experience joy and camaraderie in ways quite similar, if not identical, to us. Outward appearances can indeed be deceiving.

The loss of a loved one, human or nonhuman, is usually first expressed as acute grief, the animal making sounds of evident distress. Some animals often show no initial reaction, but later may start to search everywhere, become more vigilant, apprehensive, and pensive—sitting and waiting by a door or window as though expecting the loved one to return.

"My cat Speckles," writes Nancy Falzone-Cardinal of Springfield, Massachusetts, "was six years old when our ten–year-old terrier, Whisky, died. They had been very close and friendly with each other. When our darling Whisky died, Speckles spent every day of weeks searching our home. She wandered from room to room, looking around and over everything, all the time meowing a dreadful cry. My husband and I decided to remove our living room recliner from our home because Whisky had spent his last month lounging there, and we thought his aroma might be torturing the cat into looking for him. After doing so, she stopped the entire apartment search, but Speckles then went to the front door every late afternoon, pacing and lounging within two feet of it. And meowing until 10 p.m.! For four entire months she waited for her 'brother' to come up the stairs from a very, very, long walk. One day she just stopped her ritual. She lived another eight years. She tolerated our Shih Tzu, Randi, who joined our family, but she truly never loved him, as she had Whisky."

Kirstin L. Wesfall in Washington, D.C., wrote: "I had purchased two Blue Point Siamese brothers, Sparta and Troy. From a kitten, Troy had battled liver disease for several years and was the first to die. Upon his death, Sparta would go to the basement and let out gut wrenching screams. He would do this several times a day for an entire month and it just broke my heart. I have never heard a cry like it—I quickly realized he was mourning his brother. I have always believed pets grieve and I was certainly witness to that."

D.K., from Hollywood, Maryland, had two German shepherd dogs, Princess and Shep. "Princess was a year older than Shep and was the first to go. Shep was devastated; at times during the day he would go into the dark garage and moan the saddest moans that you can imagine. We got another adult female dog right away, but that didn't help. It took a few months for him to get over his grief."

Sometimes animals seem to know when another is going to pass on and will be especially attentive, like the account of Kisses, who comforted Orville in his last days. "I had a yellow Lab, Orville, who was quite old, and growing more feeble every day. I had adopted a one-and-a-half-year-old chocolate Lab, Kisses, only weeks before Orville died, but they barely knew one another due to Orville's advanced age. Kisses had a soft, stuffed goose, which she carried in her mouth constantly; she slept with her head on it every night . . . it was obviously her comfort/security thing.

"One evening Kisses took her precious goose and placed it at Orville's head. For the remaining three days of Orville's life, Kisses would come by and sniff the goose and push it toward Orville but she never made any move to take it from her new friend. The goose was at Orville's head when he went to sleep for the last time. Kisses took back her goose only after Orville was buried."

Sometimes the grief may be so intense that the suffering animal behaves in a totally disoriented and even reckless manner, like the cat BooBoo belonging to Sabrina Campbell of Alexandria, Virginia, who bit off his tail when the older cat in the family died, and Jean W. Burdell's cat in McLean, Virginia, who became aggressive toward her, "with many ambushes and frequent puncture wounds" immediately following the sudden death of her husband. "Ever since then, whenever guests come to the house, the cat roams around excitedly, reaching up to the men present to attract their attention. His attitude toward me has progressed slowly to tolerance, acceptance, and even affection. Today I saw him again, as I have seen him many times, sitting in the closet beneath some of my husband's clothes looking up at them. I believe that in his primitive fashion he remembers, he waits, and he hopes," she writes. I would say, not so primitive—and get rid of the clothes!

I am reminded of my days studying the behavior of wild canids—foxes, coyotes, and wolves—and the morning I found one beautiful little kit fox dead in her enclosure. Her mate had piled food and various toys around her lifeless form and threatened me when I entered the enclosure, clearly being protective of her. This makes me reflect on the suffering that hunters, trappers, and others who kill wild animals actually cause to the animals that are not killed. How many grieve the death of a mate, parent, pack leader, or beloved offspring?

Wildlife managers have repeatedly witnessed the grief of elephants (who, like us and some dogs, actually cry when they are stricken with unbearable emotional pain and anguish) after herd-mates were shot as part of wildlife conservation management policy in East Africa, according to the culling protocol. Wildlife managers now kill entire herds so there will be no survivors to suffer. Or the whole herd—a nexus of close family ties between mothers, daughters, fathers, sons, grandparents, uncles, aunts, and cousins—is moved to another area to repopulate and reduce the local overpopulation problem, which is a management dilemma in many wildlife parks, elephant ivory poachers notwithstanding. Elephants have been seen to protect injured and dying herd-mates, bury the dead under dirt and brush, and gently touch the bones of the deceased when they come across them in their ever-shrinking domain.

Sometimes the grief animals experience over the death of a loved one is so intense that they die from what we call a broken heart. D.R. from Moorhead, Minnesota, wrote to me about two horses, Pete and Florie, that she and her husband kept to plow their fields. "They were well up in their years and 'retired.' One morning as my husband was doing chores he noticed that Florie was staggering by the barn and promptly toppled over and died. Pete walked over to her and paused for some time, then took a walk through the pastures and returned to Florie. He paused again and then put his front foot upon her body and fell over beside her and died, too. That showed me how sensitive animals really are and that in their own ways they do grieve also. As I'm writing this it still brings tears to my eyes."

June Baker in Arlington, Texas, witnessed a similar event with her father's dog: "Family members would take turns staying at the hospital with my father. Every time we returned home, Dad's little brown dog (mixed breed) would meet us and smell every inch as though he knew we had been with Dad. When we all went to the funeral and returned home, his little brown dog came to every one of us and sniffed at each of us. Finally, he asked to be let out of doors. When he did not come back to the door and ask to get in, someone went out to look for him and found him dead under a bush outside. There were no marks or injuries and he was known to be in perfect health. We consulted a vet about this strange happening and he told us that sometimes, when a master dies, the pet will suffer a brain hemorrhage due to grief."

How this dog died was probably due to what is termed *vagal syncope*, the vagus nerve being part of the autonomic (subconscious) nervous system that slows the heart down and can even stop it. This is what often happens when people faint from shock: the heart rate slows or momentarily stops and the blood pressure plummets, resulting in a blackout (the opposite of a brain hemorrhage). So Dad's little brown dog died from cardiac arrest—a broken heart indeed.

Dorathea Rubsky from Miami, Florida, wrote a letter to me about the collie dog in her family that moped around the house for weeks when her father was hospitalized. "At first, we thought she might have been sick but upon being examined by the veterinarian nothing could be found to cause the problem. Needless to say the night before my father passed away our collie died. Thus we figured she was mourning for him."

Other species can suffer, too, from the death of a loved one, showing clear evidence of depression. Doris Addenbrook's male canary in Virginia Beach, Virginia, fell silent after Mr. Addenbrook passed on. The widow says the bird, who has not sung now for eighteen months, "will peep if a male comes into the house or if I put him on the porch on a sunny day. I have played canary song recordings for him and I try talking to him. It is so sad to have lost his songs."

My friend from Adirondack, New York, psychologist Dr. Emmanuel Bernstein, tells me that he knew a goldfish named Gertrude who was used to Pierre, the parakeet, visiting her every day and pecking on the bowl. Gertrude would wiggle her tail in response and stayed opposite the bird wherever Pierre moved around the bowl. When Pierre died, Gertrude visibly mourned, facing away from the side of the bowl where there was movement for many weeks before relating to anyone else.

The Wake and Viewing the Body

Some years ago I met a neighbor walking her three dogs. She was crying. Her fourth dog had just died in her home, and she was not only grieving the loss of her old dog, she was worried how the others would take it, for they had not yet seen the deceased animal in her upstairs room. I advised her to let the dogs in from the yard when she got home and let them see the body, because they needed closure. If they never saw the dead body they might wonder where the old dog had gone and be anxiously awaiting his return home. I saw her a few days later and she told me, "Doctor, it was just like a wake, when people come to view the dead. I called the dogs into the room and they walked slowly up to their dead companion lying on a blanket, sniffed him all over, then slowly and quietly walked away. I think that really helped them not miss him so much and understand what had happened to him."

Norma Nelson of Tenafly, New Jersey, writes, "After one of my cats died I left him in his burial box for our other cat to see. He stayed by the box for twenty minutes, then slowly walked away and was fine after. Animals have to mourn their friends in the 'casket' before burial just like people do."

In Bloomfield Hills, Michigan, Janise Stoneman's bichon frise stopped eating and searched the house looking everywhere for their deceased rabbit, with whom the dog had become friends. After the rabbit died, it was put in the garage because the earth was too frozen to dig a grave. After a friend suggested her dog would be less distressed if it was allowed to see the dead rabbit, she wrote: "We took our dog into the garage and showed her the rabbit. She stood totally still, not even moving her tail. She did not make a sound. She once turned to look at me with a sad expression on her face and immediately turned her attention back to the rabbit. After about ten minutes, she came back into the house. For the next couple of days, by habit, she would look to the empty cage and, as if reminding herself the rabbit was dead, would walk away. She no longer searched for the rabbit and resumed eating."

Jean Styles of Punta Gorda, Florida, sent me the following touching story about her husband with a terminal illness who decided to die at home. "Our miniature poodle, Mitzi (now deceased), loved us both but had an especially close bond with my husband. During the final days I would zip home at lunch hour to see if my husband needed anything and I would always find Mitzi parked right beside his chair like a good little nurse. When I would get home after work each afternoon it was the same story. Mitzi sitting close where she could keep careful watch over him.

"One day, while he could still communicate, he told me he didn't want Mitzie to die of grief when he was gone. To prevent this he made me promise that, when the time did come, before calling to report his death I would put Mitzi up beside him and let her check out the situation for herself. He was a very wise man but I still didn't see how this could help. . . . On the fatal morning, after making sure he was no longer breathing and before calling for help, I put Mitzi up beside him. She sat looking at him for several minutes and then slowly got down and lay on the floor beside the bed.

"Mitzi had always known just when one of us was expected home and waited, perched on the back of the couch by the front window, for his car to pull in. I was afraid she would wait for him still but, to my amazement, she seemed to completely understand and never again sat there waiting for him to come home, although she still kept to that practice till I got home each day.

"I can't help feeling that she is now with him and the two are waiting for me to join them."

What a reunion that will be!

Jean Milnor of Minneapolis, Minnesota, has a similar story. Her husband was dying at home from cancer and their dog, Hinny, insisted on getting up on the bed with her husband a couple of hours before he died. She writes, "Hinny snuggled up by his shoulder, she licked his neck, the hollow of his cheek, and then settled down to snuggle right next to him. She hadn't done this before. She laid in this spot until my husband passed over to heaven. After his last breath, she got up and moved down to his feet to lie there. There is an emotional connection—perhaps spiritual—between our dog and our spirits. I am honored to have witnessed the sacredness of the experience."

A story about a bull named Barnaby made the international news in 2004. This bull left his field in the German town of Roedental and found his way somehow to the cemetery, over a mile away where his farmer-owner, Alfred Gruenmeyer, had been just buried.

Apparently the eccentric farmer treated his animals like pets, allowing them to have free run of his home. The bull had to jump a wall to get into the cemetery and insisted on staying there for two days, despite the best efforts to get him to move out.

Carol A. Ross of Lincoln Park, Michigan, writes that some time after her father had died and was buried, she took his dog Rusty to the cemetery, "and like a rabbit, the dog ran directly to my Dad's gravesite. Remarkable, or just plain dog sense?"

There can be no doubt that animals possess some understanding of death, and from my own personal experience, I can vouch for the importance of letting an animal see its loved one, human or nonhuman, when laid to rest. But they should not witness the burial. I made that mistake with my

Old Quincy, an expired Seeing Eye dog, is laid to rest in our garden so the surviving dogs of his "pack" can view him before burial.
Photo: M. W. Fox

dog Tanza, who saw me burying Quincy, my brother-in-law David's Seeing Eye dog. My wife Deanna and I had taken Quincy in for a year, after he became too old to help David anymore. Tanza as a puppy looked up to him as her patient playmate and comforter. But when she saw me putting him into the grave she screamed and frantically tried to dig and pull him out of the hole. Needless to say, I was devastated by my own insensitivity, taking the notion of closure too far. Tanza had been lying beside Quincy's body for half an hour after I euthanized him (and she and the other dogs did not witness that). I should have simply led her away before burying dear Quincy.

Animals not only grieve the loss of a loved one, some clearly know when the loved one has just died, as the dog Hinny did. Sometimes, as in the case of cat Boo from Schenectady, New York, written about below, they are able to anticipate death.

Jaqueline Rosenbaum's husband was dying from lung cancer, and she writes that, "A couple of days before my husband passed away, Boo (an eight-year-old Scottish Fold) was sitting on an end table at the head of his bed and howled the most horrible cry I ever heard (like he was in extreme pain). I know at that time my husband's system was shutting down and I'm sure my cat sensed it. . . . I recently bought a kitten to help Boo (and me) through our grieving. Occasionally Boo will play with him, so I hope things will improve."

Boo's prescience—an ability to foresee impending death—leads us into the deep heart of animals that, as this next chapter documents, are able to somehow know that a loved one has just died—even though they are not present at the time of death. So does this mean that animals have "psychic" powers? Make up your own mind after reading the next chapter.

8.
| "Psychic" Animals and Their Super-Senses |

The more we learn about the mysteries of the animal kingdom that science explores, and the mysteries that animals reveal to us in their behavior, the more we stand in awe of the inherent wisdom and complexity of manifest life. Some of the abilities that animals reveal still baffle science and plunge us into the realm of the inexplicable, even the spiritual. Psychic trailing, or psi-trailing, is one of these.

It is quite distinct from *homing*, a superficially similar phenomenon that was for a long time thought to be "psychic." Homing is an animal's ability to find his way home after he has been deliberately released (like homing messenger and racing pigeons) or lost (like a cat or dog that slips out of the car on vacation with the family). Once thought to be psychic behavior, scientists have demystified homing by showing that various animals can use the sun, moon, stars, and the Earth's geomagnetic field as clocks and compasses.

Dogs and other animals are sensitive to electromagnetic and geomagnetic fields, and they possess an internal directional compass and an internal time clock that enables them to have a sense of time in relation to where they are and the position of the sun.

There are iron (ferrous) salt deposits in the frontal brain region of birds, cats, humans, and probably dogs and other animals, which act like a magnetic compass and thus provide an inborn sense of direction. This sense may be architecturally and technologically disrupted by, for example, people living and working indoors for extended periods surrounded by an electrical field and metal structures, and possibly by people sleeping in an East-West rather than a North-South direction. Animals also possess an internal circadian time clock that enables them to fine-tune the position of the sun (time of day) with the internal setting of their circadian clock.

This internal clock is integrated, I believe, with the compass-sense to give animals an awareness of their place in time-space.

This time-space information is actually communicated by some animals to each other. For example, honey bees with their elaborate dances tell fellow workers how far away a particular food source is, and what its direction is. Scientists first discovered that bees are aware of the position of the sun and then that they are also sensitive to gravity. Bees, like birds and humans, have iron deposits in their nervous systems.

Displays of "Psychic" Power

Dogs and other species can sense when an earthquake or tsunami is coming. They may detect changes in barometric pressure and air ionization and be more sensitive than we are to tremors and the reactions of other animals in their vicinity.

Dogs can even detect by scent various cancers, such as melanoma and cancer of the bladder. Dogs can predict heart attacks, on-coming epileptic seizures, cancer, and detect other ailments.

One example of this is an account by Candy Killian from Davie, Florida, who shared an anecdote about her father's dog, a shepherd mix named Duchess, who was devoted to him. "Dad was fifty-five years old and had no apparent major health problems. I visited my father every Friday evening. The dog had taken on a new, odd habit in the spring: she'd all but climb onto my father's lap and lay a paw on his chest, looking him straight in the eyes. We all passed it off as another cute habit of hers. To make a long story short, my father passed away in his sleep during the night. The dog lay at his side with her paw on his chest, and had to be literally pried away from him. The cause of death was chronic lung disease. None of us knew; but she did."

This account of Duchess's prescience could be explained on the basis of animals being acute observers of others' behavior—noting any change in normal behavior and in body odor that may be early warning signs of illness—rather than invoking some psychic explanation. Dogs are so observant that they are now used, with a little training, to warn their epileptic human companions when a seizure may be coming; some have helped by alerting their diabetic human companions when their blood sugar is getting dangerously low.

But science has not yet demystified psychic trailing. This phenomenon has been well documented, especially in the United States, and objectively investigated by the late Professor J. B. Rhine of Duke University, a world-renowned parapsychologist.

Several cats and dogs have performed the miraculous feat of locating their loved ones in places where they have never been before, traveling sometimes hundreds of miles. A psychiatrist friend of mine told me the story of a German shepherd he was given as a boy, by neighbors who moved to the other side of New York City. The dog ran away after they left; within a few days, they found him in their new neighborhood, a part of the city he had never been before.

There is one documented case of a cow that was sold at an auction in England. Her little calf was also sold and went to a different farm. The cow escaped from her new farm home and was found the next morning many miles away—on the farm where her calf was, in a place she had never been before.

The Empathospere

I have a rational explanation for this phenomenon: it is neither metaphysical nor mystical, but has been explicit in many spiritual teachings. Simply put, we are all connected psychophysically with the sun, moon, Earth, the stars, and with each other through the realm of the senses and the emotions. It is the emotional connection with his owner or family that forms a point in the space-time continuum that enables the animal to reorient from his home-base and find his family. I propose that the animal's internal sun-time clock and geomagnetic compass are used, like a directional feeling-sensitive antenna, once the animal has aligned himself toward the emotional field of its owner/family. This field, which I call the empathospere, makes the space-time continuum a unified field.

Albert Einstein theorized the existence of this unified field, but he failed to express it mathematically. It is doubtful that the subjective element of being and emotion can ever be expressed in objective mathematical terms. The existence of this field—in which all things are interconnected and interdependent—has been demonstrated by the modern sciences of ecology and quantum mechanics.

Animals have demonstrated the existence of this unified field of being in another way. I have received many letters from readers of my syndicated newspaper and magazine columns about their pets reacting "psychically" to the death of a companion pet or human family member. A typical example is that of an old Siamese cat who suddenly began to cry loudly in obvious distress at around 10:00 a.m. The veterinarian called the cat's owner about an hour later to inform the woman that her beloved German shepherd, which had been admitted to the veterinary hospital early that morning, had expired on the operating table at 10:00 a.m. The coincidence of this event with the cat's distress at exactly the same time is the kind of phenomenon that we generally refer to as *psychic*.

I have heard from other cat and dog owners whose animals have suddenly become agitated, distressed, or scared at around the same time that a human companion or close friend had died.

I have also received accounts from people reporting that their cat or dog becomes excited at around the time their spouses are due to arrive home. The animals have no specific cues, such as the sound of a footstep, the distinctive noise of the car engine, or a set time of arrival. These animals seem to be able to *feel-see* their human companions when they are some distance away, or just leaving their place of employment.

For example, a veterinarian's dog sensed when his owner closed the hospital for the night and took a fifteen-minute walk home. The animal doctor's wife never knew the exact time of her husband's arrival, but the dog would always wag his tail and go to the door in anticipation of his arrival. When the vet's wife started taking note of the time, it coincided precisely with his closing up of the hospital door, fifteen minute's before he was at the front door of their home.

An Ability to "Feel" Across Time and Space

I have a partial explanation of this "psychic" awareness. It is based on the notion that animals, when emotionally connected to each other and to their human companions, can "feel" across time and space and sometimes sense another's activities and emotional state.

This empathetic connection is the feeling-world, the empathosphere, of the animal kingdom from which most humans have become separated. Indeed, some people have become so alienated from this realm that they actually doubt animals have any feelings at all.

As for cats and dogs who are able to engage in what is termed *psi-trailing*, again I believed the empathosphere theory, which I will discuss shortly, seems to explain the phenomenon. Psi-trailing refers to an animal's documented ability to locate its owners who have moved to a new home, sometimes hundreds of miles away, and have left the animal with other people at the old home or neighborhood.

Those of us living in Western industrialized society are unfamiliar and out of touch with these supra-sensory powers: the animal powers that our shamanic ancestors understood and utilized. These powers also include cats' and dogs' exquisite sense of smell and superior auditory, visual, and earth-magnetic, or geokinetic, sensibilities.

Our senses are beginning to atrophy, to close down. Aboriginal people of high order in precolonial Australia used these powers to heal, and to live in harmony for health's sake—both for the sake of personal health and the health of the environment, which they considered inseparable.

These so-called primitive people have "psychic" or supra-sensory abilities. They are able to attune themselves to the unified field of being—a state they refer to as the *dream time*, and, for example, "feel-see" the presence of a particular animal over the next hill, or a kinsman coming toward them from a particular direction who is still a two-day trek away.

These above examples of animals' higher powers should make us not only question the nature of reality as we perceive it physically and emotionally; it should also make us realize how sensitive and aware animals are and lead us to question the morality of certain practices. For example: killing animals for their fur and meat; raising them in factory farms and zoo prisons; keeping them in small cages in laboratories where they are made to suffer in order to find cures for diseases (most of which we bring upon ourselves).

If animals are emotionally connected, in some kind of sympathetic resonance with us—as witnessed by the phenomenon of psychic trailing—then we should consider how we might be affecting the entire animal kingdom by our actions and our state of mind that collectively permit so much animal exploitation and suffering, wholesale destruction of nature, and the pollution and poisoning of the environment. Since everything is connected in this unified quantum field, we might also consider the adverse consequences to us—medically, psychologically, and spiritually—of what we do to animals on the illusory grounds of human necessity.

The medical and psychological benefits of a positive, loving attitude toward animals have been proven: they help heal us. Scientists have shown that petting an animal lowers one's blood pressure and reduces the incidence of coronary heart attacks. The medical, psychological, and spiritual benefits of simply being in the country, reconnected with nature, are also being more widely recognized.

As we lose touch with nature, the animal kingdom, and even with each other, we lose these abilities and their associated sensitivities. Our survival may well depend on all of us reawakening these abilities, rather than upon new medical miracles and technological fixes. We are part of a far greater miracle that beckons us to have reverence for all life, which Albert Schweitzer saw as our ultimate healing revelation and ultimate solution to the ills of society, body, and mind. As the Book of Job advises, "Listen to the animals . . . for they shall teach thee." A good beginning would be to empathize with the present holocaust of nature and the animal kingdom, to stand up and defend the rights of all animals—domestic and wild, captive and free—to achieve equal and fair consideration. Their being, their behavior and "psychic" abilities that affirm our biological and spiritual kinship with them, surely make this the first ethical imperative of a more enlightened humanity.

What our animal companions have shown us in this chapter as our spiritual teachers is that there are realms of feeling and consciousness of which we humans are an integral part. Other animals share with us some remarkable, some would say psychic, abilities that set us neither apart from them nor above them, but rather affirms our biological and spiritual kinship with all beings.

9.
Entering the Deep Heart's Core: The Empathosphere

Regardless of my training as a scientist—with a doctoral degree in science as well as another doctoral degree in the faculty of medicine from the University of London, England, plus a veterinary degree from the Royal Veterinary College, London—I have been able to keep an open mind to things that cannot be weighed and measured, objectified and quantified. Such subjective elements are feelings, beliefs, intuition, and the inner mysteries of life and consciousness. A scholarly approach—and by that I mean one that is impartial and unbiased, rather than one with a scientific or religious bias—is needed for when dealing with issues that are in the realms of the spiritual and the metaphysical. When it comes to evaluating animal prescience and remote sensing—what is commonly regarded as psychic communication or clairvoyance—an open mind is called for. Let the facts speak for themselves, from which we can draw our own conclusions and upon which we can then variously construct or deconstruct scientific and philosophical hypotheses and theories, religious doctrines and dogma, and test our personal beliefs.

In my earlier book, *The Boundless Circle*,[1] I first raised the probability, on the basis of my own observations and the anecdotal data of others, that all living beings have an innate sympathetic connection to each other through our emotional consciousness—our awareness of how we feel toward another living being, human and nonhuman, animal and plant.

---

1. Michael W. Fox, *The Boundless Circle* (Wheaton, Ill.: Quest Books, 1996).

This connected state of awareness, in harmonic resonance with other living sentient beings through empathy, is a state of being that forms what I call the *empathosphere*. This is a sphere of being that we all share and essentially participate in, like the physical atmosphere. I proposed that humans and all living beings are in a state of sympathetic resonance. This hypothesis is supported by the sensitivity displayed by many animals of different species toward us: how they avoid those of us who are afraid or would harm them; how they approach or do not flee from or attack those who have a deeper equanimity radiating toward them.

In other words, our emotional state and how we perceive, react to, and value animals—and each other—is communicated in this empathosphere with profound consequences in terms of our own mental and spiritual well-being and the well-being of others, leading to euphoria or dysphoria, mutual harmony or conflict.

Dogs have long been thought to possess empathic, psychic powers—although some of their abilities, such as their homing ability and early responses to approaching earthquakes and tsunamis, can be partially explained on the basis of physical sensation and physiological response. But there can be no immediate physical sensations associated with the following reactions in dogs and cats: with our present, limited, scientific knowledge we cannot ascribe any known physiological process to explain how an animal can react to an event occurring at the same time, but in a totally different place.

Take, for example, Edna L. Thorstensen's letter from Hollywood, Florida, about her father's cat that she was allowed to take to the hospice unit of the hospital to visit her father. "The last night we were there I knew my Dad would not be with us too much longer. That night when kitty and I came home, she started running through the house howling. I had no idea what was wrong with her. A few minutes later the hospital called and said that my Dad had just passed away. She knew it. It took her a long time to get over my father's death."

A letter from Angela in Minnesota tells of her husband dying in a nursing home, whom they visited daily. "One night around midnight our eighteen-year-old cat, on my bed, gave a strange sound that woke me up and I sat up. A second later the telephone rang telling us to come to the home. The cat knew just when the Lord took my husband."

Kathy Rector from Mellenville, New York, writes: "My husband's grandfather found a stray golden retriever and named her Penny. They were inseparable for many years, until he went into the hospital. One day Penny began to howl and howl, and my grandmother knew her husband had past before she got the phone call from the hospital a few minutes later."

According to Stephanie N. Abdon from Winston-Salem, North Carolina, her grandmother used to pet-sit for various peoples' animals. "One of those pets was my brother's dog Dixie," she writes. "When my mother called to let my brother know that Granny had passed away, he replied that Dixie had already let them know. Apparently Dixie had come into the bedroom and began to moan, as if she were mourning. This is apparently the only time she whimpered in such a way. I think this is a perfect example of your 'empathosphere' theory."

Karen Beloncik from Schenectady, New York, gives a similar account. She was taking care of her uncle's boxer dog, Champ, while he was in the hospital. "One evening," she writes, "Champ was sound asleep when he suddenly woke up barking and running back and forth throughout the house. A short time later, I got a call telling me my uncle had died. When I found out what time he had died, I realized it was the exact time that Champ had been carrying on. I truly believe that Champ knew what had happened."

Delyne E. Eddins from Joshua, Texas, remembers an event that occurred when they lived in Nebraska. Her family dog had become very attached to her grandfather, whom they visited in Kansas for a couple of weeks every summer. She writes: "One day my mother received word that her father was very ill, so she went down to Kansas to be with him. One day the dog started acting very strange and was crying, howling, and acting like he had lost his best friend. The remark was made, Do you suppose grandfather died? A few hours later my mother called and said her father had passed away. We asked what time and she told us. It was the same exact time that the dog was crying and howling."

Bay was a mutt who was adopted by the uncle of Cindy Weldon of St. Paul, Minnesota, when he was serving in the Peace Corps in Antigua, West Indies. Bay's family included Cindy's grandfather who, at 101 years of age, was flown to Baltimore for heart surgery, accompanied by her uncle. Her aunt stayed at home with Bay, who "kept a vigil by grandfather's chair by day, and by his bed at night. He would not eat. My aunt had to carry him outside to go to the bathroom. This went on for five days. My aunt was worried Bay might die. My grandfather died about 1:00 in the morning shortly after surgery. That morning Bay gave up his vigil. He ate and went outside on his own. Somehow he knew that grandpa had been released from this world. Bay has been his usual self ever since."

Bay himself.
Photo: Cindy Weldon

Sometimes the animal's prescience has a happier outcome, like that of a little black mongrel dog named Bubbles, who pined for months while his beloved master George was posted abroad during World War II, "taking prolonged naps in his bed," according to George's niece Candy Killion from Davie, Florida. She writes, "When my grandmother got mail home from the front, the dog would go wild; apparently, she picked up his scent on the letters he wrote. But strangest of all, as the war was ending up, one morning my grandmother heard the dog pacing back and forth, whining and crying at her front window. There wasn't a thing in sight to provoke the animal. This went on about a half hour until a city bus that stopped at the corner made its next drop. When the bus came into view, Bubbles went completely hog-wild, barking and scratching at the window. When my grandmother went back to scold the dog, she nearly fainted. George, in his uniform, was walking down the sidewalk with his duffel bag. No one knew he was coming—except the dog."

One sad reading of human behavior by a companion animal was shared with me in a letter by Dianne Payne of Palmetto Bay, Florida. Her husband, a veterinarian, suffered from depression, especially toward the end of his life. "A couple of weeks before he died he told me that he didn't know what was wrong with Lacey [their Labrador retriever], that she wouldn't 'Come' to him anymore like she used to. Although she would still wait to greet him at the door, once he came in she would retreat under the kitchen table. My husband unfortunately took his own life and I have always wondered if Lacey 'knew' that he was going to do that. I have no other explanation for why she started distancing herself from him in the two weeks prior to his death." Ms. Payne described a regular ritual she had with Lacey in the evening, saying "Daddy's home" when she heard her husband enter the garage. Lacey would always run to the family room window, look out and bark, then run to the door and wait for him to come in with a "present" in her mouth. Soon after her spouse's death, Ms. Payne once tested Lacey's response when she said the familiar "Daddy's home." Lacey dropped her ears, did not go to the window, and instead looked sad and went to lie down. The concern shown toward suffering human companions that many animals show reveals the depth of their empathy.

Mary F. Wilson from Livonia, Michigan, writes with reference to animals sensing that their owners have died or been injured: "I am a hospice nurse and have been told of many of these instances by patients' families. So often in fact that I do not consider it unusual at all. Frequently families will tell me that a beloved pet will suddenly begin staying very close to the patient, even though we can see no outward signs of a change in the patient's condition. Subsequently the patient usually declines and dies within the next few days. I also am told occasionally that after the patient has died, the animal will avoid for some time going into the room where the patient had resided. I think that this demonstrates that animals are much more 'tuned in' to physical changes in 'their' people, and also shows that animals grieve."

Mac is a Scottish terrier, and he worked as a therapy dog with Larry Underhill from Norway, Michigan, at the local Veterans' Administration Hospital. Going the rounds of the beds on Saturday, they came to the shared room of one of Mac's favorite patients, but his bed was empty. But Larry decided to take Mac in anyway to visit with the other patient in the two-bed room. "As I started into the room," he writes, "Mac would not go. It was like trying to pull a black brick someplace that he did not want to go. Absolutely, no amount of coaxing or treat offering was going to change his mind." Soon after a nurse told Larry that the patient had died just the day before. "Chills started to run down my back," he writes, "when I realized

Mac had seen/felt something that was there. Maybe he felt the spirit of his buddy was gone on, I really don't know. However, it was an experience I will never forget. Unfortunately within six months, we discovered that Mac had cancer and we decided to put him down. All his buddies at the hospital were saddened when they heard the news."

Roxanne MacKinnon sent me an interesting letter about her mother, a cancer victim passing on peacefully at home, and how her mother's dog reacted. Roxanne writes, "On the day she expired, her miniature schnauzer, Sarah, was lying on my husband's lap in the living room across the house, while he read the paper. I was in the family room watching my mother take her last breath. Suddenly, Sarah jumped off my husband's lap, ran into the family room, jumped up on the side of my mother's bed, and looked at her as she had taken her last breath, then looked up toward the ceiling, as if she could see or sense the soul leaving the body. Sarah then proceeded to get down from my mom's bed, and ran back into the living room to once again be with my husband. I have *never* seen anything like this before. Sarah came out of nowhere the minute my mother took her last breath."

The vigilance and empathy of dogs may even cross over the space-time continuum, as in this remarkable account by Lois R. Smithwick from Hurts, Texas. On a cruise with her husband, she woke one morning at 5:00 a.m.,

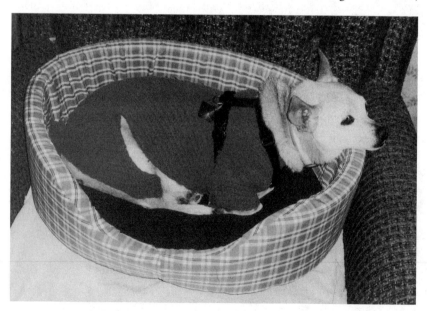

Radar, tucked in for the night.
Photo: Lois R. Smithwick

hearing their dog, Radar, scratching at the door. (Radar is her daughter's beloved rescue dog that was going to be killed by his former owners because they were moving into a new house; she and her husband took care of Radar each day while their daughter worked as a nurse.) "It was as natural, as if we had been at home with Radar getting my attention to check on 'Papa.' When I first heard the scratch my first thought was that I was missing him so much I was hearing things. Then when I became fully awake I realized all was not well with my husband. When I checked his blood sugar it was 27. If it gets below 50 it is said to be critical or the patient can go into a diabetic coma. I was able to go into immediate action and give him glucose to raise his blood sugar. When I think about my normal wakeup time I get chills down my back. It is mind-boggling to me to think that Radar's thought processes got to me when he was in Hurst, Texas, and we were aboard a cruise ship in the middle of the Mediterranean."

Radar (what an appropriate name!) and the other wonderful animals in the above testimonies affirm that animals do indeed possess super-senses of prescience, deep empathy, and remote or distance-sensing *and* communicating. This lays the groundwork for launching into the next chapter, which explores the profound realm of animals' "extraterrestrial" or afterlife communication and manifestation from beyond the grave—when beloved animals no longer exist on this mortal plane to share their lives with their human companions. But still they do, and somehow can.

The evidence to be presented raises profound philosophical, religious, metaphysical, and other challenging questions that some readers will find life- and personal-belief affirming. Others will find it unsettling and I hope life-changing—in terms of their regard for and treatment of animals sanctioned by the dominant culture's prevailing worldview in these times.

10.
| Animals Communicating After Death: The Evidence |

Humans, being aware of our own mortality, have elaborated various beliefs in an afterlife, which are part of every culture around the world and evident in the earliest recorded history of our species. But is it all hocus-pocus—the notion of life after death, of life after life, of some heaven to come?

It is all a simple fabrication of the human psyche to cushion the fear of death and the feeling that, if there is only this one life for us, then what's the point of it all? And why bother even trying to be good, if after this life there is absolutely nothing—nada, zilch? People who conclude a life after death is a fabrication through what they call "reason" are in my mind going beyond reason to embrace nihilism or nothingness.

I believe the significance of your present life is connected to your ancestral spiritual past and future—from grave to grave, womb to womb, world to world, and universe to universe. Australian aborigines call these spiritual connections through time and space our *song lines*. Christian mystics speak of the transmigration of the soul from life to life as the journey of the pilgrim soul, a vision shared by Hindus, Buddhists, and many others. This notion of the traveling of our souls or spirits from life to life, called reincarnation, was declared anathema—wrong thinking and bordering on heresy—by the early Church of Rome (for political reasons, most theological historians believe).

In Western civilization, the Age of Reason—as it is called, around the sixteenth and seventeenth centuries AD—further eroded earlier spiritual beliefs by declaring that only humans and not animals have immortal souls, because animals are our inferiors, lacking in reason and morality. This chauvinistic view of animals is alive and well today in many circles, from those involved in exploiting animals for profit and those seeking to protect the status quo of human superiority and domination over the rest of God's, or Mother Earth's, creations.

Now just suppose that dead animals could communicate and even manifest themselves physically (or, according to Theosophists, as an etheric double or astral body) to their human companions still living on this plane but grieving their departure terribly: What if this communication and manifestation could be verified? Would this not upset the apple cart of the nihilists, rational materialists, and those who think only humans have immortal souls and are special? The impact would be as profound as would the arrival of intelligent life-forms visiting us from outer space.

As for the evidence that I have gathered of the persistence of animals' spirits after their death, the following letters provide irrefutable proof. First, there is the partial manifestation and communication with the human loved one in the form most often of familiar touch. The veracity of this after-death communication is reinforced by the fact that several people have independently experienced *the same thing*. Second, further affirmation of after-death communication—and therefore existence of the animal's spirit after physical death in this dimension—comes from more than one individual seeing the manifestation of their beloved animal, partial or complete, together at the same time, or separately at different times in the same place.

No matter how much parsimony, skepticism, scientific objectivity, and impartial judgment I apply in assessing the following accounts of "visitations" by deceased companion animals, the accounts speak for themselves. They give no intimation of some mental creation and projection, or associative conditioning, in which the person claiming to have experienced such a visitation/communication is simply hallucinating or imagining that their beloved animal has returned from beyond the grave in order to help make them grieve less from the loss. While such manifestations are clearly comforting and affirming of the belief in life after life, I find no evidence in these letters that the people involved "called up" their deceased animal companions to comfort them. Rather, they appeared spontaneously and unexpectedly, thus ruling out the possibility of psychic conjuring and imaginative creation. (But this is not meant to imply that the deceased, human and nonhuman, cannot be "called" in times of need through prayer, meditation, ritual, and dream states.)

Many people believe there is a Heaven and a Hell, and that bad people go to Hell, while angels and our beloved animals (whom some people regard as angelic beings) abide in Heaven. But I like what Milton wrote: "The mind is its own place, and in itself can make a Heaven of Hell, a Hell of Heaven." I believe that the notion and creation of Heaven and Hell are purely human in origin.

The love of animals reveals to us the boundless love of the Creator, just as our love of nature reveals to us the nature of love. The thirteenth-century German theologian Meister Eckhart wrote: "Apprehend God in all things, or God is in all things. Every single creature is full of God, and is a book about God. Every creature is a word of God."

Saint Francis of Assisi said that it is through animals and nature that God is revealed to us. Hence he was recently named the Patron Saint of Ecology by the Catholic Church, but has been long and better remembered as the Patron Saint of the Animals. His teachings clearly influenced Eckhart. If every creature is a word of God, then God is speaking to us through them, which is precisely what St. Francis experienced in prayer, meditation, and rapture as he preached to the birds of Assisi in praise of the Creator and all of creation.

In light of this, it shouldn't be surprising if animals could communicate with us after they have entered the Light and left our physical presence. And indeed they do.

Experiences of Those Who Have Lost Animals

Elinor Lovegrove, from Shelton, Connecticut, wrote to me about an experience she shared with her husband. She wrote in a letter: "My husband had a grey cat named Rosemary. We had her for seventeen years and she was a dearly beloved pet. When she died my husband was broken-hearted. We were sculptors together and he spent a lot of time in our studio where Rosemary sunned herself daily on a drawing table. A week after her death he called me to the next room. He asked if I had changed my cologne. As I went to the doorway, I was struck by a lovely fragrance. I said, 'What on earth is that?' He said 'I don't know.' It was suddenly gone. It was February, the windows were shut. We both puzzled over it but had no answers. That night we were watching TV in the living room. John shouted 'Ellie look!' The fragrance filled the room and his darling Rosemary was leaving the room with her tail up in the air! This was normally her sign of great satisfaction. Suddenly she was gone and so was the lovely fragrance. We both saw her, in living color. John was in tears. This episode comforted us."

That fact that two people saw the same manifestation of their deceased animal companion in the same place and at the same time certainly supports that this experience was not simply a projection from John's imagination. They also smelled the perfumed aura of Rosemary's spirit, or essence-nature, and saw her physical manifestation that could well have been willed by Rosemary as a final act of love to assuage their grief and give them every assurance that she was indeed well and in the best of spirits in her new dimension.

Another complete manifestation, this time of a dog, was reported to me by Marion V. Russo from Hendersonville, North Carolina. She writes: "It was ten days after Noelle, our German shepherd, passed away. It was dusk and my husband and I were on the deck when a large brown dog with black markings went running past us. We gasped in shock and we said to each other, 'Did you see that?' It was Noelle. We could not speak for quite a while. I said she came back to say a final farewell. My husband did not want to admit to what we both saw, but it was our dear Noelle."

Mrs. Russo's second dog, another rescued stray that was part shepherd, also manifested herself after death. "After Chrissy died I saw her vision and heard her footsteps in the house for many months. I still hear her, especially when I am in the kitchen. She loved her food and when my husband has a late snack he hears her footsteps too. In fact he looks down at the side of his chair and says, 'Chrissy, I know you are there.'"

Some photographers have claimed to have captured images on film of alleged apparitions, which may be fake or mere artifacts of light or defective processing. But one photograph sent to me by retired U.S. Air Force officer and experienced photographer Robert J. Young of Kernesville, North Carolina—which he had examined by film experts—may indeed have captured a genuine manifestation. He was in his garden with the sun behind him one early May afternoon and took two pictures of his dog Cheyenne using a Minolta single lens reflex camera and Kodak 800 film. The first picture showed Cheyenne lying beneath a Colorado Blue Spruce tree that had been planted in memory of their deceased dog Lady, who had passed on in November the previous year. The second picture revealed a light, transparent cloud hovering in the air in front of the tree just above Cheyenne.

Mr. Young wrote to me to say, "God would not call home one of his creatures and leave behind those that loved the dog without some way for them to know that the dog was safe and in his loving care. And that the dog although gone was still watching over the people she loved. I believe that He allowed our beloved Lady to visit us and let us know."

Judith A. Sellins, who lives in Westerly, Rhode Island, often sees her deceased black cat Whiskers. "But I haven't been the only one to see him," she writes. "My daughter as well as others have also seen him, asking me when I got another black cat. But I don't have a black cat. He has been seen walking into my bedroom and through my dining room."

Cathy Andronik from Bridgeport, Connecticut, sent an interesting account: "For thirteen years my family had a pet cat, Rusty, who with his temper was quite a challenge to love, but who could be affectionate when he chose. After a long, good life, he was euthanized well over ten years ago. One thing he loved was to jump on my bed early in the morning and stare

The apparition above the dog Cheyenne around the tree planted in memory of the dog Lady. My close examination of this remarkable photograph leads me to conclude that this manifestation was a fine, amorphous energy field of light that could be one of the ways by which deceased animals may communicate to the living. It is noteworthy that while he was taking the photograph, Mr. Young did not actually see the apparition of light hovering in front of Lady's tree.
Photo: Robert J. Young

into my face, nose to nose, until he was satisfied that I was awake. One night last fall, I was awakened by the sensation of something about the size and weight of a cat—landing on my bed. When I opened my eyes, I clearly saw the shape of a cat's face and ears in front of me, and sensed an animal's presence. The shape was so solid it partially blocked the numbers on the alarm clock. When I blinked a moment later it was gone. While I remember Rusty frequently and fondly, I am certainly no longer mourning his loss. He was, however, the special companion of my mother, who passed away about three years ago, and I like to think that he paid me a visit to let me know that he and my mother are keeping one another company again."

Donna Ballard of Flint, Michigan, was on a trip to Greece and left her husband in charge of their cat Beau, a Maine coon, who was in failing health. She writes: "The Thursday before I was to come home I was reading in bed at three in the morning when I noticed a movement in the corner of the room by the ceiling. I looked up and there was Beau. He floated down to my book and disappeared. I did not go back to sleep so I know I didn't dream it. On my return, my husband picked me up at the airport and I said, 'You had to put Beau down didn't you?' He answered, 'Yes, how do you know?' 'Was it Thursday?' I asked. 'Yes, it was Thursday,' he replied."

Cheryl Morgan from Milford, Connecticut, wrote to say that she is a devout Catholic and all three of her beloved dogs had to be euthanized at different times because of intractable old-age health problems. First, after her border collie was put down, she says, "As I was riding my bicycle, I could see him running alongside me in spirit. He was very happy, and he was like a puppy again. This enabled me to let him go."

Subsequently, after her beloved beagle was euthanized, she saw the beagle and border collie running and playing alongside her bicycle, and she saw all three of her dogs running beside her on the bicycle and happily playing soon after she had the third old dog, a cocker spaniel, put to sleep.

Anita Perry from Anaheim, California, was regularly "visited" by her dog Barney a month after he passed on. When still living on this plane he used to bump the side of her bed with his nose when he wanted to go outside, and she was awakened by the same bump, which she initially thought, living in California, might be an earthquake. These nightly bumps went on for many months. "One night when I awakened to turn over in bed—I saw his reflection in a mirrored closet door. I was surprised but so glad that he was there. Looking closer at the floor, in front of the mirror, where he should be, he wasn't there. He could only be seen in the mirror."

Some time later she asked Barney's veterinarian if he had heard of anything like this before. "He laughed and said that his dog Charlie, who had died ten years before, is felt jumping off the bed every night by both he and his wife."

Ms. Perry has collected similar accounts of the "visitations" of departed animals, noting, "The owners of those pets said their life was changed for the better by their experiences," and that such documentation would greatly help in grief support for those who have recently lost a pet. I would add that this will also help those who are *about* to lose a loved one, human or non-human, or who are about to die themselves. Sharing some of these accounts with my old and terminally ill father-in-law Jim Krantz, a salty World War II veteran tank commander who has seen enough of suffering and death, elicited a sage response: "Animals know much more than most people give them credit for."

Alice Cruze in Holyoke, Massachusetts, was visited by her deceased ten-year-old Peek-a-Poo Austin, about a month after he was put to sleep: "I was slightly awakened by something jumping onto the bed. I recognized the familiar walk and knew this wasn't possibly Austin. Yet I reached out my hand and felt him begin to quiver all over, something he did when excited in his healthier days. I felt him kiss my cheek. I ran my hand down his back. I needed to feel the tail as he had a distinctive curly tail. Just as my hand touched his tail, he was gone. I felt my cheek and it was damp. The next morning I told my husband about my 'dream' and he said, 'I thought I heard Austin's footsteps in the room last night but realized it couldn't be.' I truly believe Austin came back to me to let me know he was happy and in a good place."

Sometimes the manifestation of the animal is only partial, like Marian West's deceased stray cat, Whitey, who lived with her in St. Louis, Missouri. One evening while reading in bed she felt "a cat jump on to the bed and begin to knead my leg. Without looking, I reached down to pet him and was surprised to find no cat on the bed. The stray loved to sleep curled around my legs and would always go through the ritual of kneading before he settled down to sleep. Since then he's visited me several times—I would see a flash of white from the corner of my eye. My other cats have acted strangely from time to time and in my heart I truly feel Whitey is popping in to say 'hello.' I might add that these visits rather than being frightening are quite comforting."

People who have experienced incomplete manifestations of their deceased companion animals have variously heard them breathing, drinking, eating, and walking on the floor, and they felt them close, especially lying beside them on the bed or jumping on to the bed. Sometimes they appear fully in a dream that can be so vivid that the dreamers may believe they were actually awake.

Awake or dreaming, Aaron Marten was in the Navy on board ship asleep in his bunk when, according to his mother Louise Marten of Galveston, Texas, he was awakened by a scratching at his door. "When he opened it," she writes, "there was Lucky, his dog. He jumped on to Aaron's bunk and Aaron went back to sleep thinking he was dreaming. In the morning Lucky was gone; but there was bits of white fur on his blanket." When Aaron was on shore leave he discovered that his beloved dog had died around the time he had the visitation on board ship. Some people feel their attachment and grief after their animal companion has died may keep the animal from passing on—and they should be allowed to be "released."

Lisa Biagiarelli from Easton, Connecticut, had a difficult time getting over the loss of her old cat Bobo, whom she often felt was around her feet and was staying around to comfort her. So she spoke to Bobo and said: "I know you are here with me. I know all you ever wanted was to be with me. But if you have the chance to go someplace better, to be with St. Francis (to whom I used to pray for Bobo's health), you should go. I will be OK—you can go. I immediately felt him leave me, and I have never felt him under my feet since that time. I know he is in a better place and I also know that someday I will see my beautiful Siamese again."

Alice Weir was sitting in her armchair beside the window in her home in Shelton, Connecticut, grieving over the loss of her old cat Chelsan. He had a habit of jumping off his bed on the bay window onto the left arm of her chair to get to the floor. "As I sat crying and thinking of him I felt a brush like fur on my cheek on the left side of my face where he jumped. I felt it was his way of telling me thanks for the good care I gave him before his passing and letting me know he was alright now."

Maryann Gallant in Stuyvesant, New York, shares a similar experience. Her mini-poodle Pepe started going blind at age eleven; until he passed on six years later, he developed the habit of following her around the house, staying close to her right leg and repeatedly touching her right calf with his cold nose. She and her husband grieved for Pepe for days and days. "One

Saturday morning," she writes, "I got up and without a single thought of him started to walk down the dark hallway to the kitchen. All of a sudden, I felt a cold wet nose on my calf. My heart jumped for joy and I looked down expecting to see him, but alas there was no Pepe."

I have received accounts of surviving animals seeming to respond to the spirit-presence of a recently deceased animal companion. Such an experience was shared by Ann Simanton from Houston, Texas, with her young cat. The evening after she had to euthanize her old cat she went to bed. The old cat had always slept with her on her bed. This evening she felt his presence in his usual place, on a bundle of covers that "started moving up and down and vibrating as though it was breathing and purring." She checked to see if the younger cat was under the bundle, but she was asleep on the couch. Going back to bed, she put her hand on the bundle. "It was moving and purring, and my hand and the bundle was covered with small 'sparks,'" she writes. Then, "I heard a scream from the other room and the younger cat, who had not yet set foot in the bedroom since the older one's departure, came screaming into the room, jumped on the bed, ran to the sparking, purring bundle of covers and started kneading it like mad and 'talking' to it, in the little 'chirpy' language they used between themselves." This was the only visitation she had from her deceased feline companion. Interestingly, the next day when Ms. Simanton described this experience to her veterinarian, the vet confided that she had seen each of her two dogs after they had passed on, but had never shared this experience with anyone before.

Karin D. Welsch from Albany, New York, was a student whose parents delayed telling her of the death of her cat Socks until her final exams were over. The night they told her she had a dream: "Socks came to me; he looked at me and I was made to understand that he had returned to give me the one last visit I had been wishing for. The images in my dream were so vivid and the message so clear, that it has forever affected my views on life, death, and afterlife."

*　*　*

Many people are uncomfortable sharing such experiences—fearing the ridicule of skeptics and the prejudices of rationalists and materialists, as well as those who do not believe in disembodied spirits and in animals being living souls, just like you and me. Others cast doubt on their own spiritual and metaphysical experiences, dismissing them as products of the imagination to help relieve grief, guilt, anger, loneliness, and other feelings associated with the loss and mourning of a beloved animal companion.

But as long as we deny the deep heart connection these animals can provide, we will continue to deprive ourselves of experiencing one of the greatest, life-changing affirmations of universal love that is manifested through the devotion shared between us and our animal companions. They are not simply our property; they are part of life universal in spirit, and part of the great mystery of the soul's journey from life to life.

It is easy to dismiss the miracles of every day and the intimacy with all that is sacred, which is invited by an open heart and mind, as the animals teach us time and time again—life after life. Many people have been profoundly moved and comforted by these afterlife communications by their animal companions, and their lives have been significantly changed by the revelation that there is more to mortal life than we know. We must all agree with Jim Krantz that animals do indeed know far more than most people give them credit for.

11.
| Delving Deeper:
Dogs as Our Mirror |

In my experience, our first impressions of animals and our reactive feelings we recall from our earliest childhood memories determine our ability to understand and communicate with animals. No matter how good our empirical sciences may be in this regard, our feelings and attitudes—our deepest beliefs, fears, and longings—ultimately determine how well we understand and communicate with each other, and therefore by extension, with other animals and nature.

My earliest memories of seeing other animals and being with dogs are of awe, wonder, and delight. They were something other, profoundly other. It was their diverse otherness that helped me realize that the world was not just for people but for myriad other life-forms. In their diversely adaptive modes of being and consciousness, they evidenced purpose, will, and intentionality. Dogs were my first teachers and closest nonhuman friends. I was never hurt or frightened by an animal. Many taught me the nature of respect, and to respect nature.

As a child, I found that every dog was a potential buddy—usually friendly and always fascinating, nontalking, yet somehow an easily understood significant other. Dogs were my companions, playmates, sometimes patients, and rescued strays—and above all, my teachers. They taught me about dogs, about what being a dog means in terms of likes and dislikes, and of expressing and understanding various feelings, needs, intentions, and expectations. Adults have to let go in many ways before dogs can be their teachers and healers. It's much easier for children who are not afraid and have not yet learned the anthropocentric catechism of adults who would delude them into regarding dogs and all nonhuman animals as inferior, irrational, unfeeling, even immoral soulless beings.

Professor Marc Bekoff has done much to encourage other scientists to examine this catechism in relation to their own studies of animal emotions. His collection of evidence in *The Smile of a Dolphin: Remarkable Accounts of Animal Emotions*[1] posits that nonhuman animals are not only our equals, but often our superiors in the domain of feelings and sensibility. His work is extremely convincing.

But as writer Isaac Bashevis Singer noted, "In their behavior toward creatures, all men were Nazis. . . . The smugness with which man could do with species as he pleased exemplifies the most extreme racist theories, the principle that might is right."

When I taught animal behavior/ethology in the 1970s at Washington University, St. Louis, I made it clear in my introductory lecture that the behavior of animals provide us a window into their minds, their consciousness, because much of their behavior expresses their motivations, needs, intentions, expectations, and especially their feelings or emotional states. In social contexts, their behavior enables us to better understand social relationships and modes of communication (or languages)—with the realization that animals understand each other and are adept ethologists themselves! Also, in various environmental contexts their behavior might reveal adaptively evolved mechanisms, patterns, and strategies. Some of these, like their communication signals, are innate or instinctual. They may not be consciously mediated or modulated (just as when we unselfconsciously and spontaneously smile at someone). But this does not mean that animals are unconscious, instinctual automatons. I call such a parsimonious "scientific" interpretation of animals' behavior *mechanomorphization*.

The Notion of Animals as Machines

The belief that dogs and other animals are unconscious, unfeeling machines has been around for several centuries. Such parsimony is part of the so-called objectivity of science and of perceiving and, unfortunately so, often treating animals as unfeeling objects of scientific investigation. This perception

---

1. Marc Bekoff, ed., *The Smile of a Dolphin: Remarkable Accounts of Animal Emotions* (New York: Discovery Books, 2000). See also Jonathan Balcome, *Pleasurable Kingdom: Animals and the Nature of Feeling Good* (New York: Macmillan, 2006).

is based on the Cartesian philosophy, the mechanistic and dualistic philosophy of seventeenth-century French philosopher René Descartes. This highly influential "Enlightenment" era thinker contended that the screams of dogs being cut open and dissected in the name of science and medical progress were simply the sounds of their clock-work mechanisms breaking down.[2]

Descartes held that only humans had rational souls, "I think, therefore I am." He followed the earlier Greek Stoic philosophers' view (that Saint Thomas Aquinas put into Christianity) that animals are not rational because they have no language. Being irrational, they lack conscience and therefore cannot be moral agents and therefore be entitled to certain rights and interests. Being brute and irrational, animals can have no consciousness of themselves either, according to Cartesianism. This means that when they are physically injured, like a clock, they become dysfunctional but are not conscious of any pain. Having neither reason nor language, they can have no real emotions—such as fear, pleasure, anxiety, and affection. Such emotions are exclusively human. To attribute such human-like emotions to animals is to commit the Cartesian taboo of anthropomorphization—of regarding animals as being more similar to us than they are different. On the contrary, when animals experience sensations, such as thirst, hunger, or pain, and associated conditional signals (a whistle or a command), their reactions are to be regarded as being purely instinctual, and therefore unconscious.

People were once burned at the stake, hanged, drowned, or excommunicated for having the "witch's power" of being able to talk to animals, and of having a way with them that other people did not possess. Such people—who were often lonely and reclusive, preferring to share their lives with many cats and other animals rather than associate with ignorantly superstitious neighbors—were seen as heretics, pagans, devil worshippers, and heathens promoting animism and pantheism. Cats especially were associated with evil, and black dogs and other animals that were black or had unusual markings (or were wild but had been rescued, healed from injury, and become tame familiars in the hands of the "witch") were seen to be possessed and under satanic control.

There is a political agenda in the purportedly more enlightened times of today behind the scientism that claims that since the subjective—the

2. Keith Thomas, *Man and the Natural World: A History of Modern Sensibility* (New York: Pantheon, 1983).

realm of emotion, cognition, soul, and spirit—cannot be measured and quantified, it does not really exist, except in our own imaginations. Only the objective and empirically verifiable is real and all else is irrational, even mystical superstition.

This is the essence of Cartesian philosophy that has been promoted as fact (and scientism as truth) in order to distance people from other animals who were seen as being inferior, lacking souls, reason, feelings, etc. Then there would be no twinge of conscience, sense of shame, remorse, guilt, or outrage over the cruel exploitation of animals for pecuniary and other selfish reasons, or over the annihilation of wildlife habitat and indigenous communities of animals and people who were inferior, pagan, and heathen.

One of the reasons why people enjoy the company of dogs, cats, and other animals, and have one or more in their lives, is perhaps because the animal is an antidote to the kind of soulless, heartless world of materialism and consumerism in which most of us are ensnared, and the superficiality and lack of intimacy. *The human spirit needs intimacy* in most human relations.

As psychotherapist and former monk Thomas Moore, in his book *Original Self*, concludes, "Politicians and the politics of normalcy contribute to the fostering of a soulless society, hell bent on materialism and superficiality. If you are normalized to a psychotic society, it is not a good place to be. . . . You've got to have one foot in and one foot out of this society, because this is a soulless society." A life without passion and meaning is no life at all. A soulless society is a society that regards animals as soulless and treats them accordingly. Moore advises, "Do things that are counter to society. It keeps you sane. Not normal but sane. You can't keep it all inward, or you go nuts."

I think I am not alone in acknowledging how my dogs, as well as my work as a veterinarian and animal rights advocate, keep me from going nuts. My dogs keep me in touch with the real, because, honest to dog, they are authentic, empathic antidotes to a soulless society—just as those people who understand their need for cats, or to be with horses or other companion animals, or to work in wildlife rescue rehabilitation will attest to.

Love for Animals

My studies of animals have taught me how unreasonable, irrational, unconscious, and terrifyingly devoid of emotion some humans, rather than animals, can be. How humans behave toward other animals reveals much about their attitudes, beliefs, and values—notably the materialistic, the mechanistic, and the scientific detached and "objective," as well as the controlling, the dominating, the fearful, the indifferent, and, yes, the caring and the loving.

I once witnessed Professor Konrad Lorenz, Nobel Laureate and one of the founding fathers of the science of ethology, address an international assembly of academics. He said, "Before you can really study and understand an animal, you must first love it." Many Cartesian scientists at the conference did not agree with Konrad, some sitting close to me said that Konrad had "gone soft," and that such a remark was unscholarly because it was subjective, emotional, and therefore unscientific.

What Prof. Lorenz was advocating was an element of human affect that he felt was as much lacking in our everyday relationships with each other and with other animals, as it was in the research laboratory and in the field. He told me that he was concerned that progress in the science of understanding animals through ethology, and in public appreciation and concern for animals, were being undermined by latter-day Cartesians, mechanistic reductionists, and "objective" behavioral psychologists. He trusted that "I couldn't disagree less" with him—which was quite true.

It was also true that mere sentimental love was not what he was calling for. Sentimental and possessive "love," with all its projections and conditionality, is no basis for acquiring a deep understanding of animal behavior and consciousness. He was calling for a deeper, empathic connection that has its origins in our own aboriginal past where our ancestors could indeed "talk" with the animals and become them. While this kind of relationship with animals may seem quasi-spiritual or mystical to our modern sensibilities—and certainly taboo to latter-day Cartesians mechanists—it was immensely practical and a survival skill for the adept hunter and, later, for the pastoralist and farmer.

The kind of love that Prof. Lorenz was advocating was both empathic and caring, which are the ingredients for a deeper understanding of animals' emotions and intentions and so critical to our relationship with animals, as well as our relationships with each other, and especially with our children. Such love makes for a mutually enhancing relationship between human and nonhuman. But where it is believed that animals are "dumb brutes," lacking in reason, intelligence, and feeling, there can be no such relationship. Nor can there be when it is taboo to infer certain emotional states in animals showing virtually the same behavior as we would under similar circumstances: the taboo of anthropomorphizing.

How People Affect Animals

Animals have taught me that how they are perceived by a person—as friendly, or dangerous, or even manipulative and untrustworthy—influences how that animal responds to that person. Further, people's perceptions, which are influenced by their attitudes and beliefs, greatly determine how an animal's behavior is interpreted. It is, of course, naïve to believe that all animals are either harmless and friendly (or harmful and aggressive) and respond to them accordingly. It is no less absurd to respond to them as if they were unfeeling automatons or mere commodities—inferior beings that are simply objects of possession. No mutually enhancing human-animal relationship could ever develop from such a mind-set, or from the mind-set of one who regards wild animals as trophies or pests, or from the mind-set of one who views domestic animals as degenerate versions of their wild ancestors.

A mutually enhancing human-animal relationship, based on the kind of love that Prof. Lorenz advocates, is enlightened self-interest—for the dairy or pig farmer, and for all who have dogs or other companion animals in their homes. As the old saying goes, where there is love there is understanding, but where there is ignorance, there is prejudice and fear. Several studies have recently documented how farm animals are healthier and more productive when they are on friendly terms with their caretakers. Sows produce more piglets, hens more eggs, and cows more milk. Gentle, routine handling of infant animals, and also of their mothers during pregnancy, amazingly enhances their resistance to stress and to various diseases later in life.

I was involved in this area of research in the 1960s and '70s, applying it for the U.S. Armed Forces in Viet Nam in developing "superdogs" that saved many lives in combat. The early handling, socialization, and environmental enrichment programs that I set up helped make these dogs more resistant to stress in combat, and better able to work under intense field conditions—spotting snipers, ambushes, and land mines.

Dogs as Mirrors

Dogs and cats, in becoming integral members of the human family, learn to modify certain behaviors and acquire others to better communicate their basic social and emotional needs. In the process, they "train" their human companions as much (and sometimes more so) than they are trained by their owners.

Through the interaction of genes (heredity) and early conditioning, dogs and cats develop different temperaments; and through the interaction of temperament with learning and social relationships, distinct personalities are formed.

Some people say there are no bad dogs—nor are there wild, aggressive, or fearful cats that can't be tamed—and that it is primarily human influences that determine how a dog's or cat's personality develops.

But genetic factors do influence temperament and certainly affect the quality of the bond we may enjoy with the animal, to the degree that no matter how much love and understanding has been given during early, critical, sensitive periods of development, the animal in question never really seems to fit in or enjoy life (just like some children). They do not, therefore, always mirror us, but most times, they do.

The fact that people often resemble the animals they live with—sometimes with striking psychological and physical similarity, especially in terms of temperament and demeanor—may be more than coincidence. A process that I have termed *sympathetic resonance* may account for this phenomenon, which cannot be dismissed as pure coincidence.

Dogs are as much a mirror of our humanity as they are subjects of our inhumanity. Dogs' well-being as our domesticated companions reflects our own well-being. This is determined less by our economic well-being than by our spiritual capacity to care for our families and communities, both human and nonhuman. Their well-being is a clear indicator of how civilized society has become. As William Blake observed in his poem, "A dog starved at his Master's Gate predicts the ruin of the State."

Just as we have different personalities, so too do our dogs and cats. They can also mirror various behaviors that we recognize in ourselves as deceptive and saving face.

Deceitful Dogs and Fair Play

To be deliberately deceptive involves a kind of reasoning and insight that the mechanists would deny dogs being capable of doing. But it is not an imaginative projection or anthropomorphization (seeing dogs as humans) to accept the following examples as deceptive behavior in dogs and to acknowledge that such behavior demonstrates self-consciousness.

- One of my first professional articles was a review of cases of *sympathy lameness* in dogs. Dogs will feign a leg injury in order to get their human companion's attention. One research colleague told me she saw her dog running in the yard and showing no sign of lameness. But as soon as the dog decided to come back indoors, she would start to limp on one foreleg. Sometimes she got the legs confused. This behavior began after the dog had recovered from a bad cut on her left front paw.

- My dog Lizzie will give two or three alarm barks. The two other, younger, natural (i.e., pariah or mixed breed) dogs from India then bark and run to look out of the window or yard fence to see what's there for Lizzie to bark at. Lizzie then goes over to the water bowl and drinks in peace, since when they are all thirsty, she's always last in the drinking peck-order.

- I've seen some dogs, and also coyotes and wolves, engage in what ethologists call *fascination behavior*, or *tolling*. There's a French breed of hunting dog that has been selectively bred to engage in this behavior on the edge of a river or lake to lure ducks and other water birds closer. The birds, or the prey of wolves and coyotes, become curious at the crazy antics of the hunter, who dives, rolls, and spins, and either draws closer and closer to the unsuspecting prey, or lures the curious prey within reach of paws and jaws.

There are skeptics who do not believe that dogs have a sense of guilt, shame, or a conscience. Again I think that such skepticism is responsible for maintaining the status quo of animals as inferior beings, and therefore making them ours to exploit, as long as the ends justify the means. Here is one ancedote that no skeptic can dismiss.

A woman who wrote to me about her family dog, who took a toy plane from her son's pillow while the boy was sleeping and put one of the dog's own chew toys on the pillow. Was this a fair exchange in the dog's mind? That's how this woman interpreted what transpired, and I can think of no other plausible interpretation of the dog's motives.

Self-Awareness

These examples of canine deception leave no doubt in my mind that dogs are self-aware. But to some psychologists like Professor Gordon Gallup, self-awareness is evident only in humans and apes. Prof. Gallup published his findings in a psychology journal, claiming that he had the key to objectively determine if animals are self-aware. He came to this fatuous claim after getting various primate species used to seeing themselves in a mirror. When he put a mark on the animals' foreheads, the apes used the mirror to try to remove the spot once they noticed it in the reflection. But the monkeys he tested had no response. So he proposed, on the basis of this simplistic test, that monkeys are not self-aware; only our closest relatives, the apes, are.

This conclusion is based on reductionistic and anthropocentric (human-centered) thinking and the inflation of a single behavioral response—self-grooming of the spot in the mirror—to be the sole indicator of whether or not an animal is self-conscious. No less a significant indicator of self-awareness in this same context is the *absence* of a behavioral response. Dogs, for example, ignore their images in a mirror after initially reacting as though it is another dog. They will use the mirror in other ways, seeing and responding to what is going on behind them while they are looking into the mirror.

I do know of some cats and Asian elephants who will use a mirror to wipe a spot off their foreheads, but maybe dogs are less image-conscious or narcissistic. The anthropocentric thinking of Prof. Gallup and others is problematic. By this I mean the act of interpreting the behavior, sociality, and learning abilities of other animals from the yardstick of how humans would think and act under similar circumstances. Such pseudo-scientific performance determinations, like those of Prof. Gallup, only serve to reinforce the speciesist and racist attitudes of those extreme rationalists, chauvinists, and supremacists who are averse to the ethic of equalitarianism: of giving equal and fair consideration to the rights and interests of all beings, no matter how unintelligent they may seem.

Animal Altruism

Being altruistic is not an exclusively human virtue. There are many accounts of the incredible feats of heroism by dogs and cats rescuing family members and strangers from fire, drowning, and from dangerous people and other animals. Often in their altruistic behavior they demonstrate remarkable resourcefulness and insight.

Through altruism and empathy, dogs care for each other and thus contribute to the greater good of their community or social group. One case of altruism that is particularly stunning—and which rationalists will surely say is an animal rightists' fabrication—involves a dog doing minor surgery on another. My wife Deanna Krantz and I discovered four pendulous warts inside the lower lip of one of our dogs, Lizzie. This dog's older canine companion, a street dog from Arusha, Tanzania, aptly named Tanza, closely inspected the warts along with the two of us. I decided to take Lizzie to the vet hospital and remove the warts surgically the next day. But next morning, all the warts had been neatly excised with no bleeding or damage to the lip. Lizzie was used to being groomed and having her whiskers nibbled to their stubs by her African dog companion. To witness such altruistic behavior in animals is indeed a humbling experience and helps affirm our biological and spiritual kinship with them.

Tanza came from a region where the medical benefits of dog licking for various human skin conditions (and their role as a diaper service, ingesting and thus hygienically recycling the feces of human infants), made dogs welcome community members. It was the licks of dogs that healed the Biblical leper Lazarus. Recently, the healing properties of animal saliva have been confirmed by scientists who found antibiotic and tissue-healing substances in the saliva—one of nature's miracles of evolution indeed.

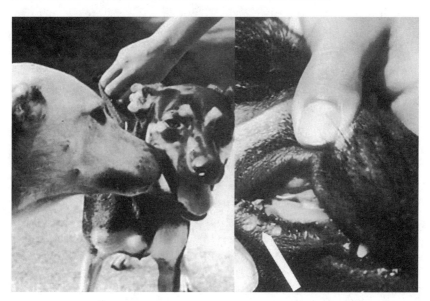

Tanza checks Lizzie's mouth the day after she removed several large warts from her lips (arrow indicates where they were).
Photos: M. W. Fox

More about Empathy

If animals were incapable of empathy, of understanding another's emotional state and having feeling for another's distress, then we would find no evidence of altruistic behavior in the animal kingdom. But we do. Ethologists use the terms caregiving (epimeletic behavior) and care-soliciting (et-epimeletic behavior) to identify those behaviors that underlie the altruism we see in various species, and that means animals do have the capacity to empathize.

Studying reactions in mice to other mice given mild noxious stimuli that caused stomachache-like pain, McGill University scientist Jeffrey Mogil and his Pain Genetics laboratory research team concluded that mice have a hardwired form of empathy that they termed *behavioral contagion*. Mice showed more empathy toward a familiar cage-mate than to a strange mouse in distress.[3]

Skeptics continue to dismiss evidence of animals' empathy as anthropomorphic and scientifically unproven, and it disturbs me to read some professional comments on this topic. For example, veterinarian John S. Parker stated that, "Pets can and often react to their owners' distress or discomfort, but that is not to be confused with experiencing the emotion of empathy."[4] Aside from contending that animals "do not have the cognitive capacity to put themselves in our place," he incorrectly sees empathy not as a process or affective state but as an actual emotion, which it is not. Animal ethics philosopher Dr. Bernard E. Rollin's response in this same journal[5] stating that "there is some very suggestive evidence that at least some animals, such as higher primates and elephants, do [empathize]" begs the question. The evidence from countless instances of empathetic behavior in companion animals is a red flag and not some anthropomorphic red herring, putting us all on notice that animals are far more aware than many people would like or accept, for reasons best known to themselves.

Here are some of the many accounts that people have shared with me about their empathetic animal companions.

Esther Schy from Fresno, California, writes, "When I returned from the Cancer Center following treatment, I was extremely weak and ill. My two Airedale dogs would each take up their positions, like two bookends,

---

3. *Science* magazine (June 30, 2006): 1860–1861.
4. Letter in the *Journal of the American Veterinary Medical Association* (June 1, 2006): 1677–1678.
5. *Journal of the American Veterinary Medical Association* (June 1, 2006): 1678.

one on either side of me in bed, and would lie there unmoving for hours, except for their taking turns laying their heads gently where I hurt the most."

One night two years earlier one of her dogs named Robbie "suddenly jumped up in bed next to my husband, almost plastered to his side. . . . He normally never did this preferring to sleep on his cushion next to my side of the bed. He kept trembling for one hour, and then went downstairs by himself, which is another action he did not normally do (leaving the bedroom at night). My husband suffered a massive heart attack and died a few minutes later. I believe that Robbie knew that something awful was to be."

Like the Airedales that rested their heads on where their human companion hurt most, M.S.D., from Romeo, Michigan, has a Siamese cat who picked up on her cardiac palpitations that were causing much distress and preventing her from sleeping. "My Chloe came up, got as close as she could, and placed her paw on my left chest over my heart. Within a very short time the palpitations slowed and stopped, allowing me to get a good night's rest."

Amy E. Snyder in Chesapeake, Virginia, was comforted by her Maine coon cat Bonkers, who slept at her side during her ordeal with throat cancer, giving her comfort and constant attention. Taking radiation treatment some one hundred miles away from home, Ms. Snyder was only able to come home on weekends; one weekend she found Bonkers lethargic and looking older. She took him to her veterinarian, and Bonkers was euthanized because he had developed an inoperable cancer, "completely cutting off his windpipe . . . I believe, due to the extreme oddness of similarity to our illness that my cat literally tried to take on my disease. He did get me through all of this."

This anecdote supports my theory of sympathetic resonance, where highly empathetic animals may develop the same or a similar disease that afflicts their loved one. Whether it is deliberate or coincidental, the fact remains that empathizing is not without risk for humans and nonhumans alike.

Patricia Anderson from Osceola, Missouri, had home nursing care after her sojourn in hospital, and the nurses were moved by her two cats, which she called her Guardian Angel Kitties. "My two gray tabby cats positioned themselves one on each side of me and they would not leave during the procedures the nurses needed to perform. When I was experiencing pain or feeling depressed I just had to reach a few inches and find a warm loving presence. They took turns getting down to eat and using the litter box so I was never alone. One day they both jumped down and began to romp and play in their usual manner. They knew, before I did, that I was healing and getting better."

Many other letters attest to how cats and dogs have helped their human companions cope with depression and other emotional and physical difficulties, especially the loss of a spouse or other close relative. Cary Watson from Clifton Park, New York, writes that, "Without my two dogs' companionship, dealing with the loss of my wife would have been much harder. I can see why many people die soon after losing a spouse. We need love to carry on."

Echoing this sentiment, Barbara K. Joyner of Courtland, Virginia, wrote that, following the untimely death of her husband to be, her adopted cats "make me feel wanted, needed, loved. They bring joy and happiness into my dark, sad existence."

Suffering the loss of her only child from suicide, Patricia Maunu of Sioux Falls, South Dakota, tells me that her bichon frise dog J'aime, "has given me the desire to get out of bed, and on many days given me the will to live!"

These and many other personal stories about how companion animals have helped their human guardians through difficult times and are a constant source of affection and the joy of life help us all appreciate why so many people who were victims of the Katrina hurricane disaster in New Orleans and other communities refused to leave without their animal companions. They are an integral part of the family and emotional lives of millions of people, and those who have not experienced the gifts of animal companionship, and the depths of animals' empathy, have missed a golden opportunity to enrich their lives and awaken their appreciation for all creatures great and small.

In the next chapter we will explore how animals can also play a significant role in our spiritual and moral development, as well as contributing in many ways to our emotional well-being.

12.
| Animals and Our Spiritual Development |

I have been a veterinarian for over forty years and have worked in animal protection as an animal rights and environmental advocate for over thirty years. My avocation has always been to improve the health and well-being of animals. I have learned a lot about human attitudes toward animals and I am disturbed that there is no unified sensibility. A most important and most difficult type of healing that I see needed in every country and culture—for the benefit of both the human and the nonhuman, is to restore the human-animal bond.

A healthy bond is one that is mutually enhancing. Two essential ingredients are required. First, a better knowledge of ecological and ethological science: the objective understanding of animals' environmental needs, behavior, communication, and emotions. Second, a better subjective understanding of animals as sentient, feeling beings. This requires establishing an empathic connection with animals. Empathy is the ability to share or experience another's feelings. (Many dogs I have known seem to be far better empathizers than the people with whom they live!)

Empathy is the emotional bridge that connects us with others. Scientific knowledge about animals does not establish a bond; empathy does. Scientific knowledge helps us better understand animals' needs, and gives us a greater clarity in interpreting their behavior, intentions, and emotional state. But it does not help us feel for animals. Feeling for animals comes from the heart—the core of our being more ancient and more sapient than all the factual information our intellects hold about the nature of ourselves and the sentient world.

Compassion and the Origin of Ethics

As Pascal observed, "The heart knows what reason knows not," meaning that wisdom comes not from the intellect alone, but also from our emotions. It is from our feeling for others that our moral sensibility and ethics arise.

Ethics and moral codes cannot make us feel for others. Our feeling for others comes through caring concern or mindfulness. The antithesis is to not be *mindful* of others, to be ignorant because of selfish preoccupation. Selfishness is thus the root of ignorance and makes empathy impossible.

Psychiatrist R. D. Laing[1] discusses the debasement of our humanity, the true nature of human beings, when we harm animals:

> *A woman grinds stuff down a goose's neck through a funnel. Is this a description of cruelty to an animal? She disclaims any motivation or intention of cruelty. If we were to describe this scene "objectively" we would only be denuding it of what is "objectively" or, better, ontologically present in the situation. Every description presupposes our ontological premises as to the nature (being) of man, of animals, and of the relationship between them. If an animal is debased to a manufactured piece of produce, a sort of biochemical complex—so that its flesh and organs are simply material that has a certain texture in the mouth (soft, tender, tough), a taste, perhaps a smell—then to describe the animal positively in those terms is to debase oneself by debasing being itself. A positive description is not "neutral" or "objective." In the case of geese-as raw-material-for pate, one can only give a negative description if the description is to remain underpinned by a valid ontology. That is to say, the description moves in the light of what this activity is a brutalization of, a debasement of, a desecration of: namely, the true nature of human beings and of animals."*

Poet Gary Snyder[2] wrote, "All creatures are equal actors in the divine drama of awakening. The spontaneous awakening of compassion for others instantly starts one on the path of ecological ethics, as well as on the path to enlightenment."

But what awakens concern for others and ignites the passion needed to sustain compassionate action? Perhaps the awakening is in our sudden

---

1. R. D. Laing, *The Politics of Experience and the Birds of Paradise* (New York: Penguin Books, 1967).
2. Gary Snyder, *A Place in Space: Ethics, Aesthetics and Watersheds* (Washington, D.C.: Counterpoint, 1995).

recognition of the universal nature of selfhood and of the capacity of all living beings to be harmed and to suffer. Other beings reflect something of our own selfhood in their fears and hopes, pains and pleasures. Through empathy we experience what others feel.

One reader of my syndicated newspaper column "Ask Your Animal Doctor," after he had caught, but not killed, a mouse in a spring trap in his kitchen, wrote: "I hastened to take it outside and as I was about to fling it to the ground, I just then caught a glimpse of the mouse's face. I swear, I could *see* the pain and fright in the mouse's eyes."

The late biologist and noted author Loren Eiseley[3] wrote, "We do not find ourselves until we see ourselves in the eyes of those who are other than human."

When we more fully empathize with each other and with other animals, we achieve a higher resonance of being and a greater refinement and clarity of spirit. We discover the value of other beings to our own spiritual growth and self-realization. Animals as *kin* extend our sense of community. Animals as *others* deepen our understanding of evolutionary and adaptative processes. Animals as companions enrich our lives, and their healing powers have been shown to benefit us physically and psychologically. Animals as totems and icons have served humanity for millennia as revelatory symbols of divine creation—as mystical, metaphorical, and mythological images have awakened our imaginations, inventiveness, and religious sensibilities. Animals can take us outside ourselves into other realms of being and consciousness. We return from the journeying into the empathosphere like the shamans, seers, and healers before us, a little more enlightened and inspired by our communion with other animals, some of whom are our allies, familiars, significant others, and also our teachers and healers.

Animals as objects and subjects serve our many needs and appetites, often reflecting in their plight the dark side of human nature. They teach us that when we demean them, we demean our own humanity.

Through reason we acquire objective knowledge. Through empathy we acquire subjective knowledge. When these two modes of understanding are integrated, then we have wisdom. When we understand animal behavior and empathize with animals, allowing compassion to be the ethical compass

---

3. Loren C. Eiseley, *All the Strange Hours* (New York: Charles Scribner's Sons, 1975).

of reason and action, then animals help us grow in wisdom—and help us evolve into a more humane species, worthy of the name *Homo sapiens*.

As the "unfinished animal," I see my species on the threshold of an evolutionary transformation into a panempathic being, having feeling for all life, provided we can divest ourselves of the anthropocentric (human-centered) worldview of human superiority and dominion. Humility is a prerequisite for the birth of our empathetic powers and faculties, as we replace arrogance and fear with compassion and love. Compassion is the ethical compass for our power of reason, without which the human intellect cannot function optimally, and will continue to cause more harm than good.

In the presence of another animal we can experience the oneness of existence, of both being alive, sentient, vulnerable, and mortal. Yet in the same gaze or breath we can experience also the profound otherness of a different species across a vast distance not in the dimensions of time or space but of consciousness. The animal looks into our eyes, and there is a moment of recognition, of affirmation perhaps. Then the gaze seems to pass through and beyond us. At this moment the animal mind becomes incomprehensible, something profoundly other, part of a deeper mystery that this sentient universe unfolds and enfolds. What is revealed in one moment of communion is veiled in the next. The ancient Indian text, the Brihad-Aranyaka Upanishad, puts it this way: "The immortal is veiled by the real. The Spirit of Life is the immortal. Name and form are real, and by them the Spirit is veiled."

So in the reality of an animal's presence, the immortal Spirit of Life is unveiled when we enter into communion. The paradoxes of oneness and otherness, of unity and diversity, and of duality and nonduality, are transcended. Such is the magical, transformative power of animals on the human psyche when we allow ourselves to be open to their presence and when our being-in-consciousness resonates with theirs. However fleeting the moment and forever enduring the memory of such sympathetic resonance with another living soul, we know that what was unveiled was indeed the Spirit of Life immortal embodied in the archetypal form that we know by name as eagle, whale, or wolf.

Some spiritual teachers, mystics, and poets advise that when we see the universal in the particular, and the particular in the universal, then we will enter the Kingdom of Heaven, or what others call the enlightened state of Samadhi or Nirvana. Those who believe or assert that this is a state of blissful liberation from sufferings and tribulations of the sentient world are wrong if they speak only of the liberation of the particular (one's self) and not of universal liberation. After personal enlightenment, then what? There is no lasting enlightenment when empathy with other sentient beings is severed and one is no longer connected to the unified field of being and part of the boundless circle of compassion.

Those who are enlightened about the universal nature of self ask themselves how can they sustain their own lives with the least injury to the lives around them. How can they help prevent and alleviate the suffering of the world in which they live? Personal liberation and animal liberation from cruel human exploitation are part of the same spiritual activism that arises out of radical compassion that is boundless in its empathic embrace of all life.

The ultimate value and significance of animals to us, other than their roles in the wild contributing to the health and functional integrity of aquatic and terrestrial ecosystems, is to facilitate the evolution of our humanity, our spiritual development. When we empathize with them, we become more humane and aware. In the process, they ennoble us in spirit as our respect and devotion for them grows from generation to generation, and from age to age.

Animal-Insensitivity Syndrome: A Cognitive and Affective Developmental Disorder

Animal-Insensitivity Syndrome, an impaired sensitivity toward animals, is a disorder that I see as part of a larger problem of insensitivity and indifference to the Earth.

Ethical blindness that comes from a lack of empathy with other living systems and beings is linked with a lack of respect and understanding that when we harm animals and the Earth, we harm ourselves, especially in our production of food and fiber, and indirectly in our dietary choices, consumer habits, and lifestyles.

We harm animals by destroying their natural habitats, and in making them suffer so that we may find new and profitable ways to cure our many diseases. The actual prevention of disease is in another domain based on an entirely different currency from what is still the norm in these sickening times. The currency of unbridled exploitation and destruction of natural resources and ecosystems, and the wholesale commercial exploitation of animals, cannot continue because it is not sustainable. One of the greatest sicknesses is the proliferation of factory livestock farms—the intensive confinement systems that are stressful to the animals, promote disease, are environmentally damaging, and also put consumers at risk.

These animal concentration camps of the meat, dairy, and poultry industries will only be phased out when there is greater consumer demand for organic, humane, and ecologically sustainable animal produce for human and companion animal consumption.

So I was heartened to see that author Richard Louv has written a book entitled *Last Child in the Woods: Saving Our Children from Nature-Deficit Disorder.*[4] This is the flip side of the coin that shows: heads, nature; tails, animals. Both are in our hands, for better or for worse. Louv contends that in modern industrial consumer society, children are being raised and educated without meaningful contact with or any understanding of the natural world, and that this will be bad for them and for the future of the Earth. This has caught the attention of educators and parents around the world. Long before this important book was published, my friend Jane Goodall, the famed chimpanzee biologist, had recognized this issue and initiated her "Roots and Shoots" program in schools in many countries to educate children about nature, ecology, and the inherent value of wild plants and creatures.

In the common currency of compassion and respect, our transactions and relationships with each other, with other animals, and with the Earth or natural world are framed within the Golden Rule. This rule, embraced by all world religions, is to treat others as we would have them treat us—and in the Golden Rule, gold alone does not rule. This currency includes ancient coins including: wisdom as *altruism*, that is, enlightened selfishness; *ahimsa*, Sanskrit for not harming in any way; and *karma*, having prescience and understanding that what goes around, comes around. All our choices and actions have consequences.

Sustainable rates of exchange are based on mutual aid, a point emphasized by Russian Prince Peter Kropotkin (circa 1900) who envisioned the ideal human community like a functioning ecosystem of interdependent, democratically integrated individuals and species creating mutually enhancing, symbiotic, micro- and macro-communities—a concept he discovered in his studies of the co-evolved flora and fauna of the vast wild Steppes of his native land.

Nature-Deficit Disorder leads ultimately to regarding and treating the living Earth as a nonliving resource, just as the Animal-Insensitivity

---

4. Richard Louv, *Last Child in the Woods: Saving Our Children from Nature-Deficit Disorder* (Chapel Hill, N.C.: Algonquin Books, 2006).

Syndrome can lead to animals being treated as mere objects without feeling. Insensitive, indifferent, and cruel contact and experiences with animals during the early years (probably a critical sensitization/desensitization developmental stage between eighteen and thirty-six months of age) can mean a poorly developed and extremely self-limiting capacity to empathize with others; to be able to recognize, anticipate, experience, and share other's feelings; and to express and deeply consider one's own. Adult denial and ethical blindness are rooted in early childhood conditioning and desensitization.

In some countries where I have worked with my wife Deanna Krantz, like India, we have both witnessed how people simply turn a blind eye to the suffering animal and the polluted stream because they themselves are struggling to survive. Individuals who feel helpless become resigned fatalists, or are either too lazy, busy, desensitized, or blind to lift a finger to try to make a difference. In some contexts intervention to help a suffering animal, or to stop a stream from being poisoned by a tannery or a slaughter house, could mean death threats and violence.

Observing another's suffering, and being unable to do anything to help, leads to learned helplessness. Seeing other's suffering, and being indifferent about it, is the next step toward the total disconnect of empathy, called *bystander apathy*. The next step is to observe and derive vicarious pleasure in witnessing another's plight. This is but one small step away from deliberate torture and calculated cruelty, either perpetrated alone or in participation with others—in the name of entertainment, politics, sport, quasi-religious or cult ritual, and, as some see it, experimental vivisection.

Why does it matter if animals must be made to suffer and die and the natural environment is obliterated, as long as human needs and wants are satisfied? For many people it obviously does not matter—even when their values and actions harm those who do care and feel it *does* matter and that it is morally wrong to harm and kill animals and destroy the natural environment. The ethics of compassion and *ahimsa* mandate that we find the least harmful ways to satisfy our basic needs and relinquish those wants, appetites, and desires that cause more harm than good. Such renunciation is seen by some as the only hope for humanity and for our sanity: to live simply so that others may simply live.

Animal suffering matters because it is a matter of conscience. Deliberate cruelty toward animals and acceptance and indifference toward their plight is unconscionable: this is a *zoopathic* state of mind. This parallels the behavior—and cognitive and affective impairment—of the sociopath and of the *ecopath* who has no twinge of conscience over the destruction of the natural environment. Where there is a lack of empathy, of feeling for others, there can be neither concern nor conscience.

Becoming desensitized to animal suffering and then treating animals as mere things, as objects devoid of sentience, is part of the same currency as treating fellow humans as objects. Such dehumanization, coupled with demonization, can lead to genocide, and more commonly to *speciesicide*. This is the annihilation of animal species and their communities that are perceived as a threat. Our attitudes toward other animals—our degree of ethical concern and moral consideration—can mirror our regard for each other, for better or for worse. When collectively our hearts and minds are open to the tragedy of reality, and we really see and feel all that is going on around us and empathize fully with the suffering of others, times will begin to change for the better.

The antidotes are many. Those in Richard Louv's book should be coupled with meaningful contact with companion and other animals, with parental supervision and humane instruction to foster respect, self-restraint, gentleness, patient observation, and understanding.

A child's sense of wonder, if it is nurtured and not crushed or left to wither, blossoms into the adult sense of the sacred: an ethical sensibility of respect for the sanctity of all life.

A child's sense of curiosity leads to natural science and instrumental knowledge. Combined with a sense of wonder, curiosity leads to imagination and creativity, while the sense of the sacred is the foundation for an ethical and just society, and for empathetic, caring, and fulfilling relationships, human and nonhuman. This empathy-based bioethical[5] and moral sensibility that gives equally fair consideration to all members of the biotic community—human and nonhuman, plant and animal—is an ideal that may yet become a reality, provided the potential for such development is properly nurtured and reinforced by example in early childhood.

Like our physical health, our mental health and Earth health are deeply interconnected, and for us to be well and whole in body, mind, and spirit, our connections with animals and the Earth must be properly established in early childhood in order to prevent the harmful consequences of the

---

5. See Michael W. Fox, *Bringing Life to Ethics: Global Bioethics for a Humane Society* (Albany, N.Y.: State University of New York Press, 2001).

Nature-Deficit Disorder and Animal-Insensitivity Syndrome. Our collective inertia over doing anything constructive to address such critical issues as human population growth, overconsumption, pollution, global warming, and the plight of animals domestic and wild will then become something of the past. Then initiatives—local and international—to promote planetary CPR (conservation, preservation, and restoration) and to promote the humane treatment of animals, will become a reality, because, in the final analysis, it is in our best interests to do so.

When we harm animals and the Earth, we harm ourselves, and the generations to come will all suffer the consequences of our actions and inaction. As the Iroquois Confederacy advised, the good of the life community mandates that, "we think seven generations ahead, and seven generations back." This translates into the bioethical consideration of consequences and in practice means that those who do not learn from the mistakes of their ancestors shall live only to repeat them.

Animals and the Politics of Compassion

It is a bioethical imperative for us humans to develop the wisdom, which in other animals is primarily instinctual, that enables us to live in harmony with all beings. This means not causing harm to others and therefore to oneself, because the self is realized fully through the love it gives rather than seeks only for itself. As the Buddha advised, the only true religion is maitri (loving kindness or benevolence) toward all creatures. He also taught that the end of suffering is in suffering itself, meaning that when we embrace the suffering of others through empathy, the communion of suffering becomes a communal response to the plight of others, human and nonhuman, who are then helped because the pain of one is the pain of all.

There is a wonderful story of a Buddhist monk who did not become enlightened until he put compassion into action. Geshe Kelsang Gyatso writes:

> *Asanga, a Great Buddhist Master who lived in India in the fifth century AD, meditated in an isolated mountain cave in order to gain a vision of Buddha Maitreya. After twelve years he still had not succeeded and, feeling discouraged, abandoned his retreat. On his way down the mountain he came across an old dog lying in the middle of the path. Its body was covered in maggot-infested sores, and it seemed*

close to death. This sight induced within Asanga an overwhelming feeling of compassion for all living beings trapped within samsara. As he was painstakingly removing the maggots from the dying dog, it suddenly transformed into Buddha Maitreya himself. Maitreya explained that he had been with Asanga since the beginning of his retreat, but, due to the impurities in Asanga's mind, Asanga had not been able to see him. It was Asanga's extraordinary compassion that had finally purified the karmic obstructions preventing him from seeing Maitreya.

That which purports to be spiritual must translate into compassionate action, loving relationships, and understanding. If it does not, then it is not spiritual because the essence of spirituality is to live ethically "in a sacred way," as the late Sioux medicine man Black Elk advised. The ethic of what Albert Schweitzer called reverence for life is the key directive. In our relationships with other animals, we have a duty to respect their fundamental entitlements of being, such as the freedom to be themselves: for birds to fly and not be in cages; for whales and dolphins to swim the oceans and not be in aquariums; for pigs and cows in factory sheds to run in the fields; and for dogs to be dogs in off-leash parks with each other. All creatures under our control and stewardship have a right to freedom from pain and fear arising from how we humans so often treat them. Some moral philosophers call these entitlements *animal rights.*

I received the following question from a reader of my Web site (www.doctormwfox.org):

Question: A friend of mine says dogs don't have souls. Even so, he says they should be treated humanely because otherwise it's a sign of bad character. God gave us dominion over them, to use as we choose, but it should be kindly used. What is your opinion?

Answer: *Kindly use* can be a slippery slope. I interpret dominion as loving kindness, as in God's dominion over us. If we are created in God's image, then we should treat dogs and all fellow creatures as we would like God to treat us.

As the late and controversial Pope John Paul II has said, all creatures, like humans, are enspirited "with the same breath of Creation." Being part of the same Creation, we should therefore give animals equally fair consideration. In my recent book, *Bringing Life to Ethics*, I call this cardinal bioethical principle *equalitarianism*.

I don't believe animals *have* souls. Like humans and plants, they *are* living souls. In my metaphysics of what I call *biospiritual realism*, the spirit is not in the body. The body is in the spirit. Through this primal and sacred duality, souls are born to experience life in different forms. Many people embrace this spirituality of the oneness, individual sanctity, and interdependence of all beings—but many don't. That is why some find it morally repugnant to put human genes into pigs and to conceive a biotechnology industry dedicated to cloning organ-donor pigs, endangered species, and people's pets and children. But many don't, and I believe that these unfeeling and therefore unawakened people are not fully compassionate humans. They are responsible, I believe, for what Charles Darwin implied in the title of his book *The Descent of Man*.

In other words, the human species has become an ethically degenerate, morally challenged, and empathically impaired species that is a blight, a parasitic infestation, on Mother Earth. The late Prof. Konrad Lorenz, one of the founding father-scientists of ethology, the study of human and nonhuman animal behavior, and an avowed pantheist who believed that all animals were as much a part of the sacred as we are, wrote: "Far from seeing in man the irrevocable and unsurpassable image of God, I assert—that the long-sought missing link between animals and the really humane being is us!"

In his seminal book, *The Eternal Treblinka: Our Treatment of the Animals and the Holocaust*,[6] Charles Patterson writes: "Throughout the history of our ascent to dominance as the master species, our victimization of animals has served as the model and the foundation for our victimization of each other. The study of human history reveals the pattern: First, human beings exploit and slaughter animals; then they treat other people like animals and do the same to them."

Columbia River Tribes activist Ted Strong echoes these sentiments, stating, "If this nation [the United States] has a long way to go before all our people are treated equally regardless to race, religion or national origin, it has even farther to go before achieving anything that remotely

---

6. Charles Patterson, *The Eternal Treblinka: Our Treatment of the Animals and the Holocaust* (New York: Lantern Books, 2002).

resembles equal treatment for other creatures who called this land home before humans ever set foot on it."

The misinterpretation of Darwin's theory of the *survival of the fittest* links his findings with the inverted morality of *might makes right*. This misunderstanding violates the cardinal principle of Natural Law, namely, mutual cooperation. The notion of some God-given—and socially, politically, and religiously condoned power over others—needs to be dispelled. Charles Darwin's use of this term was in reference to environmental fitness or adaptability, not power and competition. He recognized how important cooperation was within and between species. Survival through fitness is quite different from survival through power and control over others. Yet his theory of evolution through natural selection and survival of the fittest was seized upon by a very class-conscious English society that condoned industrialism's power over nature and colonialism's imperial power over and enslavement of other cultures and nation-states. Darwin's theory was twisted out of context to give scientific credence to a survival-of-the-fittest mentality (read superior) that sanctified competitive individualism that was encouraged in children from kindergarten on. Coupled with the religious (Judeo-Christian) belief in man's superiority over lesser beings and nature (that were made by God for man's use), this mentality has made us the least fit species on Earth because of the harm done to others, to the Earth, and ultimately to ourselves.

A spirituality that does not bring love to life is like a philosophy that does not bring ethics to life—like a religion that sees no spirituality in nature, and a spirituality that has no immediate social and political relevance. The kind of ethics that we need to bring to life, like equalitarianism and reverential respect for all living beings, are the intellectual fruits of reason that are ripened by emotion, especially our empathic and intuitive sympathies, passion for justice, and our power of love rather than the love of power. If our love for fellow creatures and for nature has no social and political relevance, then it is not true love but selfish attachment (for various reasons such as emotional, esthetic, and pecuniary). It would be pedantic and preachy for me to document why: But why isn't everyone who lives with a dog or a cat concerned about the welfare of all dogs and cats and actively supporting at least one reputable animal protection organization or local animal shelter? Why isn't everyone who eats animals concerned about how factory-farmed food animals are generally raised for human consumption and how a meat-based diet impacts wildlife habitat and biodiversity, and are then moved to do something about it? Any dominant species that chooses not to think or to empathize deserves to become sick, to be afflicted by a host of the so-called diseases of civilization—suffering the consequences of their own actions and inaction and, for the greater good, become quickly extinct.

To love the universal in the particular, and the particular in the universal, is to embrace, nurture, and defend the freedom for the particular to be, and for the universal to become. When we protect all our animal relations (or biological ancestors) with the same passion and commitment as we might protect our own kith and kin, then the human will become a humane and ethical animal. Some call this *self-realization*, while others call it human evolution.

In other words, such love respects, protects, and nurtures the freedom of all living beings, which leads to animal and human rights and liberation. It also seeks to secure the integrity and sanctity of creation and universal becoming, which is the spirit of the deep ecology, Earth First!, animal rights, and holistic health movements—which are seen by some as anti-establishment, terrorist organizations that are a threat to both the economy and to national security!

A deeper understanding of the primordial, co-evolved, empathic relationships between bee, flower, and meadow, and deer, wolf, and forest, means a deeper appreciation and respect for the creative dimensions of love where life gives to life to sustain a greater whole—the biotic community. Where in relation to this ecology and spirit of mutual cooperation that is self-sustaining and self-affirming are our lives functioning, with faster and bigger gas-guzzling vehicles and other insatiable, media-hyped appetites that are laying waste to the environment and pushing countless animal and plant species into extinction as the others we exploit suffer the consequences of our greed, ignorance, and need?

These ethical, economic, environmental, spiritual, political, and metaphysical concerns of the deep ecology, Earth First!, and human and animal rights movements opponents seek to discredit them in order to protect their own vested interests by preserving the status quo. Opponents call such concerns anti-progress, and anti-human. But it is an Earth- and life-centered love and respect that provide the ethical basis for environmental and public health, for conservation agriculture and organic farming practices, and for a sustainable economy that places the human within rather than above or outside the Earth community. Such spirituality sees the human as part of the creative matrix of self-organizing, intelligent, and transformative processes that some call God, or nature, or sacred creation. When we submit to and learn to live in harmony with what Sioux medicine man Black Elk called "the Sacred Power of the world as it lives and moves," all will be well. The way of harmony is therefore the way of loving kindness and selfless service.

13.
| Feeling for Animals and Healing the Bond |

Millions of people enjoy the company of animals because they give so much pleasure— expressing affection, playfulness, concern, interest, joyful greeting, and grateful satisfaction. These and other emotive behaviors we do not imagine. They are as real as the feelings they evoke in us. The subjective state or feelings of humans, cats, dogs, and other sentient beings when expressing various emotions must be similar, since they evoke similar responses.

The gulf that separates us from other animals is not our intelligence but our disbelief: our inability to accept their similar sentience and their emotional affinity with us. We should not demean their affinity as pathological dependence, or as the subversion of unconscious instincts by domestication. It is too narrow a view to believe that adult cats regard their "owners" simply as parent-providers and that dogs would sooner be with other dogs but are bonded to their "masters" as substitute pack leaders.

As our understanding of the *ethos* of cats, dogs, and other creatures wild and tame deepens, so must our understanding of the human-animal bond and of people's attitudes toward animals in various cultures. Otherwise our knowledge will be incomplete, and we will fail to comprehend fully much beyond self-serving utilitarian horizons. The "objective" language of the psychobiological sciences are not much help, tending to limit our horizons with mechanistic terminology. It is recognized more widely now that animals often display behavior patterns that communicate to us— empathetically and via their emotion-evoking distress calls, expressions, and postures—a whole range of subjective states, such as separation anxiety, despair, grief, terror, as well as relief, playful good humor, satisfaction, concern, and even empathy, compassion, and altruism. But the semanticists of scientism have no objective synonyms for these subjective states. And so it is considered unscientific to allude to such states, but in truth we have no other words that do not sound anthropomorphic. Alternative, terms like *approach, avoidance, satiation,* and *consummation* are unacceptably simplistic and give no intimation as to emotional or motivational state.

Some of these very human emotions I felt and witnessed in a Kashmir, India, village some years ago, when I saw a male pariah dog licking the sores and snapping at the flies around his mate's infected face. Both were emaciated, and he let the old bitch feed before him after I had thrown them some food. Such empathy and altruistic behavior is common to many animal species, not only to the human species. This ethologically documented evidence of deliberate caregiving behavior to others that are not simply immature offspring is proof of a highly developed empathic sensibility in animals. Some investigators have claimed such sensibility, albeit rudimentary, in trees and other plants, as well as in insects, other invertebrate, and protoplasmic life-forms. Be that as it may, when we begin to appreciate the significance of the sentient nature of other animals and of the universe itself, our attitude toward and treatment of animals changes radically toward what might best be termed *panempathic communion.*

But when we do not live close to animals in their natural environs and see them only in the altered states of domestication and captive confinement, we can become alienated and unfamiliar with their ways, their ethos. So we deny them feelings, awareness, even sentience as well as intelligence, and in the process of denial we *mechanomorphize* them, seeing and even treating them as unfeeling machines. Or we anthropomorphize them, unable to see them as they really are through the cloudy lens of sentimentality and objectification.

People who really see animals for the first time as fellow sentient beings become humane because they experience in other animals the kinship of sentience that includes the capacity to suffer and to experience pleasure. This is not some deluded anthropomorphic projection, but a fact of rational human experience and responsiveness and the consequence of feral vision. I recall reading of the entire change in attitude of an Australian government dingo exterminator, who was hiding in the bush near a spring where tracks indicated to him that dingos came to drink at dusk. He was to shoot whatever wild dogs came. A pair came to drink, and he killed one, who was slower and seemed to be led by its mate to the water hole. The government agent was shocked to find that the dingo he had shot was blind, had been blind for a long time and was in excellent physical condition. Without the empathy and concern of his mate, this old blind dingo would have long perished. Realizing how caring dingoes can be for each other in the Outback, the man never killed another dingo from that day on. There are instances of wild animals seeking human assistance, like a bobcat that crawled out from cover to lie across the skis of a cross-country skier and allowed itself to be wrapped in a jacket and taken to a veterinary hospital to have festering porcupine quills removed. And what of the behavior of a rehabilitated orphan bobcat who brought her cubs, born in the wild, back to show the woman who had rescued and healed her?

There are also accounts of dogs who had been treated at a veterinary hospital, taking an injured stray animal back to the same hospital for treatment. These and other eye opening anecdotes reveal a degree of intelligence or sapience as well as sentience. They move us to establish a new covenant of compassion with the entire sentient world. And until we are so moved and our empathy and feral vision close the distance between us and fellow creatures, the possibility of a truly humane society will forever elude us. We will also fall short of realizing our full human potential to be humane. To be humane means treating all living beings—human, plant, and animal—with compassion and reverential respect, including their environments and communities. It is not simply a name for animal welfare or protection, but a state of being in awareness that is the hallmark of a truly civilized society.

Healings Shared

The many benefits that animals provide people are being recognized by mainstream healing fields that involve the use of animals as pet-facilitated cotherapy, such as animal-assisted living for the physically handicapped. Many have realized the benefits of hippotherapy—therapeutic horse riding. Even simply observing wildlife, and enjoying a well-maintained aquarium of tropical fish, can be therapeutic in many ways to adolescents and nursing home residents respectively.

These new fields I call *zootherapy* are complemented by *anthrozootherapy*, where humans benefit animals in many ways (and often themselves in the process): for example, by being a volunteer dog walker or cat groomer at the local animal shelter, or by helping raise infant wildlife at a rehabilitation and wildlife conservation center or zoo. Many good people take their animal companions to nursing homes, children's hospitals, and to correctional facilities (some of which have animals already living with and being cared for by inmates).

Taking your own animal companion to a local grade school—or taking a calm, friendly, healthy one from the animal shelter—and talking about what makes animals happy and about animal care, respect, and understanding is part of such therapy.

By helping to promote compassion and humane values to children, the human-nonhuman animal bond has a chance of being formed at an early age during what I believe to be a critical period in the emotional and ethical development of our species. When that bond is either not established, or is malformed, the empathic, emotional sensitivities of adulthood are limited, and thus also our emotional intelligence and ethical sensibility.

The emotional intelligence of various companion animals was recently documented and celebrated in *People* magazine in an article entitled "Superpets!"[1] For example, Zion, a yellow Labrador dog, was playing fetch with a stick thrown into the river when he rescued a boy he did not know. Eight-year-old Ryan Rambo was being swept down Colorado's swift Roaring Fork river, and Zion let the boy grab his collar and swam with the boy holding on for dear life to the shore.

Then there's Daisy, a 150-pound potbellied pig living in Las Vegas who saved one of her human family members, seven-year-old Jordan Jones, from being attacked by a neighbor's free-roaming pit bull. Daisy sustained serious injuries but eventually made a full recovery.

Gary Rosheisen of Columbus, Ohio, who is severely handicapped, tried to teach his orange tabby cat Tommy how to paw the speed dial on his speakerphone to call 911 in case he needed help. But he stopped, because he thought Tommy might start making unnecessary calls. But one day he did collapse on the floor and needed help, and could not reach the phone. But help arrived quickly in response to a 911 call from his number. The only other being in the home was Tommy, who must have made the call.

Super-bunny Robin, living in Illinois, had been purchased by the Murphy family at a garage sale. Ten days later the little rabbit awakened Ed

---

1. "Superpets!" *People* magazine (Sept. 2006): 168–176.

Murphy by making a ruckus in her cage, and continued when he went back to bed. He then discovered that his pregnant wife Darcy, who had gestational diabetes, was barely breathing, and he called 911. Darcy is convinced that she and her baby would not be alive today if Robin had not known something was wrong and had not made such a noise in his cage.

Steve Werner of Brentwood, Missouri, is grateful for his old Golden retriever Wrigley. She started repeatedly sniffing into his right ear; after seeing a TV report about dogs being able to detect cancer in humans, he decided to get a medical checkup. An MRI scan revealed a tumor the size of a Ping-Pong ball near his inner ear that was surgically removed and was, fortunately, benign. If not detected early, thanks to his dog, it could have caused serious problems.

As Hippocrates, one of the fathers of modern medicine, advised, "Physician, first heal thyself." We see in the human-nonhuman animal bond such wisdom affirmed where the human is healed, made to feel more whole and happy, and in the process the animal feels good, enjoying life by giving and receiving affection. Well-being and welfare depend on physical and mental health, and in the mutually enhancing symbiosis between people and their animal companions or therapy animals, a kind of reciprocal healing may occur in the feel-good interaction between two sentient beings.

Healing Animals, Animal Healing

I quickly learned as a veterinary student some forty years ago—working on various farms and zoos and seeing large and small animals, wild and domesticated—that many of the health and welfare problems of animals were caused by:

1. How they were treated;

2. How they had been selectively bred to have various desired traits and acquired genetic abnormalities;

3. How they had been raised;

4. The kind of environment and relationships they had during early development with their own kind and with their human caretakers;

5. The kind and quality of food they were fed; and

6. The living conditions they were provided to satisfy their basic physical and psychological needs.

I came to realize that the healing of animals and their well-being entailed healing the human-animal bond. This bond was in urgent need of repair because so much of the sickness and suffering of animals was due to how people perceived them and treated them. It also dawned on me that if people were not in a right, ethical, and equitable relationship (or in their right minds, so to speak) with fellow creatures, then the same probably held true for their relationships with their own kind and with the environment. So the key to preventing much human suffering and sickness was probably the same for animals: the key was one of relationship and mindfulness, of compassion and empathy, of understanding and caring attentiveness.

The Ethics of Using Animals in Biomedical Research

This realization was hammered home many times when I visited various university laboratory animal research facilities and saw the small cages and pens in which cats, dogs, rhesus monkeys, and other creatures were incarcerated. What shocked me was seeing arboreal and highly social primates being housed for years alone in metal cages measuring three by four feet; and cats and dogs, who were formerly family pets, being kept in impoverished environments in which they were clearly disoriented, deprived, and distressed.

I investigated and reported how these seriously inadequate conditions for laboratory animals created sick, stressed, and abnormal animals, making them dubious subjects for scientific study. Research findings from these animals had little medical relevance except perhaps to other creatures kept under comparable intolerable conditions.

While I saw—as a veterinarian and biomedical scientist—the *status quo* of laboratory animal care and use as being ethically and scientifically untenable, most of the U.S. biomedical research establishment rejected my findings and continued to defend all vivisection unconditionally.

The biomedical research industry has so much political, economic, and public power and influence that it can change truth and revise history. With a few phone calls and threatening letters, they demonstrated this power by making Encyclopedia Britannica alter, in subsequent editions, my contribution to the 1991 revised edition, deleting all my references to examples of cruel experimentation and to animal rights under the Dog entry.

Encyclopedic Knowledge or Convenient Knowledge?
It was no coincidence, since animals were my teachers as a child, that as an adult I should teach others about the ways and whys of animals. My formal education enabled me to acquire the appropriate scientific terminology to describe animals' behavior, and my lessons from the animals helped me interpret their behavior, develop new theories, and challenge some established and establishment views. Indeed one of the many gifts of the animals was my gaining international recognition as an animal behavior expert, which opened many doors, including the opportunity to contribute to the esteemed Encyclopedia Britannica.

I had a golden opportunity to help atone for my own sins of omission and commission, when I was given the task of writing updated revisions for the Cat and Dog entries to go into the 1991 edition of the Encyclopedia Britannica.

I decided to include the following factually accurate paragraph on the use of dogs in biomedical research, because I felt that I owed something to my best friend and teacher, the dog:

> *Another common use of dogs, especially purpose-bred beagles, is in biomedical research. Such use, which often entails much suffering, has been questioned for its scientific validity and medical relevance to human health problems. For example, beagles and other animals have been forced to inhale tobacco smoke for days and have been used to test household chemicals such as bleach and drain cleaner. In addition, dogs have been used to test the effects of various military weapons and radiation.*

Soon after the new edition of the Encyclopedia was published, the editorial offices were deluged with hundreds of letters from individual scientists, from their prestigious associations like the American Society for Pharmacology and Experimental Therapeutics, the Society for Neurosciences, American Physiological Society and Federation of Biological Scientists, and also from the general public who belonged to pro-animal experimentation and exploitation organizations such as Putting People First and the Incurably Ill for Animal Research.

The biomedical scientists contended that my statement was biased and unbalanced because it didn't emphasize how experiments on dogs have helped people suffering from diabetes, or those needing a coronary bypass or a new hip or kidney. My response was that the entry had nothing to do with the benefits of using dogs in biomedical research.

I offered to change the "offensive" statement as follows:

Another common use of dogs, especially purpose-bred beagles, is in biomedical research. Such use which often entails much suffering, has provided some scientific and medical insights, but is now being questioned on ethical grounds and for its scientific validity and medical relevance. For example, dogs and other animals have been forced to inhale tobacco smoke for days; used to safety test household chemicals, such as bleach and drain cleaner; and used to evaluate the effects of various military weapons and radiation.

But the editor of the Encyclopedia would have none of it. He insisted on substituting the following statement in the next edition to read:

Another common use of dogs, especially purpose-bred beagles, is in biomedical research, a use that dates at least to the 17th century.

I told him that this was totally unacceptable unless he added that anesthetics weren't developed until the nineteenth century. Otherwise, in simply stating that dogs have been used in biomedical research since the seventeenth century, he would be ignoring the fact that this means two hudred years of vivisecting dogs (and countless other creatures) without any anesthetic, which is illegal today. Also such a statement implies some kind of ethical acceptance based on historical precedence. The fact that dogs have been experimented upon by scientists for three hundred years is no basis for justifying, or not even questioning, the continuation of animal experimentation and the continued suffering of animals.

Clearly, I had offended the academic establishment, yet my scientific credentials and long list of scientific and popular articles and books on cats and dogs is what qualified me as an expert to write for such a prestigious encyclopedia. Ironically, the censorship exercised over my entry was widely publicized in newspapers and radio stations across the nation and hundreds more letters poured in from those who supported my position. One of these from the actress Kim Basinger read as follows:

> *Dear Dr. Fox,*
> *I am writing to thank you for your dedication to the truth where animals are concerned. I recently read about the attention drawn by your writing for the Encyclopedia Britannica in the January 23, 1992, issue of the Los Angeles Times. As I am sure you know, the real truth scares people, especially when these same people make money off the lies of animal research. I wanted to let you, the Los Angeles Times, and the Encyclopedia Britannica know how much I appreciate everyone's attempt to speak for those that cannot speak for themselves.*
>
> *Sincerely, Kim Basinger*

This controversy illustrates how fact and truth have become disjointed, the same facts leading to one conclusive truth—that dogs have suffered in the name of biomedical progress and that the scientific validity and medical relevance of experimenting on animals today *is* being questioned—offends the truth that others live by. That truth is that the exploitation and suffering of animals is justified in the name of scientific knowledge and medical progress. The facts, to the proponents of biomedical research, of documented animal suffering are not really facts but rather unavoidable means to the vaunted ends of medical progress.

Unlike many of the people who wrote letters in support of keeping my statement intact in the 1993 revised edition of Encyclopedia Britannica, I actually accept using dogs and other creatures in biomedical research, but with the proviso that we learn only from those that are already sick or injured, in order to benefit them and their own kind—and our own in the process. I do believe that it is unethical to harm any creature deliberately in the name of scientific knowledge or purely human-medical progress without any reciprocal benefit to fellow creatures. No good ends can come from evil means.

The problem with biomedical research on animals, as in our other dealings with the animal and plant kingdoms, is that the boundless ethic of compassion has been replaced by the boundless imperatives of human needs and such human-centered values as progress and superiority over all life.

If this were not true, then the biomedical research community would not have reacted so vehemently to my "unbalanced" encyclopedia statement.

There is a world of difference between violating the ethic of compassionate respect for all life when we kill fleas for dogs' sake or mosquitoes (infested with malaria parasites) for peoples' sake, as opposed to when we turn animals into alcoholics or cocaine addicts or give restrained dogs inescapable shocks day after day as a way to study aspects of human depression. Testing a birth control or a new rabies vaccine on laboratory cats (and killing and dissecting them) and devising new hip joints for crippled dogs are arguably ethically acceptable "uses" of animals in biomedical research, because other animals and people may benefit from the new knowledge that may come from such research.

Many people, scientists and nonscientists alike, believe that only humans and not other animals have souls, minds, and feelings. One of my early mentors, the late Nobel Laureate Konrad Lorenz, summed up the attitude that arises when there is a lack of unified sensibility as follows:

> The fact that our fellow humans are similar, and feel similarly, to us, is evident in exactly the same sense as mathematical axioms are evident. We are not able not to believe in them. Karl Buhler, who to my knowledge was the first to call attention to these facts, spoke of "you-evidence."

We have the same axiomatic certainty for animals' souls as we have for supposing in our fellow humans the existence of a soul (which means the ability to experience subjectively). A human who truly knows a higher mammal, perhaps a dog or a monkey, and will not be satisfied that these beings experience similarly to himself, is psychologically abnormal and belongs in a psychiatric clinic, as an impaired capacity for "you-evidence" makes him a public enemy.[2]

Agribusiness and Its Treatment of Animals

I have also experienced the lies, denial, ridicule, and concerted opposition from the agribusiness establishment that wants the status quo of intensive

---

2. "Tiere und Gefuhlmenschen," *Der Spiegel*, 47, 1980.

industrialized animal agriculture—so-called factory farming—to be maintained to further the economic interests of a powerful few. The many hidden costs are neither revealed to the public nor to shareholders. These include farm animal sickness and suffering; ecological damage; loss of nonrenewable natural resources from topsoil to fossil fuels; loss of family farms and the socioeconomic demise of rural communities and once-sustainable agricultural practices. The role of animal-based agriculture in contributing to increased consumer diet- and food-safety-related health problems is also denied.

I have visited factory farms and feedlots and documented how livestock and poultry are raised for human profit and consumption. Having seen alternative, more natural ecological farming systems in the United States and in many other countries, I do not accept food (and fur) animal factories as normal and progressive "state-of-the-art." I regard them as pathogenic environments for the animals, and *as being symptomatic of a seriously defective human-animal bond.* To develop and accept livestock and poultry production systems that entail treating animals as mere production units and deny them their basic rights and behavioral needs is surely indicative of an aberrant mutation in human consciousness, an attitude or state of mind that lacks empathetic sensibility. It is ethically blind because it has no vestige of what I term *feral vision,* of perceiving the thing in itself, a purity and clarity of perception devoid of self-interest, and appreciating the intrinsic value of all living beings and our kinship with them.

While this mutation is such that we are neither in our right minds nor in the right relationship with animals and nature, it does not mean that we cannot change our minds and behavior and recover our feral vision to establish a more equitable relationship with animals and nature—a relationship that is based more on compassion, symbiosis, and service than on domination and exploitation. Then the possibility of building a global, humane, and sustainable society may be realized, but not until the liberation of animals from human bondage is seen as a spiritual and ethical imperative linked with our own survival and well-being.

The human-animal bond is as ancient as our earliest ancestors emerging from the dawn of time. Animals were the reference that helped us define what it means to be human and what it means to be "other."

As Professor Calvin Schwabe has shown in his seminal book, *Cattle Priests and Progress in Medicine*, the first veterinarians were also priests and healers of people. This noble tradition of the veterinarian as a latter-day shaman, or interlocutor between humankind and the animal kingdom, is best expressed when we begin to examine the human-animal bond and seek to correct it wherever and whenever the basic bioethical principle of *ahimsa*, of avoiding harm or injury to an animal, is violated.

Animals have served us in myriad ways over millennia and we owe them a great debt of gratitude. This gratitude we have yet to express fully in a more compassionate, egalitarian, and mutually enhancing symbiosis, since this bond today is primarily one of domination and exploitation rather than of service and communion.

Scientific research is rediscovering the many human benefits of a strong human-animal bond—or what I prefer to call the *human-nonhuman animal bond*, since we humans are animals after all. As other animals have been shown in a variety of documented studies to help people overcome great emotional difficulties and physical and psychological handicaps, we can in turn help them—by saving endangered species, by restoring and protecting their habitats, and by alleviating the suffering of animals through the art and science of veterinary medicine.

Humaneness Pays

Several studies have revealed how a positive affectionate social bond with animals helps enhance disease resistance in laboratory animals, the productivity of farm animals, and the trainability of dogs and other species.

It has now been scientifically documented that when animal caretakers express a negative attitude toward farm animals, and when the animals under their care are afraid of humans, then such animals are under a chronic state of stress. This stress has been shown to reduce the numbers of offspring that sows produce, the number of eggs laying hens produce, and the amount of milk dairy cows give. Meat quality and growth rates in broilers, piglets, and beef calves may also be adversely affected. In contrast, where farmers, farmhands, ranchers, and cowboys treat animals gently and with understanding so as not to trigger fear reactions and induce a chronic state of stress, and especially when there is a strong social bond between caretaker and animal, the animals are healthier, more productive, and profitable. In sum, humaneness pays.

But this evident fact may be discounted in favor of the cost-savings of developing large-scale, labor-saving, intensive livestock and poultry systems where one person is in charge of hundreds, even thousands, of animals. Such labor-saving "efficiencies" have been criticized for decades by those who believe that farm animals need individual attention or at least regular daily inspection. It may be argued that a good stockperson with a positive attitude toward animals on a large factory farm will do a better job than one who is indifferent or whom the animals fear. However, working in large intensive production systems has been shown to affect the behavior and attitudes of stockpersons adversely, notably causing increased aggressive behavior, which has a detrimental effect on the animals' welfare and productivity.

There is a distinction between humanely directing an animal's *telos* (final end or ecological purpose) for one's own benefit and disregarding both telos and *ethos* (or intrinsic nature) and manipulating both, as in factory-farming and genetic engineering, for exclusively human benefit. The good farmer and pastoralist knew how best to profit from the telos of plants and animals without harming either their ethos or the *ecos*—the ecosystem—as a creative participant or symbiote. This distinction between kindly use and selfish exploitation is the difference between sustainable and nonsustainable living. The difference between treating animals and other life-forms as ends in themselves, respecting their ethos and ecological role, and of using them as a means to satisfy purely human ends is a central issue of bioethics.

The consequences of this latter utilitarian attitude and relationship are potentially harmful economically, environmentally, socially, and spiritually. The keeping of wild animals in captivity for public entertainment, the selective breeding of genetically defective "bonsai" pets, and the genetic engineering of animals for various commercial purposes also illustrate how one-sided the human-animal bond has become.

In sum, natural living, like natural or organic farming, has its own integrity. Ironically, in the process of "denaturing" animals under the yolk of industrial-scale domestication, we do no less to ourselves and suffer the consequences under the guise of "civilized" necessity and progress. But there is nothing civilized or progressive in this utilitarian attitude toward life, since it ultimately reduces the value of human life and all life to sheer utility, which is the nihilistic telos of technocratic imperialism and materialistic determinism.

Until we fully address and repair the human-nonhuman animal bond *and this is, I believe, the primary task of veterinarians and humanitarians*, the world will continue to suffer the adverse consequences of a pathological human attitude toward fellow creatures and nature.

A society that destroys nature's biodiversity and resources will become materially bankrupt. Similarly, we will become spiritually bankrupt if there is no collective regard for the intrinsic value and ethos of animals, and of their telos or purpose in the ecological community. It is this Earth community—and not simply the human community—that we must all come to serve if we are to survive, prosper, and evolve.

In the final chapter of this section, I want to share a personal experience I had with a pet rabbit that turned my life around, and in many ways inspired me to write this book and to dedicate my life toward the betterment of all creatures great and small.

14.

My Rabbit and the Light: Some Personal Reflections

Companion animals can have a profound influence on young children, even when they pass on. I had a pet rabbit when I was about three years old. Thumper was a dwarf Dutch bunny—gentle, warm, and quick. He was housed in a fine wooden hutch my father had crafted, with a warm nest box and a wire enclosed porch and walkway.

I would go and see him every morning before breakfast and always had something to tell or a question to ask of him. One morning I went to greet him and found him lying flat on one side, as though he were asleep. I had never seen him behave like that before. I called his name, but he did not move an ear or open his eyes. I was scared. I opened his hutch, and found a stick to touch him gently with. He didn't move. I felt him with a shaking hand. His body was cold and no longer moved when I pressed his thigh gently.

I was bewildered, rather than sad and tearful. Those feelings came later. The evening before he was so alive and well, but now he was gone. But what was gone, I wondered, since his body was still there, as though simply asleep. Maybe he could be warmed in the sun.

I ran to tell my mother that Thumper was dead and she must come and help. His death was confirmed, and we buried him after a little ceremony in the garden later that morning. From then on, cold and death were linked in my mind.

It was a mystery to me, the question of where the life of Thumper, which once animated his body, had gone, leaving his body behind. I had heard about Heaven and someone told me that Thumper would be there waiting for me when I died. But I wondered how could he be? In what form would he appear in, since his body was buried in the garden? I knew that the skin and flesh would be taken into the soil by a host of insects, leaving only his bones, for I had often found the bones of little creatures while playing in the grass and bushes, and maggot-filled, cat-killed voles and songbird carcasses. His body returned to the earth, so where did the rest of him go?

A few days later, with Thumper still alive in my mind, I went into the back garden early one summer morning. The flowers were head-high and the mist was thick with their perfume and the buzz of myriad insects. As I breathed in this fragrant light and looked up through the mist into the heart of the hazy sun, I had a frightening but exhilarating experience and one that remained with me forever. Suddenly I became a mere particle in that misty light. I felt connected with every particle that light embraced, and its embrace was infinite. I didn't see Thumper in the light. I didn't need to. The warmth of the morning sun reminded me of the warmth that my parents had always given me. But it was so much more intense. I felt it enter into the very core of my being.

It was all knowing and all loving and made me feel infinitely secure in its embrace. I no longer missed my friend Thumper because he was part of the light. I saw and felt how every living being in the garden, every flower, herb, shrub, insect, and bird was part of this light. It was within them and around them all. In that moment of realization, I had no sense of my own self being separate from anything else. From that time on, I never feared death or dying. Even during some of the most difficult, heartbreaking events in my life, I would find strength and trust in life by thinking about Thumper and how his light and warmth had returned to the source of all being from which all things arise.

Many years later I thought of Thumper as I mercifully stomped dozens of diseased rabbits to death. It was one of those perfect Saturdays in early June, ideal for a walk over the moors and through the limestone dales of Derbyshire. I let the wind take me wherever it would, feeling it pushing me up the hills as I kept my back to it all the time. I felt as though I was flying, my body, thanks to the wind, keeping up with my soaring spirits. I was elated because I had the letter in my pocket that I had been waiting for. It notified me that I had been accepted for the 1956 first academic year at the Royal Veterinary College, London. My childhood dream was coming true.

I had always wanted to be an animal doctor, and if I passed all the examinations, I would be qualified in five years' time.

Five years, I was thinking. For the past five years, I had already been helping local veterinarians on their farm and on house calls. How much more to learn—to know how to treat sick animals, diagnose their ailments, perform surgery, deliver calves. Five years seemed like a long time, and even longer if I failed some of the exams. I groaned to myself as I scaled an old limestone wall, startling a ewe and her young lamb who were napping in the sunlight on the other side. I apologized to them and they trotted off, bleating briefly before stopping and turning to give me a look of curious disdain. The wind pushed me up the hill and at the top I breathed in deeply, enjoying the day and the boundless promise of exhilarated, youthful spirits. I readied to race down into the dale below, noting the sheep trail between the limestone rocks and boggy reed beds that I needed to skirt to avoid a bad tumble. Then I saw a rabbit moving beside an outcrop of limestone. She was not moving normally and appeared drunk and dazed. Perhaps she had been poisoned, I thought, as I moved slowly and cautiously toward her.

She disappeared behind the rocks and I followed her into an open glade that was pocked with rabbit holes. It was a large warren, but the eerie thing was that she just kept wandering around and didn't bolt down one of the holes. She seemed oblivious to my presence.

Then I saw rabbits wandering aimlessly and dying slowly by the score in the bright sun of this warm summer's day. The innocence and verdant beauty of this limestone dale was shattered. There was no breeze, and the buzz of carrion flies filled the heavy air. I walked slowly and quietly, so as not to frighten any of the less sick rabbits who seemed vaguely aware of my presence, but made no effort to escape. One so blindly sick, hobbled toward me, without seeming to be aware of my presence. Or was she asking me to kill her?

I picked her up. Bloody mucous from her mouth and gasping nostrils splattered my face and parka jacket as the pathetic creature struggled weakly in my hands. Her eyes were so swollen I felt they might burst. I could not save her, nor any of her other dozens of warren relatives, who were circling, crouching, and convulsing, as far as my eyes could see. I quickly dispatched the poor creature with a "rabbit punch" at the base of her skull. I went on killing automatically until my hand hurt too much from striking and dislocating their necks. So I used the sharp heel of my boot, placing each rabbit on a rock so that the skull would implode instantly rather than sink, possibly uncrushed into the soft ground.

Eventually there were no more rabbits alive and I was surrounded by the carnage of my own compassion. Perhaps the rabbits stayed aboveground to save others in the warren from becoming infected. I doubted, however, that there were any survivors. I sat down in their midst as my senses slowly returned. I heard a skylark's spiral song rising above some distant meadow as the breeze returned and rustled in the reeds close by.

Needing to vent my rage at the plight of the rabbits, I walked and walked until I could walk no more and collapsed on the wide upland moor, lying with my back on the soft, warm earth. I let my mind lift into the clear sky, following the cadence of motion and sound so perfectly balanced in the spiraling and trilling of the larks. I was able to weep then for the tragedy behind and below me: so many slow dying rabbits with heads swollen and protruding eyes from a disease that I had read about—myxoematosis, or rabbit plague. This disease had been deliberately introduced by government agents to reduce the rabbit population. It ensured long suffering before death, leaving behind a resistant population that gradually increased in numbers. But unaccounted numbers of foxes, owls, and hawks had died from starvation when the rabbit warrens were decimated by this disease. A few years after this mass extermination of rabbits, they became even more of a problem because these natural predators had died of starvation and were not around to help keep their numbers in check.

Such a cruel, futile, and perverse attempt at biological warfare by man had made the valley, and dozens more, a festering trench of blind, starving, disoriented, and dying rabbits. What right had I to end their suffering: better perhaps to let the disease take its course and leave the valley. But their suffering was mine, and I would have been a coward to have left them alive.

On my way home, the evening breeze brought its cool sweetness from across the distant moors and my sadness turned again to the rage and humiliation (for being human) that I had felt as my hand and boot snapped and crushed life out of rabbit after rabbit. I remembered then that none of the rabbits had screamed: their death was perhaps a merciful release from their silent suffering. The scream of a rabbit in pain or fear I know was a penetrating and distressing emotional tone, at least to my ears. I caused them neither pain nor fear when I assumed responsibility for their suffering that day. Perhaps it was my first real examination, to test if I really had the right qualities and potential to become a veterinarian and, first and foremost, to be able to put compassion into action.

Part Two
Dog Body

15.
Trends in Companion Animal Care, Health, and Welfare

Animal Care and Welfare: A Snapshot

A recent American Pet Products Manufacturers' Association National Pet Owners' Survey conducted for the $31 billion pet product industry includes some basic, as well as some interesting and unsettling, information.

Demographics

A total of 64.2 million U.S. households own a companion animal, up over 10% from a decade ago. There are 65 million companion dogs. Two out of ten dogs are kept outdoors.

Spay and Neuter Statistics

Nearly thirty states have laws mandating that animals adopted from shelters be spayed or neutered.

National Nutrition Statistics

Sixteen percent of dogs are obese or overweight, up from 12% found in the 2000 survey.

Cats and dogs are receiving better nutrition, according to the 2003–2004 study. More people are feeding their pets higher quality commercial pet food as well as home prepared diets, which I regard as a significant improvement.

Animal Protection

Over thirty states now have laws making animal abuse a felony. Six states have laws granting immunity from civil or criminal liability to veterinarians reporting suspected animal cruelty. Forty-five states have made dog fighting a felony offense, and several have enacted the posting of bonds to ease the financial burden on shelters holding animals for the courts.

More judges, prosecutors, and social workers are aware of the link between family, animal, and spousal abuse, as well as childhood cruelty toward animals to later violent criminal behavior.

As of 2000, only three states mandated pound seizure (allowing cats and dogs to be taken from shelters by research labs for experimentation). More than a dozen states now prohibit this practice in most municipalities and dropped the practice because of public outcry.

Both common and statutory laws are now increasingly acknowledging the loss of an animal companion as a basis for recovery of damages above and beyond the fair market value of the animal.

Euthanization Statistics

According to the Humane Society of the United States (HSUS), animal shelters are euthanizing fewer animals. An estimated 4.6 million (4.5%) of the 120 million dogs and cats owned are euthanized at this time (2005–6), down from 5.6 million (5.5%) of the 110 million dogs and cats owned in 1992.

Canine Cosmetic Surgery

The deliberate mutilation of certain breeds of dogs' ears and tails, routinely performed in the United States for cosmetic purposes but outlawed in England and many other countries, should be abolished. The American Animal Hospital Association is on record as being opposed to the cosmetic tail docking and ear cropping of dogs.

Deforming dogs' ears and removing their tails, regardless of the pain, are unconscionable practices that deprive dogs, for their entire lives, of body parts that are important to their body language communication.

Show Breed Cosmetic Surgery

Surgical and other cosmetic alterations of show breeds should be prohibited, such as ear cropping and tail docking, and veterinarians should be professionally disciplined for performing cosmetic alterations to cover

Young Doberman with recently cropped ears bound in splints—a painful and unnecessary mutliation.
Photo: M. W. Fox

up superficial genetic and developmental defects such as eye, lip, and ear abnormalities (even an undescended testicle by implanting a plastic one!).

Animal-Based Industries

The high regard in the West for certain animal species, variously regarded as food or vermin in other cultures (most notably, cats and dogs), is an irony that some critics see as sheer overindulgence and misplaced emotion—particularly when billions of dollars are spent annually on the care of such animals. That such animals are considered human companions and family members has helped promote the social acceptance in the West of animals having rights and being worthy of moral consideration. This is seen as a significant threat to various animal-based industries in the United States—particularly the factory-farming, fishing, animal research, and wildlife trade and fur industries.

These animal industries erroneously dismiss pet lovers as sentimentalists who anthropomorphize their animals, having no real understanding of what really goes on in these "vital" industries.

These exploiters of animals do not wish to accept the fact that animals have feelings and emotion mediating neurochemical pathways virtually identical to ours. There is scientific evidence demonstrating these phenomena in such animals (see chapter 10).

We are now seeing an about-turn, a radical change in human-animal and Earth relations, with the realization that we are part of the Earth and the Earth is part of us. When mankind harms the Earth, mankind harms himself. When mankind demeans animals, human rights are ultimately eroded as well.

Commercialization Issues

While the conscientious veterinarian tries to balance the interests and needs of the client and the animal (often a difficult challenge), market research by the pet food, pharmaceutical, and supplies industries are primarily focused on selling ever more products and services.

From drugs, insecticides, and snacks to toys, training collars, and invisible fences, critics see these companies catering more to owner/caretaker/guardian needs, fears, and phobias rather than to the animals' needs and best interests.

All these insecticides that are injected, fed to, and put on companion animals finish up in the environment via their stools and urine. This effect profoundly affects the entire ecosystem. It is imperative that the government address this serious issue.

Vaccination Practices

Until recently, dogs and cats have been given far too many vaccinations, and too often. While many veterinarians are now changing their vaccination protocols and owners are becoming more aware of the risks, too many kennels and catteries that board animals still insist on up-to-date vaccinations. A safe alternative to unnecessary repeat-vaccinations is to have blood titers taken to determine if any revaccinations are needed.

Annual booster shots are now being shown to often cause more harm than good. They have often resulted in a variety of autoimmune diseases, chronic immunodeficiency, endocrine disorders, and cancer (fibrosarcoma) in cats.

The Dark Side

Many people enjoy a deep sense of communion with their animal companions. This special relationship has led to a plethora of books celebrating this bond, as well as the spirituality of the animal connection and its healing and transformative powers. Companion animals are even regarded as angelic beings.

But there is a dark side to our relationship with companion animals that love and respect alone will never eliminate.

Education, legislation, investigation, and prosecution are called for when addressing the cruelty suffered by animals in a society where closed-door institutions like the pet food industry contract out to test animals to develop, for example, a new diet for cats with kidney disease. This research is all too often conducted at the animals' expense.

The public is not aware of how such research is carried out. Most of the cats' kidneys are surgically removed, and experimental dietary products are tested. The "special" diets that are developed are done at many animals' expense and suffering.

I do not believe this is the way to proceed to sell market commodities. The pet food industry obviously disagrees.

That a scientist, lab technician, or student can design and perform experiments on cats and dogs that outside of the institutional setting would be a violation of anti-cruelty laws points to the power of situational ethics over the ideal boundless ethic of compassion.

Laboratory animals are being bred with specific diseases to facilitate development of new drug tests and screens for genetic disorders. Modern science is experiencing an explosion of biomedical research, especially on genetically engineered rodents.

Genetic engineers are now eyeing the purebred dog as the next laboratory rat. The U.S. government has provided researchers with $50 million of taxpayer dollars to sequence the canine genome for the purpose of identifying genetic abnormalities (of which there are close to four hundred) that are analogous to those seen in Homo sapiens.

Dogs will be deliberately bred to have genetic disorders; while this may help breeders eliminate defects from the gene pool of afflicted breeds, it is clear that dogs will be made to suffer in this new service for humanity as models of similar hereditable diseases in man.

I have advocated for years that sound science can demonstrate that animal experimentation is not necessary.

It is ethically wrong, and, I believe, unnecessary to deliberately induce illness and injury in healthy animals. There already exist many sick and injured animals. More ethical animal research can be done in collaboration with veterinarians and their clients.

With good liaison and collaboration between veterinary schools and veterinarians in private practice, much can be learned from testing such new diets, surgical procedures, medications, and diagnostic procedures (with the owners' informed consent) on animals who are in need of such advanced treatment.

I firmly believe that these methods are the way to progress humanely toward better companion animal health. Much unnecessary laboratory animal research would be eliminated.

The Essence of Companion Animals

One of my classmates, the late Derek Pout, a British veterinarian, wrote to me, "Animal lovers seem to love animals for their own personal needs, rather than for the animal and all its qualities." This is, I believe, somewhat an overgeneralization. I am finding that more people are much more responsible animal caregivers. They extend themselves to provide their animal companions with not only the best nutrition and veterinary care, but also an environment in which they can enjoy being animals. They thus allow their companions to experience their own dogness, catness, guinea pigness, birdness, and fishness; animals are no longer simply regarded as emotional surrogates and extensions of their human caregivers.

Animals are not just intelligent beings; they also have feelings. I was recently asked in a television interview, "What is the most highly developed ability of companion animals, Dr. Fox?" I answered, "Their ability to empathize."

We must be very mindful of the emotional "vibes" we emit to these highly evolved, very empathic beings. Just like humans, they have emotional intelligence.

Categorically, animal rightists believe that animals should not become a means to human ends because they have their *own* lives, interests, and ends in of and for *themselves*. For this reason, it is argued that keeping animals as pets is morally wrong. This is a contention that must be addressed.

Humans enjoy mutually enhancing, symbiotic relationships with other animals. We should really celebrate this bond; but we must develop and nurture it with understanding and education. A healthy human/nonhuman animal bond is, by its nature, mutually enhancing; each being meets, in part, the other's interests and ultimate well-being.

The America Kennel Club

I am concerned about the American Kennel Club (AKC) and its ties to major pet food manufacturers, openly advertised at its shows. The AKC should be censored for its seeming endorsement of the practice of ear cropping and tail docking. It collects hundreds of millions of dollars selling required pedigree registration papers. It now has a DNA testing program because of the degree of falsified breeding records that has allegedly put their pedigree records in jeopardy. Of particular concern to me is that the AKC continues to register dogs from commercial breeders, or puppy mills. The puppy mill business is a huge one. I advise all people not to buy purebred dogs and cats unless they can see the animal's parents, and personally evaluate their care and temperaments.

I strongly encourage them to adopt animals from their local shelter or get a mutt, a mixed breed that is less likely to have the health and behavioral problems often seen in purebreds. Large commercial breeders of puppies and kittens that primarily market through pet stores and via the Internet, and also export animals abroad, cannot engage in the essential ethic of sound breeding practice through progeny testing, which means keeping track of all offspring to monitor for genetic disorders and heritable behavioral problems such as extreme timidity, hysteria, and aggressiveness.

Canine breeding stock in a typical puppy mill, confined in narrow cages on wire floors above piles of their excrement.
Photo: Foxfiles

In Our Companion's Best Interests

Fortunately, many of my close colleagues are holistic veterinarians. They are a new breed of professional animal health and welfare advocates, focusing not just on physical manifestations of animal health, but the emotional and social aspects as well.

These colleagues stress the following principles for basic animal companion health.

1. Get a mixed-breed dog or cat; adopt a healthy companion from the shelter. The in-breeds and purebreds generally come with a host of genetic defects unless you can find a reputable breeder who keeps impeccable progeny testing records.

2. Provide a healthy social and emotional environment, including compassion and respect for a species with needs different from our own.

3. Provide healthy (organic, if possible) nutrition. Avoid the highly processed foods containing additives and condemned animal parts.

4. Obtain holistic veterinary treatment and set up a health care and maintenance program that means a regular (ideally every six-months) consultation with a veterinarian who will spend time talking about optimal care, nutrition, minimal vaccination, and ways to deal with and prevent common health and behavioral problems.

Thoughts on Progress

The movement to protect companion animals has made considerable progress since I first became involved more than thirty years ago. Much of the credit goes to the public: its concern for the welfare of animals, both through individual efforts and through the support of the local shelters and the various humane societies, has blossomed. Improved shelter facilities, well-trained and more dedicated staffing, behavioral counseling programs, spay/neuter and adoption programs, improved anti-cruelty investigations and stricter law enforcement, coupled with more humane education outreach programs in schools throughout the country are to be applauded.

Society is serving the needs, rights, and interests of the animals with which it coexists. Their time has come.

A mother dog and her pups in an anmal shelter awaiting adoption or death.
Photo: Foxfiles

Onward

The social environment and relationships of dogs, cats, and other companion animals, however, is of continuing concern to me.

More open green spaces for dogs to run safely and play with each other are needed. A more liberal attitude by landlords and property owners toward renters and retirees who wish to live responsibly with the companionship of one or more animals is vital. People with companion animals must understand that it is inhumane to keep them crated all day to "protect" the house.

Owners must appreciate the fact that having two animals, be they cats, guinea pigs, parakeets, or goldfish, is more humane than simply having one animal who is left alone during long workdays, living a life of extreme social deprivation.

One must avoid the genetically engineered "Frankenpets"—a startling example of genetically engineered fish that glow in the dark.

Cats, dogs, sheep, and other animals are now being cloned. The unknown health ramifications of these experiments with nature are frightening. There is a repugnance factor here, and the general public has a gut feeling that this aspect of commercialized bioscience is morally and ethically wrong.

Before we can hope to move federal and state governments to enact more effective animal and environmental protection legislation and enforcement, we must educate the legislators to see the connections, the big picture. They must acknowledge that the plights of the natural environment and exploited animals mirror the plight of the human condition, with its lack of compassion and respect for life, both human and nonhuman.

The greatness of a nation can indeed be measured by the status it has accorded to every life—human, nonhuman, plant, and animal.

Just as the security of a nation is tied to the fate of the Earth, so the future of civilization is tied to effective education, legislation, and law enforcement that functions to protect all animals, the natural environment, and the last of the wild.

But as long as other animals, from puppies and kittens to parrots and potbellied pigs, are regarded primarily as commodities, and there are no laws to prohibit lawmakers from winning elections funded by those vested interests responsible in part for the holocaust of the animal kingdom, the ethical and spiritual erosion of society will continue unabated.

Evil flourishes where good men do nothing.

16.
A Holistic Approach to Health and Behavior

From March 2004 to March 2005 I kept a record of the hundreds of different health and behavior problems that readers of my nationally syndicated *Animal Doctor* newspaper column wrote to me about. Many of these problems had received veterinary attention, and for various reasons had not been resolved.

The top five health problems for dogs were:

1. Itching, hair loss, hot-spots/raw areas, acral-lick granulomas (inflamed benign growths due in part to excessive licking)

2. Adverse reactions to vaccinations and anti-flea and tick medications

3. Lameness/arthritis

4. Tying for fourth place were seizures and congestive heart failure

5. Cancers

Reasons Why Dogs Visit Veterinarians

The American Veterinary Medical Association recently published the following facts and figures on the most prevalent health problems in dogs in the United States that caused owners to seek veterinary treatment. This was compiled by the Veterinary Pet Insurance Company of Brea, California.

- Veterinary visits for skin "allergies" resulted in the most claims for dogs in 2005.

- Ear infections topped the list for dogs in 2004.

- Claims by incident for dogs in 2005 were: (1) skin allergies; (2) ear infections; (3) stomach upsets; (4) bladder infections; (5) benign tumors; (6) osteoarthritis; (7) sprains; (8) eye infections; (9) enteritis; (10) hypothyroidism.

Aside from the few health problems in dogs from being allowed outdoors to roam free (eating garbage, getting into fights, and contacting sick animals), all of the above medical conditions are worth careful scrutiny considering the fact that they occur in animals that are essentially confined indoors most of their lives.

So what is brought into their environments from the outside to cause so many health problems demands some consideration? At the top of my list for consideration are the kinds and quality of food, water, and routine preventive medicines—especially vaccinations and anti-flea and parasite drugs.

Most of these health and behavioral problems, as I have long advocated, can be prevented. In many instances, this can be achieved by a more holistic approach by veterinarians who include behavioral counseling and preventive health-care education for cat and dog owners—especially those with a new kitten or puppy. Many animal shelters are now doing this, and veterinary colleges are including this in their curricula and students' in-field experience and community outreach.

There are genetic susceptibilities of certain breeds of dogs and cats, individual genetic abnormalities notwithstanding. However, most of the above health and behavioral problems—which result in much animal suffering and emotional and financial cost to the primary caregivers/owners—should and *can* become something of the past when the basic principles of holistic veterinary preventive medicine and responsible animal care are applied to the companion animal-human relationship. These translate into caregivers/guardians/owners providing animals with not only the right nutrition, but, most important, with a right relationship based on an understanding of the animals' behavior and emotional, social, environmental, and physical needs, which boils down to providing the right environment for the animal.

The other right of all animals under our care is proper veterinary care, which must begin with a more conservative approach to prescribing and administering potentially harmful and often unnecessary vaccinations and other drugs, especially those used to control fleas and ticks. These are wrongly toted under the banner of "preventive" medicine[1] for pecuniary if not misguided reasons. It is not unlike the wholesale use of antibiotics in intensively farmed animals that put consumers at risk worldwide from antibiotic-resistant strains of bacteria in contaminated meat, eggs, poultry, and dairy products. (Those who have read Ivan Illich's book *Medical Nemesis* may well see a parallel in this veterinary nemesis that I have been seeking to rectify for many years. And I am not alone[2] in this deep concern for animal health and well-being, for the good of every society, East and West.)

Vaccination Protocols

The practice of giving dogs and cats several different vaccinations against various diseases all at the same time early in life and then again every year as *boosters* for the rest of their lives is coming to a close. This is for two primary reasons: animals can have adverse reactions to vaccinations that can impair their health for the rest of their lives; routine booster shots are not needed since earlier vaccinations have given animals sufficient immunity to the diseases in question.

Very young kittens and puppies (i.e., before twelve weeks of age) should not be given vaccinations since this can interfere with the natural immunity in their systems conferred by the colostrum or first milk of their mothers.

---

1. Adverse vaccination reactions resulting in disease (so-called vaccinosis) include encephalitis, seizures, polyneuropathy (weakness, incoordination, and muscle atrophy), hypertrophic osteodystrophy (shifting lameness and painful joints), autoimmune thyroiditis and hypothyroidism, liver, kidney, and bone marrow failure variously associated with autoimmune hemolytic anemia, immune mediated thrombocytopenia. Certain breeds are more susceptible than others. The increased recognition of vaccinosis means a more conservative approach to vaccinating dogs, cats, ferrets, and other companion animals.

2. For more information contact the Association of Veterinarians for Animal Rights (PO Box 208, Davis, CA 95617-0208) and the Holistic Veterinary Medical Association (2214 Old Emmorton Rd., Bel Air, MD 21015). For beginners in the quest for a more holistic approach to companion animal care see Donna Keller, *The Last Chance Dog* (New York: Scribner, 2003); Richard H. Pitcairn and Susan Hubble Pitcairn, *Natural Health for Dogs and Cats* (Emmaus, Penn.: Rodale Press, 1995); Franklin D. McMillan, *Unlocking the Animal Mind* (Emmaus, Penn.: Rodale Press, 2004). More advanced texts for veterinarians include Allen M. Schoen and Susan G. Wynn, *Complementary and Alternative Veterinary Medicine* (St. Louis, Missouri: Mosby, 1997); Susan G. Wynn and Steve Marsden, *Manual of Natural Veterinary Medicine* (St. Louis, Missouri: Mosby, 2003); Cheryl Schwartz, *Four Paws and Five Directions* (Berkley, Calif.: Celestial Arts, 1996).

Other animals that should not be vaccinated include adult animals in a compromised immune state (for example, those who are ill, injured, or being given an anaesthetic and operated on for being spayed, castrated, or any other surgical procedure); animals that are pregnant or nursing; animals that are old and infirm.

The following protocol for vaccination has been published in slightly different form in the American Holistic Veterinary Medical Association journal.[3] A different protocol is called for in animal shelters where a mother's vaccination history is unknown.

The Minimum Vaccination Protocol

- Twelve weeks or older—give MLV (modified live virus) distemper, adenovirus and parvovirus only ("core" vaccines), and none thereafter.

- Twelve to sixteen weeks—give rabies vaccination and then only every three years if permitted by law. (State and municipal laws that do not permit the use of a three-year rabies vaccination should be challenged and changed).

- For dogs at risk, Leptospirosis vaccine should be given at twelve and fifteen weeks and repeated one year later.

- Lyme vaccine should be given to at-risk dogs but the bacterium vaccine can cause immune-complex disease so the recombinant Lyme vaccine is preferred.

- Blood serum titers should be taken to assess a dog's immune status where there is doubt, rather than simply giving booster shots. Repeat "core" vaccines at one year if titers are not determined.

Studies have shown that in normal, healthy dogs at the time of vaccination, Parvovirus vaccines are good for seven years, Rabies vaccines for three to seven years, Distemper vaccines for five to fifteen years (depending on the strain), and Adenovirus 2 vaccines for seven to nine years.

---

3. *Journal of the American Holistic Veterinary Medical Association* (Vol. 22, Numbers 2 & 3, July–December 2003): 47–48.

No vaccine can guarantee immunity, since different strains of infective agents may be involved, and animals who are stressed, suffering from poor nutrition, genetic susceptibility, and concurrent disease may have impaired immune systems and lowered resistance to disease. But this does not mean that they should never be vaccinated or be routinely revaccinated just in case, because vaccinations can cause further immune system impairment and a host of health problems—the so-called vaccinosis diseases—that these new vaccination protocols are aimed at minimizing.

Urine as a Vector
Dog urine can kill trees, bushes, and other vegetation, which is a problem in many high dog-density urban and surrounding suburban communities. In such areas where dogs are living at high density, their scent-lines can also become sickness and death-lines. Certain viruses, like distemper and canine hepatitis, and parasites like leptospirosis that can infect humans, are rapidly spread via an infected dog's urine to other dogs in the neighborhood. Often by nosing into the urine while sniffing it, and sometimes even licking it, dogs are at risk from these diseases if they have no natural immunity. Hence the need for effective vaccines, coupled with safer vaccination protocols.

Prevention or Profit?

The love that is shared between most people and their animal companions makes both parties vulnerable to the exploitation of those whose vested interests in making a profit from selling some new product or service is only too often frivolous and contrary to the best interests of the animal and those of the animals' caregivers. Those who resort to a kind of emotional blackmail (saying, If you don't give this new pet food or disease-and-suffering-preventing product to your pet, you are an uncaring and irresponsible person) operate in a money-driven ethical vacuum in total disregard of the real costs and consequences.

In the final analysis, we are beginning to make amends for our limited appreciation and understanding of what wellness in body, mind, and spirit means. With a deeper understanding of the health and behavioral problems that afflict our companion animals—which mirror, in so many ways, our own afflictions and disease—we may find the way to wholeness, health, and fulfillment.

An Ethical Issue: Debarking Dogs

Many people have asked me what I think about debarking dogs. They asked if debarking might be a way to appease neighbors who complain about their dogs' barking.

On ethical grounds, I am strongly against this surgery of cutting a dog's vocal cords just so the animal won't make a lot of noise. Dogs need their vocal cords to communicate. More than one dog has rescued his or her owners from a burning house by awakening them with barking. A barking dog tells you when someone is at your door. Dogs who bark excessively often do so because they have been left alone too much. Leaving a radio or TV on during your absence, or getting a second companion dog or cat for your dog to play with, can calm and quiet your dog down.

Drastic surgical measures are not the solution to a pet's behavioral problem. Understanding what is troubling your companion animal and showing compassion most assuredly are.

17.
| Preventing Fleas, Ticks, and Mosquitoes Naturally |

I was recently shocked by an article in the Spay/USA magazine, *Paws to Think*. The Companion Animal Council, a group of expert veterinarians, stated that cats and dogs should be administered "pharmaceutical" insecticides to control fleas and ticks. Veterinarians and animal caregivers alike should be extremely cautious about using the new pesticides, such as Frontline and Advantage, which are now routinely given to dogs and cats.

I have received volumes of mail about animals going into seizures, their immune systems being impaired, and their thyroid glands being adversely affected shortly after treatment with these products.

I consider it malpractice for veterinarians to advocate the regular administration of such pesticides, from kittenhood and puppyhood on, as prophylaxis against fleas or ticks.

Physicians do not prescribe antibiotics and other medications *just in case* one might get pneumonia.

The pharmaceutical industry is a mighty one, and, like any commerce, has a vested interest in selling its products. I believe it puts companion animals at risk from excessive and unnecessary medications.

In addition to the adverse reactions many animals have to the new antiflea and tick medicines, there is an environmental risk of these chemicals in part associated with climate-change/global warming. Since these chemicals (and also the heartworm preventive medicine, ivermectin) are excreted in treated animals' stools, fecal material should not be left in the open or flushed down the toilet, but should be bagged and put in with separated, biodegradable household garbage to go to the hopefully well contained and managed municipal landfill.

The holistic approach to flea and tick control detailed below helps reduce the need to give cats and dogs potentially harmful new anti-flea and tick medicines (as pills, spot/drops on the skin, sprays, dips, and collars). These new medicines do not actually eliminate ticks and fleas, and when there are many, the additional control measures detailed below must be adopted anyway. Any and all control measures are jeopardized when cats and dogs are allowed out to roam free in the neighborhood. Collars are especially risky, since the chemicals are inhaled as well as absorbed by the animals, to the dog and anyone sitting close and petting the animal, especially children.

These systemic insecticides that variously kill and disrupt the development of these and other parasites have to be ingested by ticks and fleas for them to work. This means that they must have at least one meal of the animal's blood before getting the poisons in the medicated pet's blood into their systems. Hence these new treatments do not stop infected ticks from transmitting Lyme disease, as well as Ehrlichiosis, Q-fever, Babesiosis, Tick paralysis, and Rocky Mountain Spotted fever, or stop fleas from spreading the plague and Murine typhus or from causing allergic hot-spots in animals allergic to the insects' saliva.

Cold winter is the best control, but in warmer states where it never gets cold enough to kill off fleas, the convenience of using these new anti-flea and tick meds should be weighed against the risks to the animals. Any animal showing any adverse reaction—lethargy, nervousness/irritability, nausea, poor coordination, and more severe neurological symptoms—should be taken off the drug at once. Very young, aged, sick, and nursing animals may be especially at risk, as well as those that have been recently vaccinated, since these drugs could compound any adverse effects of vaccinations on the immune and neuro-endocrine systems of companion animals.

A Holistic Approach

My holistic approach to keeping fleas and ticks at bay consists of:

1. Check daily with a flea comb.

2. Closely examining between the animal's toes and ear-folds.

3. Note any telltale shiny, black, coal-dust-like specks that turn reddish-brown on a piece of wet white paper, indicating flea droppings of digested blood.

4. Fleas and unattached ticks caught in the comb can be quickly disposed of by dunking the comb in a bowl of warm, soap-sudsy water. Attached ticks should be removed by grasping the tick with tweezers as close to where it is attached, using a straight pull; twisting will break off the neck of the tick and leave its head buried in the animal's skin.

5. Vacuum all areas where the animal goes in the house every week, thoroughly.

6. Put cotton sheets over favored lying areas, such as sofas, carpets, and floor surfaces with deep cracks or crevices where flea larvae can hide and mature.

7. Roll up and launder these sheets in hot water every week.

For an already infested house, use insecticidal aerosols or "foggers" following all operator instructions, or call in a professional exterminator and put your animals in a boarding facility or motel during home-extermination *only* after each has been treated with a relatively safe pyrethrin-based anti-flea shampoo, or with an emulsion of neem and karanja oil rubbed into the fur. A second round of fogging the house and shampooing/dipping the animals may be needed, since flea pupae developing in cracks and crevices in the house may not be killed during the first treatment and may subsequently hatch out and start biting people and animals in the home. Dusting the animal with diatomaceous earth—a superfine, harmless powder of fossilized microscopic sea creatures—purportedly kills fleas and their larvae by desiccation. (Birds often dust-bathe, probably to get rid of feather mites in this way.) Liberally sprinkling this same material (or borax powder) to act as a flea desiccant on floors, carpets, and in wall crevices, then vacuuming up after twenty-four to forty-eight hours, and repeating every two to three weeks during flea season, will help keep the home environment clear—provided animals living there do not roam free and come home infested. Some animals may not react well to this dust, which should be applied outdoors.

When control-measures break down and fleas are found on the animal and cannot be kept at bay with regular flea-combing and other controls in the animal's environment, one of the safer flea-control products are those containing the oils and essences of chrysanthemum flowers, which paralyze fleas and are considered the least toxic to animals of all the insecticides, namely natural pyrethrins and synthetic pyrethriods. Repeated spraying, powdering, or shampooing is often needed since not all paralyzed fleas die on the first exposure.

Clean all porch, yard, patio, and garage areas of old mats, debris, brush, and dead vegetation where fleas and ticks may hide and flourish, especially in those areas where animals like to lie. Remove all old tires, plant pots and other objects where rainwater may collect— including clearing blocked gutters and drain or fill areas where water pools—in order to control mosquitoes. Please avoid using ultra-violet light, electrocution bug-zappers, and spraying insecticides that kill millions of beneficial insects. Instead, put citronella candles out on the patio and in garden areas as repellants, put up insect screens on porches, and repair door and window screens.

A small lamp with a 20 or lower wattage bulb angled low over a large flat dish of soapy water or vegetable oil will become a heat-magnet and trap for hungry fleas in an empty house. This can be an alternative, when set up in different rooms, to fumigation while you are on vacation or purchasing a new home where there were animals.

Spritz your dog or cat daily with a floral-scented shampoo or hand soap, diluted in warm water; rub it into the fur and let it air-dry. This will change the scent signal of your companion animal and may help deter insect pests. Putting a few drops of oil of lemon and eucalyptus, neem and karanja, or cedar and peppermint (or trial a mixture of various combinations of the same) in a cup of warm water, then shaking vigorously and spraying on the animal's fur, especially around the ear tips to repel biting and flesh-eating flies, may significantly help repel fleas and ticks and mosquitoes. The lemon and eucalyptus oil combination has been recently approved for human use by the FDA as a safe and effective alternative to DEET to repel mosquitoes. But be prudent, especially with cats who should not be allowed to lick off these various sprays or hand-applied emulsions. Slicing a lemon, placing it in a cup of boiling water, and letting it stand overnight will provide a quick emergency potion that can be rubbed into a dog's fur and allowed to dry to repel fleas and other insects.

A bed for the animal stuffed with cedar shavings, mixed with crushed neem leaves and bark, and dried bunches of rosemary and lavender may help deter fleas and keep them off an animal lying on such a bed. Few animals to my knowledge are allergic to these various plant materials. Pennyroyal has been advocated as an herb that helps repel fleas, but it has fallen into disuse because it can be toxic if ingested.

Healthy animals are less attractive, for reasons that science has yet to determine, to fleas and other external and internal pests and parasites whose whole existence is one of opportunistic survival and multiplication. I have received many letters affirming this from readers of my "Animal Doctor" column. A classic example is one reader who wrote to me to say that her cat never gets fleas because she feeds her cat a natural home-prepared whole-food diet and supplements his diet with Brewer's yeast. Her neighbor's cat, which also goes outdoors like hers (a practice I deplore if it is not into a cat-confining and -excluding backyard enclosure) always gets fleas in late summer (she lives on the East Coast).

I advise giving Brewer's yeast or nutritional yeast (not Baker's or bread-making yeast). Adminster about one teaspoon per thirty pounds of body weight, mixed into the animal's food every day. This, like taking B complex tablets, is the hunter's and fisherman's way of avoiding bug bites (though I would wish that as nonsubsistence hunters they might find more compassion-filled modes of recreation!).

Flaxseed oil, a teaspoon full per thirty pounds of body weight, will also help improve skin and coat condition for both dogs and cats, though cats may do better on an organically certified fish oil. For most breeds of dogs (but not for cats) one garlic clove per forty pounds of body weight, chopped up daily and mixed into the food, may also help increase resistance or deterrence to fleas and other opportunistic bugs from the invertebrate world.

Fleas, ticks, mosquitoes, biting flies, and other insects we hate and fear are far more ancient than humans and their animal companions. Our irrational flea-phobias and tick-terrors are fanned and inflamed by the profit-driven, multinational, petrochemical-pharmaceutical industrial complex that advertises nightly on TV to billions of viewers worldwide to convince us of the need and wisdom of buying their poisons. We should try to keep these creatures at bay with the least harm to all—and that entails a holistic approach to animal health, a kind of ecological diplomacy based upon the ultimate empathy of enlightened self-interest, which includes companion animal's emotional/psychological as well as physical well-being (the two being inseparable in making for a well-functioning immune system).

The best medicine is prevention, and a holistic approach to companion animal health in this twenty-first century calls for a revision of vaccination protocols, of feeding highly processed commercial pet foods, and of over-medicating—especially with so-called preventive medications like those sold to keep fleas and ticks at bay, as there are safer and cheaper alternatives with far less risk to animals' health.

18.
Endocrine-Immune Disruption Syndrome

Chemical compounds called endocrine disruptors may play a significant role in various chronic diseases in both companion and other animals, and also in humans. These diseases include allergies; chronic skin diseases; recurrent ear, urinary tract, and other infections; digestive system disorders such as chronic colitis, diarrhea, and inflammatory bowel disease frequently associated with immune system impairment; and metabolic and hormonal disturbances expressed in a variety of symptoms, from obesity to thyroid and other endocrine disorders, especially of the pancreas and adrenal glands.

Veterinarian Dr. Alfred J. Plechner's clinical findings that link elevated serum estrogen levels, thyroid dysfunction, and impaired synthesis of cortisol with a variety of health problems in animals warrant careful consideration, more detailed research, and randomized clinical trials. His claimed benefits of very low doses of cortisone, often in combination with thyroid hormone replacement, may hold true for some patients suffering from what I term the *Endocrine-Immune Disruption Syndrome* (EIDS). But long-term cortisone treatment may aggravate the syndrome, especially in the absence of a holistic approach to improving the animal's immune system and overall physical and psychological well-being.

Adverse reactions to vaccinations, anti-flea and tick medications, and other veterinary drugs, as well as hypersensitivity to various foods and dietary additives, may be consequential and contributory elements in what I interpret as a widespread and not yet well-recognized Endocrine-Immune Disruption Syndrome. I receive many letters from readers of my syndicated newspaper column concerning dogs and cats with the kinds of chronic, complex, multiple health problems that conventional veterinary treatments have at best only temporarily alleviated.

The primary cause of these hormonal imbalances and associated neuro-, endocrine, and immune system dysfunctions is most probably environmental in origin, specifically the endocrine-disrupting compounds (EDCs), such as dioxins, PCBs, arsenic, and various pesticides, in animals' food and water. Through bioaccumulation, these compounds become concentrated in various internal organs of companion animals, in farmed animals raised for human consumption (including aquatic species), and also in wildlife and humans at the top of the food chain. Many EDCs are *lipophilic:* they especially accumulate in animals' fatty tissues, brains, mammary glands, and milk.

An Internet search and review of the existing literature and ongoing research in the field of environmental toxicology will reveal the ubiquitous presence of endocrine-disrupting compounds (EDCs) in the environment, especially from industrial pollutants (from power plants and municipal incinerators, to paper mills and chemically dependent industrial agriculture) and from untreated and inadequately treated sewage water (some 850 billion gallons of which are dumped annually into U.S. waters). EDCs are also being identified in a host of household and medical products, especially plastics, in clothing, floor materials, and lining of food cans, (notably phthalates and Bisphenol A), and in the food and water we share with our companion animals and give to farm animals.

New EDCs are being identified, detected in human breast milk, infant umbilical cord blood, and in "signal" wildlife species, from alligators to Artic seals. Researchers with the U.S. Geological Survey (USGS) Contamination Biology Program have found that PCB-treated fish have lower resting plasma cortical titers and disrupted stress responses, impaired immune responses, and reduced disease resistance. PCBs disrupt glucocorticoid responsiveness of neuronal cells involved in the negative feedback regulation of circulating cortical levels. I link these and other research findings on EDCs with Plechner's findings of low serum cortical levels in his patients, exposed undoubtedly to a number of EDCs that can have enhanced toxicity through synergism. Ironically the USGS has found human birth control estrogens in river waters.

EDCs not only disrupt endocrine signaling systems (estrogen, progesterone, thyroid, glucocorticoid, retinoid, etc.) and immune system functions, they can also cause profound behavioral, neurological, and developmental disturbances. They may play a role in obesity and in animals' adverse reactions to vaccines, other biologics, and pharmaceutical products.

There is an urgent need for the veterinary profession to address this Endocrine-Immune Disruption Syndrome, and to consider it when treating a variety of chronic diseases in animal patients. For a start, all veterinary practitioners should encourage animal caregivers to provide sick (and healthy animals, as part of holistic health maintenance) with pure water and organically certified food, including diets with animal fat and protein derived from young animals fed and raised organically and not exposed to herbicides, insecticides, and other agricultural chemicals, and veterinary pesticides and other drugs (even synthetic pyrethrins are powerful endocrine disruptors). Seafoods in the diet, especially of cats, should preclude species high on the food chain, like tuna and salmon. Also livestock that is organically certified should not be fed fish meal because of the bioaccumulation of EDCs. Many commercial dog and cat foods are high in soy/soya bean/vegetable protein. Since soy products are high in plant estrogens (those from genetically engineered soy being potentially extremely problematic in this matter), it would be advisable to take all animals suspected of suffering from EIDS off all foods containing phytoestrogen-laden plant proteins, and for healthy cats not to be fed any diet that relies on soy as the main source of protein. Healthy dogs, who are more omnivorous than cats (who are obligate carnivores), may not be at such risk.

The use of so-called xenobiotic detoxification enzyme and other therapeutic nutrient-supplement treatment, as detailed by Dr. Sherry A. Rogers and Dr. Roger V. Kendall (see references, p. 184), is worth consideration for chronically ill animals that may have EIDS. These include essential fatty acids, as in flaxseed oil, digestive enzymes (e.g., papain and bromeliad), and vitamins A, B complex, C and E, alpha-lipoic acid, L-carnitine, L-glutamine, taurine, glutathione, dimethylglycine, CoQ10, bioflavinoids, selenium, copper, magnesium, and zinc (with caution as per breed susceptibility to toxicity).

Homeopathic practitioners use Nux vomica and Sulfur to help detoxify a patient.

Detoxification can also include a bland, whole-food, natural diet for three to five days (individual food-hypersensitivity being considered), including steamed carrots, sweet potato and other vegetables, cooked barley or rolled oats, and a little organic chicken or egg, plus a sprinkling of kelp (powdered seaweed), alfalfa, or wheat grass sprouts, and milk thistle. For cats, the amount of animal protein should be at least two-thirds of the diet, while one-third is sufficient for dogs. After this cleansing diet, a whole-food, home-prepared balanced diet is advisable. In some cases, fasting for twenty-four hours may also be beneficial prior to giving the detox diet. But caution is called for since this could put some cats at risk.

The use of lawn and garden pesticides and other household chemicals, especially petroleum-based products, which could be endocrine disruptors should be avoided, and also plastic and water food containers for all family members, human and nonhuman. New carpets, plastic chew-toys, and stain-resistant fabrics and upholstery may also be potential hazards

The medical and veterinary evidence of an emerging EIDS epidemic is arguably being suppressed for politico-economic reasons: witness the U.S. government's foot-dragging from one administration after another to take effective action to phase out hazardous agricultural chemicals and industrial pollution to protect consumers from dioxins, PCBs and PBBs—all potent EDCs. These compounds in particular contaminate through bioaccumulation the foods of animal origin—the discarded and condemned parts of which are recycled into pet foods and livestock feed.

References

Theo Colborn, et al, *Our Stolen Future* (updates at: www.ourstolenfuture.org/ NewScience/new sources/newsrce.htm; see also: www.ourstolenfuture.org/ New/recentimportant.htm).

"Body Burden2: The Pollution in Newborns" (Washington D.C.: Environmental Working Group, 2005): www.ewg.org/reports/bodyburden2/.

R. V. Kendall, "Therapeutic Nutrition for the Cat, Dog and Horse," in A.M. Schoen and S.G.Wynn, eds., *Complementary and Alternative Veterinary Medicine* (St. Louis, Missouri: Mosby, 1997): 53–72.

Sheldon Krimsky, *Hormonal Chaos* (Baltimore: Johns Hopkins Press, 1999).

Alfred J. Plechner, *Endocrine-Immune Mechanisms in Animals and Human Health Implications* (Troutdale, Oregon: New Sage Press, 2003).

T. G. Pottinger, "Topic 4: 10 Interactions of Endocrine-Disrupting Chemicals with Stress Responses in Wildlife," *Pure and Applied Chemistry* (Vol. 75, 2003): 2321–2333.

S. H. Rogers, "Environmental Medicine for Veterinary Practitioners" in A.M. Schoen and S.G. Wynn, eds., *Complementary and Alternative Veterinary Medicine* (St. Louis, Missouri: Mosby, 1997): 537–560.

U.S. Dept. of the Interior, U.S. Geological Survey, Summary of Endocrine Disruption Research in Contamination Biology Program. Updated 11-10-04: www.cerc.usgs.gov/.

19.
| Pure Water for All |

It is difficult to find pure water almost anywhere on the planet, because of chemical contamination. This contamination stems from pesticides, heavy metals like lead and mercury, copper from pipes, arsenic compounds, radioactivity in some regions, excessive amounts of nitrates and phosphates, potentially harmful bacteria and other microorganisms, pharmaceutical products excreted by humans and other animals given various drugs, and also industrial pollutants, especially dioxins and PCBs. Pollution of the air means contaminated rain, and polluted lakes and oceans mean contaminated rain through the hydrological cycle of evaporation and poison-cloud formation.

Water treatment facilities and most water-purification systems (like reverse osmosis, ultraviolet and ozone disinfection, ion exchange, and activated carbon filters) do not get rid of all of the contaminants that can pose serious health problems to us and to our animal companions. The widespread chlorination of water to kill bacteria causes further problems, especially when there are high levels of naturally occurring organic contaminants; by-products such as chloroform and trihalomethanes are formed, which are highly carcinogenic—causing kidney, liver, and intestinal tumors, and also kidney, liver, and brain damage, as well as birth and developmental defects in test animals. Alternative water disinfection with chloramines, a hoped-for safer alternative to chlorine, also results in the formation of highly toxic iodoacetic and holoacetic acids.

Fluoride and Other Problems in Water

Compounding these health hazards of water treatment of already contaminated water is the addition of fluoride, a by-product of the phosphate fertilizer industry, ostensibly to strengthen people's teeth and prevent cavities. But in order to do this, fluoride must be in direct contact with the teeth. That means the fluoride must be applied topically. Studies have shown no benefit from ingested fluoride.

On the contrary, fluoride can mottle the teeth and cause a host of health problems—notably osteoporosis, arthritis, kidney disease, and hypothyroidism. Fluoride has also been linked with gastrointestinal ailments, allergic skin reactions, impaired cognitive ability in children, harm to the pineal gland that helps regulate the onset of puberty, and possibly cause cancer. Flouride in tap water has been linked with osteosarcoma, particularly in young boys.

Of particular concern is when there is some already-existing kidney disease, the kidneys' ability to excrete fluoride becomes markedly impaired, leading to a buildup of fluoride in the body.

I am also very concerned about the widespread use of aluminum chlorhydrate and other aluminum compounds, implicated by some to play a role in Alzheimer's disease, and various anionic and cationic emulsion and powder polymers, especially polyacrylamide, for waste-water treatment. Used to cause flocculation and coagulation of various wastes, including the effluent from poultry slaughter/packing plants, some wastes that contain these added agents may be variously used as fertilizer and livestock feed. Acrylamides are carcinogenic and can cause genetic damage, neurological problems, and birth defects, and may therefore finish up in our food chain and drinking water. Flouride can combine with aluminium to form aluminium fluoride, which is implicated in Alzheimer's disease and can interfere with many hormonal and neurochemical signals. Clearly trading one or more health risks from contaminated water for others created by water treatment processes is ill advised. Safer, cost-effective, organic, microbial, and ecologically based alternative systems of water treatment, recovery, purification, and waste management/disposal are most urgently called for.

It is for the above reasons that I advise all people to drink pure spring water (that usually only requires sand-filtration to meet with U.S. National Sanitation Standards certification) *and to provide same for their animal companions*, particularly those who, for various health reasons, are drinking more water and who have impaired kidney function.

The mineral content of most spring water, and water from remote, often high-altitude, glacial and other isolated sources far from industrial and agricultural activities, are generally extremely beneficial, but excesses need to be closely monitored because of possible trace-nutrient imbalances that they may cause, as well as urinary calculi or stones. Purified, distilled water, lacking in these essential minerals, may actually cause osteoporosis and other health problems.

The Risk of Free-Standing Water Sources for Dogs

Dogs, when outdoors, often want to drink from puddles and ponds. They should not be allowed to do so because standing water can be heavily contaminated with the chemical cocktail of road runoff, as well as various pathogens: giardia, cryptosporidia, botulism-toxin bacteria, harmful fungus that can cause fatal pythiosis or "swamp cancer," fecal bacteria from human, farm animal wastes that cause periodic epidemics of flu-like food poisoning in the human population, and also lawn, garden, and golf-course pesticides and other harmful chemical run-off, most especially from agriculture.

Humans have disrupted and poisoned the hydrological cycle/system on this blue water planet Earth, at great cost to our own health and to all other life-forms that, like us, need water to live. Many of them live in the polluted surface waters of the planet from which they have no escape—nor ultimately, do we.

We are drinking the poisons that we thought nature, the ecology, could somehow assimilate, dilute, and neutralize. But that is not the case, as any chemical analysis of human and whale mother's milk will affirm. But there are long-term solutions beyond the science and technology of water purification and desalinization that alone cannot guarantee a safe and sustainable source of drinking water for the generations to come. These include not using pesticides (herbicides, insecticides, fungicides), and chemical fertilizers on our lawns, gardens, golf courses, and crops—organic and sustainable agriculture being one hope for the future; deconstructing the waste-disposal, incineration, energy, petrochemical, paper, plastic, and other consumer-driven commodity and appliance industries so that the fewer pollutants they release into the air and surface waters (and ultimately into our food and water chains), the more they profit; market no products or by-products that cannot be recycled without harm to the health, vitality, integrity, and beauty of this living Earth and all who dwell therein.

A Call to Action

We can no longer take water for granted as one of nature's bountiful, pure, and eternally renewable resources. Water is the fundamental life source that sustains all beings, and to our peril and the demise of this living planet, we have thoughtlessly squandered and poisoned this basic, vital element of existence. We cannot trust that the water coming from our faucets and wells is safe to drink or to give to our animals, and the science of water-safety and quality evaluation is still in its infancy.

Even so, consumer-citizen taxpayers have a right to have their municipal water authorities test domestic water sources regularly and make their findings available to the public. They also have the right to demand better monitoring and law enforcement to protect open waters from pollution runoff from people's lawns and gardens, as well as from agriculture and other human activities and various industries.

Just as the organic foods market has accelerated with increased, informed consumer demand over the past decade, so too in this next decade of the twenty-first century is a more informed public demanding pure water—some of the purest coming from ancient springs, more remote, higher-altitude, and glacial sources, and as yet uncontaminated and sustainable deep aquifers. But these sources will not last forever. It is the responsibility of all of us to conserve water, to stop polluting, and to treat this basic resource—the source that sustains all life—with respect and gratitude.

The northern states of the United States have an immediate and most urgent responsibility at this time to reduce the agricultural, industrial, and municipal sewage pollution of rivers and overexploitation of same, through diversion and dam-construction for commodity-crop irrigation and dairy and other livestock production. (This has been notably facilitated for decades by the U.S. Army Corps of Engineers, which has put the Florida Everglades on the never-glades path to extinction for the sugar and cattle industries and for industrial-scale orchard/plantation irrigation after natural ecosystems have been annihilated—along with the many wildlife species like the wolf, the lynx, the Florida panther, the flying squirrel, and the coati-mundi.) The rivers/waterways that flow south across the North American continent harm all southern states that take what poisoned water is left, which ultimately flows to the Gulf of Mexico—where an area of ocean the size of Rhode Island is so polluted that it is void of any life, according to marine biologists and the local fishing industry.

All those who care about their health, the health of their families, and the health of their companion animals will see the wisdom of purchasing the best quality water they can and stop adhering to the erroneous belief that their tap water is necessarily safe for their consumption. Water quality and safety is a wake-up call for us all, and the state of its quality confirms the truism that when we harm the earth, we harm ourselves. The health of the Earth—of aquatic as well as terrestrial ecosystems, just like the health of the human population—is interdependent and linked by air and water quality that, for the good of all, we must improve and maintain.

20.
| The Right Diet |

Commercial Nutritional Horrors

I believe if consumers were aware of the ingredients in many commercial pet foods they would be outraged. Most contain condemned parts of factory-farmed animals that are considered unfit for human consumption. One would not use them as fertilizer in one's garden, let alone feed them to one's beloved pet.

In *Foods Pets Die For: Shocking Facts About Pet Food*,[1] author Ann Martin presents more disturbing details and documentation on this issue. As Martin emphasizes, many ingredients are essentially leftovers from the human food and beverage industries, and are lacking in essential nutrients, which manufacturers compensate for by adding synthetic additives and supplements. Processing at high temperatures destroys many so-called heat-labile nutrients. Preservatives, especially in dry and semi-moist dog foods, added to stabilizers, make for a chemical soup that can lead to chemical sensitivity and food allergies. After endorsing the first edition of Martin's wonderful book in 1997, I was actually put on disciplinary probation (and essentially silenced) and my salary was frozen until my mandated retirement from the Humane Society of the United States in 2002, by the then-president of HSUS. The pet food industry had sent a letter of complaint to my boss, who was hoping to secure funds from pet food companies!

---

1. Ann N. Martin, *Foods Pets Die For: Shocking Facts About Pet Food* (Troutdale, Oregon: New Sage Press, 1997).

New Hope for Companion Nutrition

There is a niche market that is expanding now for organically certified pet (and human) food. There are several excellent books by veterinarians and other informed animal nutritionists on home cooking for animal companions. They present recipes for making nutritious and well balanced foods from scratch for dogs and cats (see Ann Martin's book for recipes, as well as my own basic recipes included in this chapter).

This new trend is by far, I believe, the best way for all conscientious consumers to provide healthy nutrition for their animal companions. Alternatively, one can purchase organic, high-quality commercial pet foods that are based on sound nutritional science. You can also feed a combination of both home-made, whole foods, and organic commercial kibble. Avoid commercial food with an ingredients list stacked early on with corn by-products. Such foods are too high in starches and too low in essential fatty acids. Avoid semi-moist commercial foods, which are full of preservatives and artificial coloring.

Many dogs develop tooth problems when fed exclusively moist or semi-moist commercial foods. Providing biscuits or a bowl of dry dog food to chew on whenever they like (provided they don't overeat), or mixing dry and canned moist food together, will help keep your dog's teeth clean and free of tartar. (Some toy breeds need a regular brushing with a toothbrush.) All dogs should be given something safe to chew on to keep their gums and teeth clean and healthy. A large dog biscuit, or a raw, uncooked marrow bone is ideal. Never give your dog any other kind of bone, since the bone may splinter and cause serious internal injuries.

A Home-Cooked Meal

Home-prepared foods for our animal companions, ideally with organic ingredients that were locally produced, are important because you then know what your animal is being fed if a food-related health problem such as an allergy to a particular ingredient or digestive upset were to arise. With most processed commercial pet foods, which contain all kinds of human food–industry by-products and ingredients that are considered unfit and unsafe for human consumption (many are of questionable nutritional value after repeated processing), you just don't know. Aside from coloring agents that may cause problems other than saliva-staining of animals' faces and paws, most commercial pet foods contain artificial preservatives like BHA, linked with cancer of the bladder and stomach; BHT, which may cause cancer of the bladder and thyroid gland; and Ethoxyquin, one of Monsanto's many allegedly harmful products that renderers (meat and poultry processors) add to the fat/tallow put into pet foods to prevent rancidity. Ethoxyquin is a recognized hazardous chemical and a highly toxic pesticide.

Dr. Michael Fox's Homemade "Natural" Diet for Dogs
Below is a recipe for my homemade natural diet for dogs.

> 3 cups uncooked whole grain rice (or barley, rolled oats,
>   or pasta noodles)*
> pinch of salt
> 1 tablespoon vegetable oil (flaxseed oil or safflower oil)
> 1 tablespoon wheat germ
> 1 tablespoon cider vinegar
> 1 teaspoon brewer's yeast
> 1 teaspoon bone meal or calcium carbonate
> 1 teaspoon dried kelp
> 1 pound lean hamburger, ground lamb, mutton, one
>   whole chicken, or half of a small turkey
> 1 cup raw, grated carrots (or sweet potato or yam)

Combine all ingredients, except the raw, grated carrots. Add water to cover the ingredients (about 8 to 10 cups), simmer, stir, and add more water as needed until cooked. Debone chicken parts and do not feed cooked bones, as they can splinter and cause internal injury. The recipe should be thick, to be molded into patties (add bran or oatmeal to help thicken). Mix well into the stew while it is still very hot a cupful of raw, grated carrots, sweet potato, or yam. Serve one cupful of this recipe for a thirty-pound dog with the rest of his/her rations, and freeze the rest into patties and store in the freezer. This can be served thawed or frozen (to gnaw on outdoors in hot weather).

For variation, you can use cottage cheese plus well-cooked lentils, chickpeas (garbanzo beans), lima beans or other legume, or a dozen eggs as a meat alternative. *All ingredients, ideally, should be organically certified.* (Note: Some dogs are allergic or hypersensitive to some foods, especially soy, beef, eggs, wheat, and dairy products.)

* For dogs under 30 pounds and for overweight and less-active dogs, use 1 cup of uncooked rice or barley in the recipe, and cut the liquid to 2 cups.

Give a half cup per 30-lbs of body weight twice daily as a supplement, and reduce the amount of regular food by the same amount. Mix increasing amounts of your dog's new food with decreasing amounts of the old food over a seven-day period to enable adaptation and avoid possible digestive upset.

As a stand-alone meal, give 1 cup per 30-lbs of body weight twice daily, adjusting the amount over time depending on the dogs appetite and weight gain or loss.

It is advisable to vary the basic ingredients to provide variety and to avoid possible nutritional imbalances, and to monitor the animal's body condition to avoid either overfeeding or underfeeding, based on the average dog consuming one cupful of the food twice daily per thirty pounds of body weight.

Please note that different animals have slightly different nutritional needs according to age, temperament, amount of physical activity, and health status.

Largest Pet-Food Recall Ever: Full Inquiry and Accountability Called For

In March 2007, millions of pet owners became aware that their pets were at risk of developing acute and even fatal kidney disease because of tainted pet food produced in one plant in Canada. The company, Menu Foods Income Fund, recalled sixty million cans and packages of contaminated, poisonous cat and dog food. Menu Foods produced more than one billion containers of dog and cat food in 2006, and these were distributed to brand-name pet-food companies and mega-stores for sale under many different labels—from so-called premium pet foods to store brands. So which labels can we trust?

And how can one trust the industry when Menu Foods, after receiving many complaints about problems with its products, took three weeks to notify the Food and Drug Administration after running feed tests on some fifty cats and dogs that resulted in the unnecessary suffering and death of even more animals. Noted in the press as a "horrible coincidence," the CFO of Menu Foods sold about half of his stake in the company three weeks before the widespread pet-food recall.

This eventually became the largest pet-food recall in the industry's history, involving about a hundred different brand names and distributors, including major well-known brands such as Iams, Eukanuba, Nutro, Hills, Nutriplan, Royal Canin, Pet Pride, Natural Life vegetarian dog food, Your Pet, America's Choice–Preferred Pet, Sunshine Mills, and store brands such as PetSmart, Publix, Winn-Dixie, Stop and Shop Companion, Price Chopper, Laura Lynn, KMart, Longs Drug Stores Corp., Stater Bros. Markets, and Wal-Mart, and a host of private labels of mainly canned (moist) cat and dog foods. Under each brand name are usually many different varieties of cat and dog foods, and this meant that hundreds of different types of pet food were recalled.

The FDA has no mandatory authority to demand a pet-food recall. All recalls are "voluntary," upon written request notification by the FDA. There is no mandatory requirement for pet-food manufacturers to inform the FDA in a timely fashion, or any penalty for not doing so.

No sooner had the recall begun, than I started to receive letters from dog and cat owners thanking me for "saving their animal's lives" because they were feeding them the kind of homemade diet that I have been advocating as a veterinarian for some years. Other letters document the suffering and death of several companion animals, their care givers' disbelief and outrage, and the financial and emotional loss experienced. Many people, including some on fixed incomes, had veterinary bills ranging from three to six thousand dollars and had to take out credit card loans and pay exorbitant interest rates.

On March 23, 2007, the New York State Department of Agriculture and Markets announced that it had found rat poison in contaminated wheat gluten imported from China, which was initially thought to be responsible for the suffering and death of an as yet uncounted number of cats and dogs across North America. The poison is a chemical compound called *aminopterin*.

Veterinary toxicologists with the American Society for the Prevention of Cruelty to Animals and American College of Internal Veterinary Medicine shared my concern that there may be some other food contaminant(s) in addition to the aminopterin that was sickening and killing many pets. Experts were not convinced that the finding of rat poison contamination was the end of the story.

On March 30, the FDA reported finding in the wheat gluten a widely used compound called *melamine*, described as a chemical used in the manufacture of plastics and as a wood resin adhesive and protective. The FDA claimed that the melamine was the cause of an as yet uncounted number of cat and dog poisonings and deaths. The FDA could not find the rat poison aminopterin in the samples it analyzed. However, a lab in Canada, at the University of Guelph, confirmed the presence of rat poison.

The Environmental Protection Agency identified melamine as a contaminant and by-product of several crop pesticides, including *cryomazine*, which is actually absorbed by plants after being sprayed and is converted into melamine after ingestion by an animal. People began to question if there was also pesticide contamination of the wheat gluten. Was there a possibility of deliberate contamination, or was this the result of gross mismanagement and lack of effective food-safety and quality controls that account for levels of melamine reported to be as high as 6.6 percent in FDA-analyzed samples of the wheat gluten?

Wheat gluten is wheat gluten, fit for human consumption. So the question remained, what was wrong with this imported gluten that made it considered fit for use only in pet food?

On April 3, Associated Press named the U.S. importer as ChemNutra of Las Vegas, reporting that the company had recalled 873 tons of wheat gluten that had been shipped to three pet-food makers and a single distributor, which in turn supplies the pet-food industry.

On April 6, the FDA's veterinarian, Stephen Sundlof, told CNN that the melamine found in the contaminated wheat gluten from China could actually have been added as "cheap filler." Melamine crystal is a urea-derived, synthetic nitrogen product that is used as a fertilizer and could have been added to the wheat gluten. But in fact it is *not* cheap. Fine Chem Trading Ltd. Special Offers lists the China melamine price indication for one metric ton at $1,130, while other sources list China's wheat gluten at around $750.

How this melamine got into the gluten is still an open question, and some toxicologists still doubt that this is the main cause of so many dogs and cats becoming sick and even dying from kidney failure.

But melamine, according to Dr. Sundlof, "is not very toxic as a chemical." Since it was found in some 873 tons of wheat gluten from China, the dilution in the vast volume of pet foods being recalled must be considerable. So perhaps melamine is a smoking gun—a symptom—and not the primary cause of so many animals becoming sick and even dying.

Pesticides are used extensively on rice crops, and many varieties of genetically modified/transgenic rice have been planted in Asia. This may account for the presence of melamine in rice protein identified in two of Natural

Balance's cat and dog foods that led to a recall on April 16, 2007, after people reported that their cats and dogs were getting sick on the dry food.

The possibility of synergism of toxic pet-food contaminants, where two or more harmful additives or contaminants resulted in this pet-food poisoning pandemic, still remains open. The massive pet-food recall in 2004 of dry cat and dog food manufactured in Thailand by Pedigree Pet Foods after reports of kidney failure in hundreds of pets, mostly puppies, in nine Asian countries is a matter of public record, but no toxic agents were ever reported to the public by this multinational pet-food company.

Until there is evidence to the contrary, the following concerns remain to be addressed by the FDA.

1. The wheat gluten imported from China was not for human consumption, because, I believe, it had been genetically engineered. The FDA has a wholly cavalier attitude toward feeding animals such "frankenfoods" but places some restrictions when human consumption is involved (yet refuses appropriate food labeling).

2. The "rat poison" aminopterin is used in molecular biology as an anti-metabolite, folate antagonist, and in genetic engineering biotechnology as a genetic marker. This could account for its presence in this imported wheat gluten.

3. Melamine, the plastic and wood preservative contaminant and the parent chemical for the potent insecticide cryomazine, could possibly have been manufactured *within* the wheat plants themselves as a genetically engineered pesticide. This is much like the insecticidal poison Bt. (Farmed animals are fed corn and other feeds from genetically engineered crops that produce their own Bt.)

4. So-called "overexpression" can occur when spliced genes that synthesize such chemicals become hyperactive inside the plant and result in potentially toxic plant tissues, lethal not just to meal worms and other crop pests, but to cats, dogs, birds, butterflies, and other wildlife.

My initial suspicion was that the FDA had been aware that the gluten came from genetically engineered wheat that was considered safe for animal consumption. To admit that the gluten came from a genetically engineered food crop could harm the U.S. agricultural biotechnology industry by raising valid consumer concerns, so better for the FDA to focus on the melamine question.

I could be wrong. But a greater wrong is surely for the pet-food industry to use food ingredients and food-and-beverage industry by-products considered unfit for human consumption; to continue to do business without any adequate government oversight and inspection; and for government to give greater priority and support to agricultural biotechnology (which requires far more food quality and safety tests and surveillance than conventional crops—all at the public's expense) than to organic, humane, and ecologically sound farming practices.

Two widely used herbicides, glufosinate and glyphosate, which have caused kidney damage and other ailments in laboratory test animals, may be part of the problem. These herbicides are liberally applied to crops across the United States and are absorbed by crops that are genetically engineered (transgenic or genetically modified), so that the crops are not harmed by the weed killers while all else growing in the fields is wiped out.

It is quite possible that these and other agrichemicals are in the pet food that made so many animals get sick and even die and are in most of the crops and crop by-products currently being fed to beef cattle, pigs, poultry, and dairy cows whose produce is not certified as organic.

Also, high levels of Bt in crops have made farmers ill and poisoned sheep. Since pet foods show no labels to the contrary, and the FDA does not even permit the labeling of human foods when they contain genetically modified ingredients, we have no way of knowing what we are really eating or feeding to our pets. (For details see my books *Killer Foods: What Scientists Do to Make Food Better Is Not Always Best*, The Lyons Press, 2004, and *Eating with Conscience: The Bioethics of Food*, New Sage Press, 1997.)

Although my theory that a melamine-like derivative insecticide such as cryomazine could have been produced within the wheat plants as a result of genetic engineering may not hold up, and we are dealing instead with a simple chemical contamination, accidental or deliberate, one fact remains: Two independent laboratories found the chemical aminopterin, which they identified as a rat poison, in samples of the recalled pet food. This chemical is used as a genetic/DNA marker and is included in U.S. Patent 6130207, filed on November 5, 1997. (Cell-specific molecule and method of importing DNA into a nucleus.)

And though the United States has resisted the temptation of genetically engineering the staff of life—wheat, our daily bread—China, in collaboration with the UK's Rothamsted Agricultural Research Center, has forged ahead to develop genetically modified/transgenic varieties of wheat, as well as rice and other commodity crops.

So it is surely incumbent upon the FDA to determine if this imported wheat gluten from China was genetically engineered. It possibly was, because it was not bought for human consumption. (Maybe an experimental crop with anti-fungus blight and viral disease genetic insertions went haywire as a result of "overexpression.") Other endogenous toxins not yet identified could well have resulted in so much sickness, suffering, and death in companion animals across North America.

The "life science" industry has convinced legislators that genetically engineered crops are safe and "substantially equivalent" to conventional varieties of food and animal feed crops. But the scientific evidence and documented animal safety tests point in the opposite direction. The U.S. government even attempted to have genetically engineered seeds and foods included under the National Organic Standards.

While scientists and environmental health experts, along with the Sierra Club's Laurel Hopwood, are pointing to agrichemicals and to the pollen of genetically engineered crops as being possibly responsible for the collapse of the honey bee population—which could mean an agricultural apocalypse—veterinarians and toxicologists are unraveling the cause of the epidemic of food poisoning and untimely death of thousands of beloved cats and dogs across the nation. My theory awaits answer from the FDA, namely that the most probable cause was the source of the poison. It had been extracted from wheat that was genetically engineered to produce its own insecticidal chemical, or an as yet unidentified biopharmaceutical or other chemical that became concentrated in the gluten after it arrived in the United States.

This latest pet-food recall in North America should mobilize the public and its elected representatives to take control of how our food is produced and where it comes from. Without labeling as to country of origin and method of production and without organic certification, prepared human foods and manufactured pet foods (which should include no ingredients considered unsafe for human consumption) can no longer be considered safe and wholesome.

Or is the FDA downplaying the severity of this nationwide pet-food poisoning scandal? One major question has not yet been answered: Why was the imported wheat gluten not intended for human consumption?

What is the pet-food industry doing to compensate people for their veterinary expenses? Evidently nothing. They are just setting up yet another expert committee.

Duane Ekedahl, head of the Pet Food Institute (PFI), which represents the pet-food industry, told senators at a hearing that the institute had set up a National Pet Food Commission, while he held up a full-page ad that the PFI had placed that day in major newspapers. He asserted that "Pet foods are perhaps the most regulated product on market shelves."

When challenged by Senator Richard Durbin, representatives for the PFI and the American Association of Feed Control Officials, whose AFCO labeling is standardized on most processed pet foods but gives no valid guarantees on quality or safety, became extremely defensive and contradicted themselves when it came to the actual inspection and testing of ingredients. Dr. Sundlof cited a federal inspection rate frequency of only 30 percent for the last three years for pet-food processing facilities, and this frequency rate was actually higher than usual because of mad cow disease.

The pet-food recall is a wake-up call to every consumer and every pet owner. The FDA has questions to answer (go to www.fda.gov/cvm). Surely it is now incumbent upon the Pet Food Institute in Washington, DC (www.petfoodinstitute.org) to coordinate with all the pet-food manufacturers involved as well as with agribusiness pet-food subsidiaries for which it lobbies and represents, an emergency fund to compensate people for all veterinary expenses resulting from their animal companions becoming sick, possibly dying, and requiring lifelong care as a consequence of this largest pet-food recall in recent history.

There are many vested interests that would like to see this poisoned pet-food pandemic forgotten because it exposes the unhealthful nature of industrial food production, processing, and marketing that harm people and their animal companions, as well as wildlife and the increasingly dysfunctional natural environment. Mercury, lead, arsenic, cadmium, dioxins, and thousands of other industrial pollutants, and especially those highly toxic petrochemicals used ironically in the production and preservation of food—from fertilizers to herbicides, fungicides, and insecticides—now contaminate our drinking water, our food, even the milk of human, polar bear, whale, and elephant mothers. And all this can lead to the untimely death, often after prolonged suffering, of our loved ones, including our animal companions. This need not be, but it will continue as long as there is public apathy and indifference rather than outrage and political action.

On April 18, 2007, Wilbur Ellis Co. of San Francisco began voluntarily recalling all lots distributed to date to pet-food manufacturers because imported rice protein from China had melamine contamination, and it is urging all pet-food manufacturers who have used this rice protein to recall any pet food that may be on supermarket shelves.

Natural Balance was the first company to respond to this concern, recalling two of its dry foods for cats and dogs on April 18. This second recall epidemic spread as more pet-food manufacturers like Blue Buffalo dry kitten food and several cat and dog dry foods manufactured by Royal Canin hastily recalled their products that contained contaminated rice protein/gluten. Then corn gluten was found contaminated with melamine in South Africa, where Royal Canin withdrew its dog foods from the market.

A hog farm in California was under quarantine because although its pigs were healthy, melamine was found in their urine. Their feed was suspect because Diamond Pet Foods in Lathrop, California, which produces Natural Balance pet food, had bought contaminated rice protein from China and had sold "salvage pet food" to the farm for pig feed.

The FDA's Dr. Sundlof stated at the onset of this debacle that melamine is used in the manufacture of plastics and may have been deliberately added as a cheap fake protein supplement to inflate the protein content. But gluten, be it of corn, wheat, or rice origin, is used in the manufacture of the new generation of biodegradable plastics.

This raises the terrible question as to whether the multinational pet-food industry, following the economic mandate of lowest-cost feed formulation, thought it could get a good deal by incorporating industrial-grade product gluten in pet foods. However, what it actually purchased on the world market was never intended for human or animal consumption; it was intended for the manufacture of biodegradable food containers, utensils, and plastic shopping bags. This is essentially what went into pet foods, causing untold numbers to suffer and many to die. Maybe industrial grade soy with melamine, imported from China, is also in some manufactured pet foods, and these will be on recall next.

The high morbidity and mortality rate in dogs and cats associated with this largest pet-food recall ever could well have been aggravated by other chemical contaminants in pet foods that can harm the kidneys, liver, and digestive, endocrine, immune, and other systems of our animal companions. And the industrial crops of corn, wheat, rice, and possibly soy, grown in China for biodegradable plastic manufacture, could well have been genetically engineered, raising additional health and environmental concerns. But the details of this may never be fully unraveled.

This debacle of the commercial processed pet-food industry puts us all on notice. Better quality controls, oversight, and testing are called for, but one must be realistic. There have been recent massive recalls of human food commodities, including ground beef, poultry, onions, and spinach. Costs aside, no system of mass production can be fail-safe. The recycling of human food industry by-products, and products considered unfit for human consumption, into livestock feed and processed pet food presents a monumental risk-management challenge.

Getting Off to the Right Start

Pups should be weaned gradually from the mother anywhere from five to seven weeks of age, or they may have behavior problems at a later age. They should be fed small amounts four times a day for the first three months, then three times daily until six to eight months of age. By one year of age most dogs require only one meal a day, though some enjoy a snack first thing in the morning. To ensure a steady appetite and regularity in elimination, always feed your dog on a regular schedule.

Pups need more protein and other nutrients for their growth requirements than the amount required to maintain the health of adult dogs. They should only be fed commercial foods that are complete and balanced. Read the label. Many dog foods on the market carry this statement on the label.

A pup should *never* be fed an all-meat diet, which is not complete and can result in serious nutritional disorders. Accustom your pup to one or two types of dog food early in life. If you keep changing brands, your pup may suffer acute digestive disturbances. Worse, your pup may become a finicky eater and train you to give him only what he likes. This will not be in your pet's best interests.

21.
The Right Health Care

Every new pup should be taken to a veterinarian for a thorough checkup, fecal tests for worms, and a series of core vaccinations against common virus diseases such as canine distemper, provirus, and canine lymphoma. At a later age, the pup will need a rabies vaccination. Depending on where you live, your pup may need vaccinations against Leptospirosis and other diseases; your veterinarian will advise you about these. A blood test and regular preventive medication against heartworm are essential for disease prevention. (Collie-type dogs can now be tested for genetic susceptibility to being poisoned by heartworm medicine. Only some collies are susceptible.)

Adult dogs should also go to the vet at least once a year for a regular physical and to receive necessary blood titer tests for vaccination/immunity evaluation, and booster shots as needed.

Until your vet says that your puppy is safely protected by the vaccinations she was given, do not take your pup out on a leash or to the park to play with other dogs, or she may succumb to a serious infectious disease from another dog. If you live in a multidog household, make sure your own dogs will be vaccinated and disease free for their and the puppy's sake.

Common Parasites

Pups are usually born with roundworms and sometimes hookworms, for which they should have their stools examined. Many people make the mistake of worming their pet whenever it seems to be sick. This can be dangerous, as real symptoms get overlooked. Avoid all home-doctoring except under your vet's instructions.

Adult dogs will often get infested with hookworms, especially if they're kept outdoors. These worms develop in the soil and then get into the dog by burrowing into the skin; from there they migrate to the dog's intestines. Regular checkups are extremely important to control this parasite.

Rice-like segments in a dog's stool indicate the presence of tapeworms, a common problem in adult dogs. Some kinds of tapeworm result from a dog eating a dead rabbit or rodent, but the most common one has part of its life cycle in fleas. When the dog nibbles and grooms herself, she picks up the infestation from the fleas. So having your dog appropriately wormed is not enough. You must also eliminate the fleas to prevent reinfestation. (See chapter 17 for further details on controlling fleas.)

If you let your dog roam free and unsupervised, the dog is much more likely to pick up fleas, worms, and more serious infectious diseases from other dogs. Your dog may also get injured in fights with other dogs or get hit by a car. For health's sake, keep your dog indoors or in a clean pen or yard outdoors, and take your dog out regularly on the leash for exercise.

Of course dogs need time outdoors off-leash to run and chase. For most dogs, running is one of their greatest joys. They take off when let loose, running circles around their guardians with bright eyes and big grins—expressions of pure canine delight. So find safe dog parks for your dogs to run and play and socialize.

When to Take Your Dog to the Vet

Dogs, like people, get ill periodically. The following signs indicate that your dog needs veterinary attention:

1. Seems less active and playful and won't eat or drink

2. Has a dry, hot nose, red eyes, and seeks a quiet, cool place

3. Has a dry cough and runny discharge from eyes and nose

4. Has diarrhea for more than twenty-four hours

5. Vomits repeatedly and has difficulty in breathing

6. Has poor exercise tolerance and fatigues quickly

7. Has convulsions (runs wildly, "swims" on the floor, foams at the mouth)

8. Scratches or paws certain areas of the body excessively, such as ears or mouth

9. Yelps when touched in certain places (abdomen, ear, paw, etc.) or is restless, irritable, and even snappy.

10. Drinks excessively

Exercise

All dogs need regular exercise. Some dogs and some breeds require more or less than others. Use a long leash for workouts in a legal dog park, and until your pup is trained to "Come" on command. Never let the pup off the leash near traffic. Don't overdo jogging with a young pup, and especially not with an older dog: the dog could have a heart attack. Never take a dog of any age on a long run in hot weather. Heat stroke is a canine killer. With strenuous exercise some dogs, especially Jack Russell terriers and some lines of bird dogs, develop severe muscle cramps that can be permanently crippling.

If you're taking your dog along in your car, always park in the shade and keep the windows partially open so that the car won't be too hot inside when you and your dog return from exercising. On a warm day, the temperature in a parked car without shade can reach 120°F quickly, even with the car windows partially open. Your dog can quickly suffer brain damage or die from heatstroke or suffocation when trapped in high temperatures. If your dog becomes overheated, you must lower your pet's body temperature immediately by applying ice packs all over, hosing with cold water, or immersing in a cold bath.

Playing with Your Dog

We know that dogs enjoy playing because they signal their joyous anticipation in various ways. A dog tells you he wants to play when the forelimbs are extended as the front end drops and the elevated rear end displays a wagging tail, with a bright-eyed, open-mouth, play-face expression. The play-bow is the cardinal signal as an invitation, a solicitation, and an initiation. The dog may also bark, pant excitedly (equivalent to human laughter), and skip backward and forward. I advise adults and children to mimic this signal when they want their dogs to play, and by so doing, learn how to use their body language to communicate like a dog. Jumping or bouncing up and down, panting, yapping, and barking are other play signals of dogs that children can easily mimic, because their own behavior is so similar when they are playfully excited.

A pup should have chewable, rollable, and tugable toys that won't splinter or break into dangerous pieces that could be swallowed. Play will give a timid pup more confidence. Play will also teach a pup not to be too rough or bite too hard during playful tugs-of-war and play-fights. Puppies will sometimes get overexcited and play too hard. With few exceptions, they will quickly learn to play gently when they are consistently reprimanded and are not played with for a while after being too rough.

Dogs also solicit play by staring and then crouching as though ready to attack, or by staring around from behind objects like a sofa or door, and then quickly hiding. The latter peek-a-boo game—like the former direct-stare showdown at hign noon at the OK Corral—are wonderful games. They can lead to games of chase, hide-and-go-seek, and catch-me-and-I'll-catch-you. With my own three dogs, I will sometimes make eye contact and then pretend to be a threatening monster, and they love it most any time.

Most dogs, but not all, love to chase a ball, Frisbee, or stick and to return it to be thrown again and again. Some dogs also enjoy a tug-of-war with an old towel or rubber pull-toy.

Play is enjoyable and a physically and mentally beneficial activity that helps establish and maintain a strong social and emotional bond between participants. People who play with their pets will have happy and alert animal companions from their infancy into old age. Our animal companions also enjoy play with each other, which is also fun to watch. Those who play together stay together.

A Guide to Grooming Your Dog

Regular grooming makes a dog look and feel better, and there is scientific proof that grooming improves the pet's health as well. For aged and convalescing animals, grooming stimulates the circulation. With any pet, grooming causes deep relaxation with a dramatic slowing of the heart rate—thus helping the animal cope better with physical and emotional stresses.

All dogs should find brushing pleasurable. Some people find it is difficult to get their dogs to submit to regular grooming. Perhaps they don't know how their dogs like to be brushed. The following guidelines will help to make weekly grooming a fuss-free occasion.

- *Get dogs used to grooming early in life.* Long-haired breeds especially should be groomed from the time they are puppies.

- *Be sensitive to your dog's likes and dislikes.* Dogs often like to flop over onto one side for brushing, so don't insist that they sit up or stand. Just brush on that side first; then gently grab hold of their front and hind legs to roll them over to brush the other side.

- *Use appropriate combs and brushes.* Use a brush with stiff bristles on one side and wire on the other. If the atmosphere is very dry and full of static, as it often is in winter, I moisten both my fingers and the brush to reduce the chances of giving the dog electric shocks. For the same reason, it is good to place the dog on a wool rug or cotton towel.

- *Be gentle and reassuring.* Before you begin grooming, stroke your dog reassuringly around the head to make the dog feel safe and secure and know that nothing unusual is going to happen. Any time you accidentally knock a knee or shoulder with the edge of the brush, stroke your dog.

- *Learn to use the brush and your fingers properly.* First, run your fingers down the dog's back quite firmly several times to loosen up any dead fur. Then use the wire brush, working down from the head to the tip of the tail, then under the chin, along and around the chest and abdomen, and finally brushing down each leg. Finish up with the bristle side of the brush, using it around the dog's face and then briskly brushing down the back to give the dog's coat a final sheen. Don't use the wire side of the brush on your dog's face, as you could easily poke him in the eye or otherwise hurt him. Also when dogs are shedding the thick under-fur that insulates them during the winter, don't keep raking hard with the wire side of the brush. You will only make your dog's skin hypersensitive. Don't brush hard on patches of fur that haven't loosened up yet either.

You may find that your dog has a very definite molting pattern, with the fur first loosening up around the legs and thighs. Work on these areas first, and wait for the shedding to spread. Tangled long fur on the legs, or feathers, are best loosened with your fingers and a stainless-steel comb. As the under-fur begins to lift, either pluck or twist it out with a steel comb. Some dogs have long guard hairs over the under-fur that tangle very easily with the fur beneath it. Such tangles are best loosened with your fingers or a steel comb. If tangles are very matted, you will need scissors to trim them out. Even though soaking a dog's coat will help to loosen the under-fur, the coat is more likely to tangle when it is wet. If your dog's coat is in the process of shedding, do not bathe the dog before grooming with a brush.

Consider coupling a regular grooming with a good massage. Massage therapy is good for dogs of all ages, and can be done in the evenings while family members are watching TV or relaxing after dinner. My book *The Healing Touch for Dogs* has been used by many who have written to me confirming the many benefits, physical and behavioral, of giving dogs the kind of massage therapy I describe in this book.

Regular Grooming

Make a weekly habit of checking your dog's teeth, ears, and toenails. The more the pup is used to being handled, the easier he will be to restrain later in life if he gets sick and needs medication. Long-haired dogs need a daily grooming and brushing. In hot and humid weather, they may need clipping or stripping out to feel more comfortable and to prevent skin problems, like a hot spot. Never shave a dog bald in summer because they can get sunburn. The summer coat may actually insulate your dog somewhat, like the lining of a thermos flask, helping to keep the body core cool.

Regular grooming will also reduce natural "doggy" odors, which are quite strong in some breeds. Grooming is especially needed when your dog starts to shed his coat for the summer. Also in summer, be on the lookout for ticks. Sometimes a species will infest your house! See Chapter 17 for ways to deal with ticks.

Winter has its health hazards, too. Salt put down on icy roads can burn your dog's paws and underbelly. A regular rinse after going outdoors will help overcome this discomfort. Also, be alert to remove painful snow and ice balls from between the pads of your dog's feet—especially in dogs kenneled outdoors.

Lack of sunlight in winter is associated with so-called seasonal alopecia, or hair loss and patchy baldness in some dogs. Set up a full spectrum grow light where your dog likes to lie, and put a humidifier in the room to make the heated, dry environment better for your dog's skin and yours.

Responsible Dog Ownership

Allowing a dog to roam the neighborhood freely can cause many problems. Your dog may be killed by a car and/or be the cause of a serious traffic accident! Each year free-roaming house dogs are responsible for thousands of people, especially children, requiring medical attention for bite injuries. Even a docile dog becomes aggressive outside, guarding his or her territory, chasing, scaring, or even biting passersby or children.

Free-roaming dogs in rural areas form temporary "packs," causing thousands of dollars of damage each year to farm livestock, as well as having a disastrous impact on wildlife.

Dog owners in heavily populated urban areas should be responsible enough to clean up after their dogs have defecated on the public sidewalk or park. A small plastic bag used as a pick-up glove that is turned inside out and tied will do the trick. Dog feces are both a pollutant and a source of disease infection, especially for children.

A responsible dog owner also respects his or her neighbors' rights and trains his or her dog not to bark excessively (one of the most common nuisance complaints in residential areas). Nor does he let his dog urinate on someone's lawn or sidewalk trees because the strong urine can eventually kill grass and young trees and shrubs.

Once they attain sexual maturity, many male dogs desire to be free to roam the neighborhood. They may become more aggressive around their home-base and also more difficult to handle. Neutering your male dog will make life much easier for both yourself and the dog. As a bonus, neutering the dog eliminates future prostate problems. There are no serious side-effects from such an operation, and he will not be "effeminate."

Female dogs should be spayed to cut down on their frustration when in heat. Spaying eliminates future problems of her reproductive system and reduces chances of mammary tumors. There is a serious overpopulation of unwanted pets (millions being destroyed each year in animal shelters). Neutering your dog is a truly responsible contribution toward reducing this problem. It is a myth that a neutered male dog is less trainable and that a female dog must have a litter to "mature" her. In fact, the opposite tends to be true.

* * *

In return for zealously upholding your dog's basic rights of a complete and balanced diet, regular health checkups, and a responsible owner who understands the dog's needs and the social responsibilities of keeping a dog, you will have a faithful and affectionate companion—and often the guardian of your property and your person. It is, really, an equal relationship.

But you are likely to outlive this relationship, and will have to face the last and ultimate responsibility for your beloved dog, namely euthanasia.

The Euthanasia Question

When a fellow being is suffering without hope of relief and recovery, those who care will opt for mercy killing (euthanasia). Euthanasia is unacceptable in some cultures and religious traditions because to kill another being deliberately, such as a holy cow in India, is taboo. This has less to do with the life and plight of the animal than with the shame of making oneself "impure" by killing another. Self-interest, in this instance, takes precedence over compassionate action. Such inaction (letting the animal continue to suffer) is more than cowardice. It is the essence of hypocrisy when euthanasia is equated not with compassion but with violence, disobedience to some religious doctrine (like ahimsa, nonharming), and personal defilement.

The attitudes in the West toward euthanasia are no less divided and divisive. While the euthanasia of animals is culturally accepted, there is no consensus over the euthanasia of people, even of the terminally ill who are able to give informed consent to caring doctors, and who have supportive relatives.

Any cultural or religious moral principle such as ahimsa, or respect for life, cannot be absolute since there are extenuating circumstances (i.e., situational ethics). Killing an animal out of compassion can be a purely selfish choice. I have been in situations where my decision to euthanize an animal was difficult to separate from my own empathic suffering. Putting the animal out of her misery would put an end to my own burden of suffering for the animal. It is difficult in some situations to be compassionate and at the same time sufficiently detached to be able to make the right decision, free of self-interest, especially when facing the decision to have a beloved companion animal euthanized and one is suffering with it. Empathy, and sympathetic identification, must be balanced by clinical objectivity and assessment of the situation in terms of the animal's degree of suffering and chances of recovery, and options for immediate, short-term relief, as with analgesics and tranquillizers.

I recall one instance in India, treating a Pomeranian dog named Snowflake who had lost most of the skin on her back (about one-third of her surface area) from an accidental scalding by her owner. My first reaction, while cleaning the massive wound, was to consider euthanizing her. But strangely, she seemed to be in less pain than I had anticipated, and with her indefatigable spirit and will to live, combined with intensive wound care and love, she healed completely in three months.

So it is important when considering if it is time to have one's companion animal euthanized to have a second opinion from a veterinarian, and ideally an impartial third-party opinion, as from a close friend who understands your connection with your animal companion but can be more impartial than you. Some people will hold on for emotional reasons, or out of some irrational hope that the animal may miraculously recover while in fact the animal's quality of life calls for letting go. Terminally ill animals in the wild will often seek solitude and a safe place to die, just as companion animals may become more withdrawn and inward, even going off if they get outside to hide before they die.

An animal who shows less and less interest in life, in food, water, daily activities, especially the routine walk or playtime and petting time, and is either more withdrawn or restless, even agitated and seeking extra attention—all signs of pain, fear, and what I call *senile dysphoria*, the antithesis of euphoria—should be seen to immediately by a veterinarian. Ideally a house-call by the veterinarian may be preferable to taking the animal to the hospital or clinic—unless the animal is very easygoing, was never unduly upset going to see the veterinarian on prior occasions, or is so out of it that a short car ride cradled in your lap would not cause the animal undue distress. Some animals do seem to know when it is "their time," and animals sharing the same home will often react by being more attentive and solicitous, or fearful and avoid contact, much like people do toward their own kind.

For many animals, in-home euthanasia is the most humane. It may be best for some family members, including animals not to be present during the procedure. But viewing the body after euthanasia may be an important closure for all concerned. Likewise at the veterinary hospital, some veterinarians do not want the animal's owner involved, but in other instances one or more human family members may be allowed into the room and help hold the animal while the procedure is undertaken.

One of the more widely adopted procedures is to first inject the animal in the thigh or other deep muscle area with a tranquillizer prior to giving an intravenous injection containing a barbiturate drug that causes rapid unconsciousness, like a general anesthetic, but from which the animal never recovers because an overdose is given, sometimes in combination with other drugs to stop the heart. As the animal passes rapidly to unconsciousness, body movements, muscle spasms, changes in breathing, including gasping, sometimes with a vocal sigh or moan, may occur. These can be extremely upsetting to the uninformed but are body reactions associated with the brain and circulation shutting down after the animal has lost consciousness and is not, therefore, suffering. Some animals simply collapse with a short sigh, as though in relief moments after the intravenous injection is administered. But because of the reactions, which can never be predicted, many veterinarians prefer not to have many of their clients witness the procedure.

Death with dignity and freedom from fear are the goals of euthanasia. The grief, guilt, and tendency to blame oneself or others for the loss of an animal companion are all part and parcel of the mourning process. Seeking the support of other family members and friends, attending support groups and grief counseling sessions, often available through veterinary referral or at your local humane society, can be well advised. The grieving over the loss of an animal companion can be unexpectedly painful and enduring, complicated by depression and despair that could even be life-threatening. Rather than focusing on the loss, on blame and shame, one needs instead to remember the good times—the unconditional love and joy the animal brought into one's life, and the final gift to the beloved animal of providing a humane death that liberated the animal's spirit from a worn-out body, preventing further pain and fear. This is all part of the recovery phase of letting go.

In the final analysis we should adopt neither a sanguine nor an abolitionist attitude toward euthanasia of animals—or of our own kind for that matter. The compassionate middle-ground between these extremes can be difficult to establish, as for instance in some non-Western countries where appeals to reason and compassion with regard to animal euthanasia can evoke violent opposition. It is indeed tragic when abandoned cows starve to death and when homeless dogs are neutered and released, only to suffer a hopeless existence on busy city streets before they are killed by traffic or are rounded up by municipal dog catchers to be killed by electrocution or with injections of strychnine and cyanide. The Western humanitarian policy of humanely euthanizing unadopted homeless dogs is anathema to many of their counterparts in the East. Surrounded by suffering, people can become desensitized to it. The attitude of live and let live can then have cruel consequences when responsible euthanasia is taboo—just as when, for purely selfish reasons, the inability to let go and let die leads to taking extreme measures to keep a loved one alive, regardless of the individual's quality of life and suffering.

22.
| In Praise of Mutts |

Cloning

Goats, sheep, cows, pigs, rabbits, mules, horses, deer, and mice have been cloned for commercial and biomedical purposes. In January 2002, it was announced that the first domestic cat had been cloned; two were exhibited at Madison Square Garden in New York City a couple of years later, with an offer by the company to clone people's cats for $50,000 per kitty clone.

In August 2005, the first dog was cloned, an Afghan hound, by South Korean researchers at Seoul National University where earlier, human embryos had been cloned and stem cells extracted. The surrogate mother of this cloned dog was a yellow Labrador retriever. One hundred and twenty-three dogs were used as both egg donors and surrogate mothers. From over a thousand prepared eggs or ova, each containing a skin cell from a dog's ear, three pregnancies resulted: one ended in a miscarriage; one resulted in a pup that died soon after birth from respiratory failure; the third was a viable clone of a male Afghan hound. Some bioethicists fear that the cloning of man's best friend is the final stepping-stone to eventual public acceptance of human cloning.

Cloning entails taking a single cell from an animal and placing the cell inside the egg case, or ovum, from another animal of the same species (the egg case having been emptied of its contents). After a procedure that activates the cell to begin to divide, the ovum containing the cloning cell is placed in the uterus of a hormonally receptive surrogate animal. Because of low success rates in getting the cloned cells to implant into the uterine wall, and because the placenta and embryo may not develop normally, several ova containing the clone cells may be put into the surrogate animal's uterus at the same time.

Should technology be perfected to the point where cloning becomes a business, people will likely be able to take a beloved dog or cat to the veterinarian for a routine health check and have a few cells removed, quickly frozen, and shipped for storage at a pet cloning center. A processing and storage fee will be charged, and when the owners want their companion animals to be cloned, the center will begin the process after a substantial downpayment is made, or full payment has been provided. Before this new biotechnology is perfected and large-scale operations set up—with hundreds, possibly thousands, of caged and hormonally manipulated female dogs and cats serving as ova donors, and others being the recipients of ova containing the cells of the to-be-cloned pet—the cost will probably be in the six-figure range for some time before mass production follows mass demand. But there are many concerns other than financial.

The cloned dogs and cats will not be exact replicas of people's beloved animal companions, and many clones will probably be spontaneously aborted, or may have to be destroyed because of various birth defects. Abnormalities may also develop later in life. Clones of other species often have abnormal internal organs, neurological and immunological problems, and may be abnormally large at birth due to a defective growth-regulating gene function. What about the origins, quality of life, and future of the thousands of caged female dogs and cats who will be exploited by the pet cloning industry, and the procedural risks to their health and overall welfare? Do the ends justify the means? There is no evident benefit to the animals themselves.

Why not adopt from an animal shelter a dog or cat that needs a good home; or donate money, equivalent to what it would cost to produce one clone, toward improving the welfare of hundreds, even thousands, of dogs, cats, and other animals in communities around the world?

What are these ends anyway? Certainly there is a commercial end that is potentially lucrative, given the right market promotion and endorsements by professionals and celebrities.

But is there real human benefit in making a clone of one's beloved animal companion? Or is it mere pandering to a misguided sentimentalism? Because of the close emotional bond between humans and their animal companions, the pet cloning business can be seen as an *unethical exploitation of the bond* for pecuniary ends. Exact replicas of people's dogs and cats will not be created because an identical environment during embryonic and postnatal development cannot be achieved. All clones may, at the time of birth, be of the same chronological age as the age of the cells taken from the to-be-cloned animals. So if a cell is taken from a six-year-old dog, because of the aging "clock," the clone may already be aged by six years at the time it is born.

From various religious and spiritual perspectives and beliefs, cloning violates the sanctity of life and the integrity of divine or natural creative processes. It is problematic from the point of view of reincarnation, or transmigration of the soul. From a Buddhist perspective, the consciousness incarnate in the body of the clone, or the consciousnesses in the bodies of many clones from the same original animal, are all going to be different from the original donor.

It is not inconceivable that dog and cat clones might also be created initially on an experimental basis, and used to provide spare parts such as kidneys, hearts, hips, and knees for ailing dogs and cats. Research laboratories may also use cloning to develop identical sets of dogs, cats, and other animals for biomedical research. Some sets and lines of clones having the same genetically engineered anomalies to serve as high fidelity models of various human diseases may be created and marketed to develop new and profitable drugs to treat these conditions in humans and other animals.

The bioethics and medical validity of these developments need to be examined. And pet owners who put out the money to have their animal companions cloned may want to think twice, since they may well be giving this new cloning business not only a financial jump start, but also the socio-political credibility it needs in order to gain widespread public acceptance and a market for human cloning and for other biologically anomalous and ethically dubious products and processes.

The fact that a venture capitalist made a grant of $2.3 million and hired an agent to find a university biotech laboratory already in the cloning business to clone his dog Missy (visit www.missyplicity.com), and the subsequent public relations and media promotion of this project, points to another agenda: the cloning of pets may be a ploy to promote human cloning. If the cloning of pets becomes a reality, the public will become desensitized to the issue of cloning and more likely to accept a highly lucrative biotechnology for childless couples and rich and selfish singles for the cloning of complete human beings, and of partial human beings (such as anencephalics or headless clones) as a source of replacement tissues and organ parts.

The Philosophy Department at Texas A&M University—where the Missyplicity Project started in another department before being spun off into a private company called Genetics Savings & Clone—developed a set of bioethical guidelines based on the ethical principle of what they called *axiomatic anthropocentrism*. This strategy was clearly designed to deflect public criticism and concern over the morality and animal welfare aspects of the project. Axiomatic anthropocentrism essentially means whatever is good for people is ethically acceptable. Anthropocentrism—human centeredness—is an outmoded paradigm that many advocates of animal rights and environmental protection see as the root cause of untold animal suffering and ecological devastation.

Several female dogs were up for adoption on the Web site, one of the company's "bioethical principles" being regardless of the source through which dogs were obtained for use as egg donors or surrogate mothers (from animal shelters, breeding farms, etc.), at the completion of their role in the Missyplicity Project, all dogs would be placed in loving homes. No funds would be expended for dogs raised under inhumane conditions, such as puppy mills. The Missyplicity Project included several goals in addition to the cloning of Missy that were published on the Web site. These included dozens, perhaps hundreds, of scientific papers on canine reproductive physiology; enhanced reproduction and repopulation of endangered wild canids; plans to develop improved canine contraceptive and sterilization methods as a way of preventing the millions of unwanted dogs who are euthanized in America every year; to clone exceptional dogs of high societal value, especially search-and-rescue dogs; and to develop low-cost commercial dog-cloning services for the general public.

These goals gave the project the kind of credibility that a gullible public, as well as organizations and professionals with a limited grasp of the inherent limitations and harmful consequences of cloning, would readily accept. Ethical concerns and the questions concerning the validity and relevance of applying cloning biotechnology to wildlife conservation, to dog overpopulation, and to the propagation of high-performance dogs were cleverly deflected by these promissory goals.

The veterinary profession has been relatively silent on this issue of the risks and ethics of companion animal cloning. I trust that my respected colleagues will not remain silent on this issue—as they did thirty years ago with the advent of factory farming that has resulted in great animal suffering, environmental harms, and increased public health risks.

A Postscript

The company, Genetic Savings & Clone, a commercial spin-off from the Missyplicity Project at Texas A&M University, launched Operation Copy-Cat in 2000. The company estimated that the price for cloning a cat or dog will drop to $25,000 within three years. In the fall of 2006, the company closed shop: they never succeeded in cloning a dog and the two cats they cloned failed to spark the market demand that they had hoped for.[1]

Ethical Questions Concerning Pure-Breed Dogs

The British Veterinary Association (BVA) has long opposed the cropping of dogs' ears. It is illegal in the UK to crop dogs' ears, so you won't see any in a dog show.

The BVA is also strongly opposed to tail docking, except as a necessary surgical amputation for a tail that is gangrenous or has been crushed. Tail docking for nonmedical, cosmetic, and breed-standard reasons is now outlawed in the UK.

Dogs need their tails not only for balance but more especially for communication. They use their tails to express their social status and various emotions. Tail docking can often lead to what is called an *amputation neuroma*. This is an inflammation of the nerves in the tail that can drive dogs crazy so they are constantly chasing and chewing their tails, which eventually need to be amputated again.

In the United States you can see more and more show dogs like Dobermans and schnauzers with their tails intact and with uncropped ears. In fact, the American Veterinary Medical Association has spoken out against ear cropping, although some veterinarians still do it. The main argument against the practice is that ear cropping is a form of mutilation without any medical benefit. It is therefore regarded as a professionally unethical and unacceptable surgical procedure. The American Association of Veterinarians

---

1. For additional information about genetic engineering, cloning, and the creation of transgenic animals, see Michael W. Fox, *Killer Foods: When Scientists Manipulate Genes, Better Is Not Always Best* (Guilford, Conn.: The Lyons Press, 2004) and Michael W. Fox, *Bringing Life to Ethics: Global Bioethics for a Humane Society* (Albany, N.Y.: State University of New York Press, 2001).

for Animal Rights have campaigned nationwide to discourage dog breeders, owners, and especially dog show people from having their dogs' ears cropped. It is a very painful operation for puppies and it often goes wrong, so the ears have to be splinted and taped for weeks. Infections are common, especially in hot and humid weather. All this means more suffering—and for what end? Along with tail docking, cropped ears should be eliminated as a standard for any breed.

There is ample evidence that dogs that have been traumatized by ear cropping during their sensitive period (around eight to ten weeks) tend to be head-shy or touch-shy later in life—and even more so if they developed painful ear infections. In my mind this mutilation is as unacceptable as giving guard dogs a permanent snarl by surgically removing part of their upper lips on each side of the muzzle. A veterinarian once did this for a company in New York City that rented out Dobermans to protect private property: it makes dogs look more threatening to other dogs, just like a permanent snarl. If you think that is cruel and unethical, then you must also feel the same way about ear cropping.

No dog benefits from having cropped ears. It is done just for human vanity, a twisted aesthetics that has no place in a civilized society and surely no place in a dog show. Dog shows are places where compassion should be evident, as well as respect for our canine companions. Such surgical mutilation is a blatant example of human selfishness and lack of compassion, and it exemplifies how we are craven to the latest fads and fashions. Dogs should not be the victims of such selfish ends.

I strongly urge all dog show judges and dog show participants to prohibit tail docking and ear cropping by making it impossible to show any dog that has been so mutilated after a given date. Dogs born before this date and having had their tails and ears cropped prior to this date would still be eligible for entry in a dog show. This way, these unnecessary mutilations would be gradually phased out.

There are other problems with purebred dogs that raise the hackles of humanitarians—and to ignore them is to use these dogs as mirrors of our own insensitivity. For example, the BVA moved to prohibit the breeding of shar-peis because their skin folds lead to chronic infections, especially in hot and humid climates. They are prone to develop eye problems because they are afflicted with entropion (turned in eyelids). This disorder can cause blindness if not corrected surgically, but then people want to breed the dogs and so the inherited disorder is passed on to the offspring.

There are other breeds that won't do well in warm climates, such as the British bulldog, who is prone to heat stress and heatstroke because he can't breathe properly, even on food days. The pushed-in muzzle and long soft palate make breathing difficult. A negative pressure may develop such that the dog's windpipe collapses. Pekingese and boxers can suffer a similar fate, called *chronic partial asphyxia*.

Other dog breeds not suitable for tropical places and seasons are cocker spaniels; their pendulous ears never dry out, so they become chronically infected. Northern breeds like huskies and keeshonds likewise do poorly in hot and humid environments and are not suitable companions for those who live in places like Miami, Florida, or Madras, India.

In fact, most pure breeds of European origin take generations to acclimate to such climates. And many mutant breeds like shar-peis, bulldogs, and cocker spaniels never will. I have seen some sad and sorry specimens in countries like Jamaica, Kenya, and India, where owners have imported them from Europe and North America. Unlike local pariah dogs and indigenous breeds, they have little or no resistance to parasitic and infectious diseases. Chronic skin problems and immune system breakdown are also all too common.

The Question of Domestication and Wolf-Dog Hybrids

The evident suffering of captured wild animals, which is well documented over the past 10,000 to 14,000 years, is a manifest reality of animal domestication. Wild stock must be captured, confined, and suffer the stresses of captivity to which they are neither adapted physically nor emotionally. Subsequent generations are selected for their ability to adapt to the conditions and demands of domesticity. Those who cannot adapt must be killed. But if, like a wolf, they mature relatively slowly, they must be kept for many months before one can tell if indeed they will adapt and settle down. Increasing instability may develop with increasing age in young, captive-raised wolves—especially around five months of age and again around sexual maturity, around one to two years of age. During this developmental and adaptation phase, the animal suffers from being deprived of freedom and space to be active and explore, from fear of strangers and unfamiliar things, and from having basic instincts confused, conflicted, denied, and frustrated. This is a form of suffering that can be avoided by not trying to turn a wild wolf into a pet or companion animal.

The same is true for wolf-dog hybrids, *especially with the first- and second-generation hybrids*. More dog-diluted wolf hybrids are generally more adaptable, but only a percentage of earlier generation hybrids are stable and adaptable. The rest do suffer, as my research on wolf hybrids and coyote-dog hybrids has shown. Many end up having to be euthanized. Is their suffering worth it so that a few people can enjoy owning a wolf-dog hybrid? Some may claim that this is their "right." But is the right of ownership greater than the right of these animals— the unstable predecessors and littermates of your stable and adaptable hybrid—to be free of suffering? I think not.

Those who keep and propagate wolf-dog hybrids may well reflect upon this. The scientific evidence for suffering they cannot deny, nor should they skirt the ethical issue claiming that it is their right to own and create such hybrids. Nor can they rationalize and avoid the issue of unnecessary suffering by claiming that they are "improving" various dog breeds. There are enough genes in dogdom to improve every breed without having to introduce wolf genes again. Neither can they abdicate ethical responsibility by focusing on their own particular hybrid animal and rationalizing that it's okay since *some* are stable and make good pets. Who is responsible for the misfits, which must be destroyed or kept in a cage or otherwise protected from terrifying strangers: who but the owners and propagators of wolf-dog hybrids? They may, and surely must, love their animals. But I contend that their love is blind and immature, lacking responsible compassion and awareness of the ethical ramifications of their self-indulgence.

While some breeders of hybrids may carefully place their creations with good owners, can we always guarantee that such sensitive and unstable (or potentially unstable) psychically delicate creatures do not fall into brutal hands—the kind of person who wants a savage wolf in his dog? You may avoid this yourself, but other mercenaries will commercialize on their hybrid creations and mass-market wolf-dogs and sell them to anyone. Suffering may then be compounded when potentially stable hybrids are sold to unstable people who are drawn to the negative wolf mythos of wolves being fierce and aggressive—people who have neither the sensitivity nor knowledge to handle a part-wild animal.

The prevention and alleviation of animal suffering is one step in the direction toward a more compassionate society, Clearly, the propagation of wolf-dog hybrids is one of many unnecessary self-indulgent activities that a more mature and enlightened humanity would not engage in. Surely we can enjoy and enjoin with other life-forms on Earth without having to create them for ourselves. To fight to conserve wolves and their wilderness habitat, for example, is better than enslaving wolf genes to create some hybrid pet.

The latter has no right to be born, for that which does not exist cannot have rights. We have the responsibility to assure that hybrids will not be born, since there can be no guarantee they will not suffer after they are born. Their right to a life of nonsuffering can never be guaranteed—and this is surely greater than someone's claim to breed, sell, and own such an animal. So let sleeping dogs lie and let wolves have sanctuary in the wild. We can respect and love both without adding to the problems of the biosphere and the burden of suffering and of human responsibility by interbreeding the wolf and the dog.

Perhaps, deep in our psyches, we are both wolf and dog ourselves, still wild and yet civilized. Or do we long for a sense of the wild and of the wilderness in our urban lives? Do we then vicariously satisfy this need by shooting a wild "trophy" animal, or keeping one captive, or incorporating a part of the animal's wild essence into a domestic dog? Or is possession simply for social status and self-aggrandizement by having something unusual?

Let us examine, therefore, not only the ethics of owning and breeding wolf-dog hybrids, but also the underlying motives. Some may feel close to God, as creators of such unique animals. But a closer look into the mirror will reveal that many of these attractive hybrids are unstable misfits. If we are to be the trustees of all that is wild and the humane stewards of our fellow creatures, we must see that everything already has its place and understand that we create further chaos and suffering when we change the natural order for selfish ends.

Wolf Hybrid Study

Between 1967 and 1974, while I taught at Washington University, St. Louis, I studied the behavior and development of many species of wild canids, including certain hybrids (coyote x beagle, wolf x malamute). Many of the canids I studied had the same rearing history—having been hand-raised—and all had much human contact and handling to ensure optimal socialization. For example, as part of the research design, social and environmental influences were kept as constant as possible so that the genetic differences in behavior and development that we were interested in would not be masked or confounded by such variables.

The wolf stock was principally from (Canadian) Mackenzie River Wolf Subspecies bred in captivity, and the domestic dog breed used in these studies was Alaskan malamute. Two hybrid litters were provided by Dr. John Schmidt (Snowmass, Colorado), which were first-generation (F1) hybrids. From one of these we bred F1X malamutes (backcross). We also studied three hand-raised wolf litters, one litter of purebred malamutes, and bred one litter of F1 wolf x malamutes. These data were not published because we did not breed an F2 (second generation) hybrid generation. However, our wolf x dog hybrid studies did reveal a consistent pattern in temperament development. The "wild" traits of the wolf were evident in those hybrids having the most wolf genes and were least evident in the more "diluted" hybrids (i.e., F1 hybrid x malamute). However, *within* litter rather than between litter comparisons showed that even in the more wolf-dilute hybrids, later instabilities in temperament emerged in some individuals. While there is little doubt that with selective breeding, stable hybrids can be produced, my concern is over the fact that hybrid animals with behavior problems can result from breeding wolf and dog and will occur unpredictably in subsequent hybrid offspring.

While to eliminate such problems is a realistic and accepted goal of wolf x dog hybrid breeders, and while admittedly there are magnificent and temperamentally stable hybrids alive today, my concern over the unstable hybrids remains. I have encountered some that are even more unstable than any timid hand-raised wolf. Hybridization may therefore intensify emotional/behavioral problems in some wolf x dog combinations. This possibility gains indirect support from our coyote x dog studies where, in the F2 hybrid generation, some individuals were indeed in this tragic category.

To take a wolf, crossbreed the wolf with a dog, and then expect the offspring to make pets and adapt to the domestic environment is something that should be outlawed. I wish every municipal authority would crack down on all breeders and traders, but not confiscate wild and hybrid pets, unless their living environments cause otherwise avoidable stress and suffering. Surely every living soul has a right to live and be well in conditions that are best for spirit, mind, and body. This does not mean captivity for wild souls unless conditions are comparable to the natural state.

We do not have the knowledge yet to create homologous habitats identical to the real. The best we can ever hope for are successively higher fidelity analogs. But such efforts should not weaken our commitment to the conservation, protection, and restoration of wild animals' natural habitat. An apartment, house, cage, or backyard is such a low fidelity environment for a wild animal that many states do not permit them to be kept and propagated under such conditions—except on fox, mink, and other fur farms or ranches that are an abomination to any normal human sensibility.

In Praise of the Natural or Original Dog

There's an irony about humankind's longest relationship—which some scientists believe to be some 100,000 years old—with its most devoted member of the animal kingdom: the dog. The civilization of ancient Egypt saw divinity in the dog as Anubis, the dog-headed god of their zoomorphic pantheon. We can still find in Egypt, and throughout much of the third world, dogs that look much like they did six to eight thousand years ago, depicted when they were sculpted and drawn in reverence as images of Anubis. But now these dogs are widely shunned and variously called all kinds of disrespectful names, such as pariahs, curs, and bastards. The Eastern term pariah is synonymous with a human outcast or member of the lowest caste. In the West, cur is synonymous with a contemptible person. The French call such dogs bastards and inferior canines, analogous to illegitimate human offspring.

One may wonder why there is such widespread prejudice toward these natural dogs, which in the West we call mongrels or mutts. Fear, ignorance, and superstition underlie most all prejudicial attitudes, and the negative attitude toward the natural dog is no exception. Yet with a little understanding, these dogs would be more widely respected and treated far better than they are generally today. They would not be given derogatory names, but would rather be called natural with respect and admiration. But this is a big step for some people to take. Natural dogs are widely feared for a variety of reasons.

While people in the West will befriend these dogs and even take them into their homes, these dogs the world over have a hard life and a difficult time surviving under the best of circumstances; all too often they become the victims of human prejudice and fear. Some fifty years ago, Mohandas Gandhi made this poignant statement about Indian dogs: "Roving dogs do not indicate the civilization or compassion of the society; they betray on the contrary the ignorance and lethargy of its members."

In some religious traditions, the dog is the embodiment of evil, a prejudice many justify because dogs are not immune to rabies and epidemics, which lead villagers to club, spear, and stone all sick dogs from fear of being bitten and contracting the diseases that are usually fatal. The superstitious belief that dogs can be possessed by evil spirits probably originated from the crazed behavior of dogs afflicted with rabies.

While the origin of the natural dog remains a mystery, their widespread, basic physical similarities from one continent to another make them a class of their own—distinct from specific breeds that have been subjected to selective breeding for various purposes. The Australian dingo is a somewhat larger type of original dog that has become feral (wild). The African Basenji is one example of a type that has been subjected to selective breeding to "fix" and exaggerate certain traits, such as the curled tail and wrinkled forehead.

The natural dog is more a creation of nature, a product of natural selection, rather than an object of human fabrication—like a toy poodle or a basset hound, a bulldog or a giant Great Dane. The natural dog could well be called the "original" dog because the dog's most prototypical form is evident, especially in the village dogs of the Andes, East Africa, and Southeast Asia.

The natural dog is characterized by a body weight of twenty-five to fifty-five pounds; a long tail carried high and curved over in dominant, confident adults; a short, smooth coat varying in color from fawn, tan, and red, to piebald, black, and brindled. The limbs of the natural dog are usually long, strong, and graceful, the haunches being well muscled for speed. The front paws of both sexes are extremely flexible, giving the dog a cat-like dexterity. Many will wash their faces with their front paws like a cat. The front dew claws are used like thumbs to hold and manipulate objects. The neck and jaw muscles of males are more heavily developed than in females. Their often almond-shaped eyes range from light yellow-gold to burnished dark copper, while the ears are either erect and pointed or slightly folded, but never heavily pendulous like a cocker spaniel. These dogs are usually deep-chested and narrow waisted, often resembling small greyhounds. Such dogs are favored for hunting (and poaching) in Africa and India, while in the Far East, stockier, more barrel-chested dogs are favored to be eaten as a culinary delicacy.

Underlying the highly adaptable nature of the natural dog are generations of rigorous natural selection. Subjected to this process, where the fittest survive, they are extremely intelligent, alert, and agile animals, with superbly developed senses. If we were to combine the best qualities of the various breeds of dog, or let a diversity of different breeds interbreed on some island for a few generations, we would probably finish up with a natural dog look-alike.

Geneticists refer to the phenomenon of *hybrid vigor*, where the genetically mixed offspring of two relatively inbred breeds of dogs are healthier than either of their parent lineages. This certainly holds true for the natural dog in developing countries, whose health is widely recognized as being superior to imported Western purebred dogs, which lack natural immunity to various local diseases and especially parasitic infections.

Natural dogs are incredibly adaptable creatures. They are able to live and multiply in the wild and in villages and towns as solitary or pack hunters and scavengers. They also take readily to living with livestock and poultry if they are raised as puppies in such an environment. These dogs become very protective of their adoptive human "pack," including the family's territory and property, especially livestock. They are often the playmates, guardians, and surrogate "diaper service" for young children (actually consuming infants' stools). And out in the bush or jungle they can be hunting and trekking companions for adolescent boys and grown men tending livestock or foraging for food. Some indigenous peoples recognize the healing power of dog's saliva, allowing their dogs to lick skin sores and wounds.

Often some of the dogs seen in a pack belong to particular families, while other dogs who make up the village guild of dogs belong to no one in particular. They are community dogs and are cared for by the people. This basic humane care is to be encouraged in third-world countries because of the clear public health and environmental benefits these dogs bring to the human community. Subsidized rabies and distemper vaccinations, routine anti-parasite treatments, and especially spay-neuter programs are urgently needed to help these dogs—animals that give so much and receive so little in return.

Roaming packs of dogs, foraging and hunting together in the bush or jungle, can pose a health threat to wild carnivores when they are infected with rabies, distemper, mange, and other communicable diseases. But where the village dogs are well cared for, they have no need to roam far in search of food and are less of a threat to wildlife.

The author's pack of rescued "natural" dogs—Lizzie (center, from Jamaica) with Batman (L) and Xylo (R) who are from the same village in S. India.
Photo: M. W. Fox

Village life in much of the third world would be impoverished without its natural dogs, and the health of the human population would likely be at risk because the village dogs are such efficient garbage removers, recycling organic wastes and rendering many potentially harmful human bacteria and other pathogens into harmless by-products of their own digestive processes. As hunters, they keep pests and pestilence at bay. They will defend their territory from intruding dogs that are driven off by the resident pack. This helps protect people from potentially rabid free-roaming dogs. In view of this important public health role that the dogs can play in poor communities that lack sewage and garbage disposal services, these dogs warrant far more respect than they are usually given.

My advice to anyone who is looking for a good dog, and who can't go to a third-world country to adopt one of the millions of homeless natural dogs, is to visit the local animal shelter. Remember, natural dog look-alikes can be found from Detroit to Delhi and from Rome to Rio. With a mental image of what a natural dog looks like, and knowing they all have good temperaments if they have been socialized and never abused, I will guarantee that there will be at least one waiting at your local animal shelter to be adopted into a good home. With a little expertise or advice, it is not difficult to pick out an adult dog or a puppy with the characteristics and potentialities of this all-natural dog breed.

Dogs and Humans Evolved Together

I believe that wolves became dogs in ways that were similar to those selection processes that turned apes into humans to differ in degree but not in kind from their ancestors. Many humans would like to believe otherwise, but it is a fact that we, like our canine companions, are in many ways degenerate when compared to the adaptability and survivability under natural conditions evident in our living wild ancestors.

But with new or more developed attributes in the realms of dog-human communication and cognition, sociability (including proximity-tolerance), and changes in fright-fight-flight and fear reactions in conjunction with altered emotional and related neuro-endocrine functions, humans and dogs stand apart from their progenitors.

They are neither superior nor inferior: simply different—respectively "civilized" and domesticated. This means that in some ways humans and dogs are more similar to each other than to their respective wild counterparts, especially in terms of their autonomic nervous system "tuning" and reactivity. Through what I call "sympathetic resonance" we began to establish social, emotional, and empathetic bonds with other animals, dogs in particular, and we began to regard animals as beings beyond something to kill and eat or wear. This sympathetic resonance, over thousands of generations under the more protected conditions of domesticity, allowed for the emergence of new physical and emotional characteristics, traits, and personalities that under the narrow selection forces of the wild would be unlikely to survive one generation. So it can be said that humans and dogs, along with other domesticated species, began to evolve *together*. Such co-evolution includes varying degrees of emotional interdependence, trust, affection, and the ideal of mutually enhancing symbioses where the best interests of both human and animal are realized.

And for us it includes an enormous debt of gratitude to all the animals that have helped us become more civilized, compassionate, and caring as a species. We all have a responsibility for the animals that share and enrich our lives as companions, that are raised for food and fiber, that are experimented upon for medical and other commercial purposes, and that are still wild and continue to enrich and sustain the natural world and remind us of our origins.

Let's Be Worthy of Our Dogs

Dogs mirror some of the best and worst qualities of the human species. "Like master, like dog" is a truism worthy of our contemplation. When we honestly and impartially look at how we value and treat our dogs, and the reasons why, we may ultimately rise to their level of dignity and integrity. What we do to dogs is indeed a reflection of our humanity—both individually and culturally. We may or may not like what we see. But when we begin to see through the dogs' eyes and put ourselves in their place—and don't do to them what we would not have them do to us—we might be more worthy of their fidelity and devotion.

Index